The Enemy Within

Also by John Demos

Circles and Lines:
The Shape of Experience in Early America

The Unredeemed Captive:
A Family Story from Early America

Past, Present, and Personal:
The Family and the Life Course in American History

Entertaining Satan:
Witchcraft and the Culture of Early New England

A Little Commonwealth:
Family Life in Plymouth Colony

JOHN DEMOS

The Enemy Within

2,000 Years of Witch-hunting

in the Western World

VIKING

VIKING

Published by the Penguin Group

Penguin Group (USA) Inc., 375 Hudson Street,
New York, New York 10014, U.S.A.
Penguin Group (Canada), 90 Eglinton Avenue East, Suite 700, Toronto,
Ontario, Canada M4P 2Y3 (a division of Pearson Penguin Canada Inc.)
Penguin Books Ltd, 80 Strand, London WC2R 0RL, England
Penguin Ireland, 25 St. Stephen's Green, Dublin 2, Ireland
(a division of Penguin Books Ltd)
Penguin Books Australia Ltd, 250 Camberwell Road, Camberwell,
Victoria 3124, Australia (a division of Pearson Australia Group Pty Ltd)
Penguin Books India Pvt Ltd, 11 Community Centre,
Panchsheel Park, New Delhi–110 017, India
Penguin Group (NZ), 67 Apollo Drive, Rosedale, North Shore 0632,
New Zealand (a division of Pearson New Zealand Ltd)
Penguin Books (South Africa) (Pty) Ltd, 24 Sturdee Avenue,
Rosebank, Johannesburg 2196, South Africa

Penguin Books Ltd, Registered Offices: 80 Strand, London WC2R 0RL, England

First published in 2008 by Viking Penguin, a member of Penguin Group (USA) Inc.

1 3 5 7 9 10 8 6 4 2

LIBRARY OF CONGRESS CATALOGING IN PUBLICATION DATA
Demos, John.
The enemy within : 2,000 years of witch-hunting in the Western world / John Demos.
p.   cm.
Includes bibliographical references (p. 297) and index.
ISBN 978-0-670-01999-1
1. Witchcraft—History.   I. Title.
BF1566.D46 2008
133.4'309—dc22   2008021427

Printed in the United States of America
Set in Dante
Designed by Francesca Belanger

To Pen and Tom

Preface

This book is the end product of an almost half-century engagement with witchcraft study.

Imagining such a lengthy prospect was impossible when, as a beginning graduate student in 1960, I was assigned the topic of witchcraft for a term paper. In due course, however, the paper became a published article. And the article spawned other articles, numerous conference presentations, and eventually the writing of a large scholarly book (*Entertaining Satan: Witchcraft and the Culture of Early New England*, Oxford University Press, 1982).

At that point I thought surely I had said my last word on witchcraft history. Yet the talk-show invitations kept coming each year at Halloween; there was still the occasional witchcraft conference to attend; there were even middle-of-the-night phone calls from people who thought themselves possessed by the Devil. To an extent, therefore, I kept my hand in.

Then, to my surprise, I was back in the thick of it—invited by the editors of Viking to attempt a broad-gauge summary and synthesis of the entire subject. The challenge was considerable, but I did feel a certain eagerness in response. It would be like returning to a house well-known from long before, but now grown through various additions into a mansion. There were old rooms to revisit, and new ones to reconnoiter for the first time. Indeed, many of the mansion's contents—nothing less than a vast output of scholarship during the past two and a half decades—were unfamiliar. The study of European witchcraft has reached extraordinary levels of sophistication; reading and reflecting on that would prove especially rewarding.

The American side of witchcraft study has also been reinvigorated; rewards would come from there as well. The range and variety of all such work did indeed invite synthesis.

But synthesis was itself an unfamiliar process for me. I have previously made my way as a historian of very specific times, places, and events. My aim in all my other projects has been depth more than breadth. Those priorities are reversed here; the coverage is nothing if not broad. The idea is to pull together histories as widely separated as the late Roman Empire, medieval Europe, colonial America, and modern-day Red scares (among others). Moreover, my synthesis seeks to bridge not only histories but also historiography—that is, the writings of literally hundreds of different scholars, each with his or her own style, presuppositions, research focus and strategy, and period of interest. Wide coverage seems an important, even necessary, goal with certain historical topics, but the risk of collapsing distinctions, oversimplifying, flattening, trivializing is formidable.

A second unfamiliar aspect of my current project involves audience. Although I have always hoped to interest general readers in the fruits of my research, my primary audience till now has been fellow scholars and students. But again, in this book the priorities are reversed. In fact, what some are calling popular history has of late achieved a remarkable growth. "History is hot," I heard a publisher say last year, and bestseller lists would seem to bear him out. Interestingly, many history books on such lists come from the hands of "writers" with no claim to scholarly credentials (as if historians were not writers themselves!); the results, in my opinion, are decidedly mixed. The finest of these books are fine indeed, the worst so crude as to seem a kind of caricature. One can only be pleased that history should become popular, even hot; but professionals, too, must be persuaded to enter that mix.

There is a third kind of unfamiliarity here which may be most compelling of all. My focus, through a long academic career, has been on people who lived and died two, three, or more centuries ago. Though I've tried to understand them, to empathize with them, and (in a way) to connect with them as fellow humans, their experience has the unavoidable feel of remoteness. In direct contrast, the current book brings its subject virtually to the present; hence the sense of connection grows far more immediate and personal. Many of the individual people described in my concluding section are still living; some are the entirely innocent targets of recent witch-hunts (in the figurative sense). For example, an unknown number of those prosecuted in the day-care "abuse" investigations of the 1980s and '90s remain in prison years later; to write about them is a new and different experience. If this book were somehow to shorten their "trials" at least a bit, or if it proved at all instrumental in forestalling similar injustice in the future, I would feel extremely gratified. Furthermore, connection with the targets of modern-day witch-hunts brings a renewed and deepened feeling for their counterparts in the old-style witch-hunts of pre-modern times. Targets then, targets now: the struggles and sufferings of them all are painfully clear.

I wish, finally, to express appreciation to various colleagues and friends who have helped move my project along. First comes the legion of previous witchcraft historians whose spadework in the many corners of this large landscape underlies my synthesis throughout; their names will be found in the Bibliographic Commentary that stands at the book's end. The names of others whose assistance was more direct and personal can be set down here. Jane Kamensky, Aaron Sachs, and Virginia Demos gave the entire manuscript a careful reading and offered many critical and constructive suggestions. James R. Green, Alexander Keyssar, and Paul Freedman read and commented on one or another section that fell within their own special areas of expertise. Numerous others responded to my requests for advice about readings or specific points of fact and interpretation: among these Robert Johnston, Beverly Gage, and Michelle Nickerson were particularly helpful. I benefited greatly from the work of three undergraduate research assistants: Jeremiah Quinlan, Adrian Finucane, and Christine Matthias. Finally, two skilled editors at Viking, Wendy Wolf and Ellen Garrison, provided invaluable late-stage counsel, and thereby improved things in ways both large and small.

And now I believe that I truly *have* said my last word on witch-craft history . . .

J. D.
Tyringham, Massachusetts
February 2008

Contents

PART FOUR: **MODERN AMERICA**

The Enemy Within

Prologue

June 1582. In the English town of Chelmsford, half a dozen elderly matrons carefully undress a sawyer's wife named Alice Glasscock and begin a search of her body for "the marks of a witch." In due course they discover several "spots . . . well sucked"—so they presume—by Satan's imps. This is part of a formal investigation that will lead to Glasscock's trial, conviction, and execution.

September 1623. In the small south German village of Marchtal, a group of farmers and their families interrupt their harvest dance to forbid the approach of a woman named Ursula Götz. "Begone! Begone," they shout together, "you shitty witch!" Branded thus, and under threat of torture, Götz will eventually confess to all sorts of "devilish" designs against persons, cattle, crops.

Autumn 1656. In New Haven, in the British colony of Connecticut, a woman named Elizabeth Godman knocks at the door of her neighbor Goodwife Thorp and asks to buy some chickens. Thorp replies curtly, "We have none to sell," whereupon Godman turns away muttering what sounds like a threat. The next day, when several of Thorp's chickens are found dead, she will charge Godman with using "evil means" against them.

May 1692. In Salem, Massachusetts (also a British colony), seven mostly teenage girls thrash wildly about on a courtroom floor, alongside a bewildered witch suspect named Martha Carrier. "There is a black man whispering in her ear!" shrieks one of the girls. A second wails, "She bites me, and tells me she would cut my throat!" while others in the group endure "most intolerable outcries and agonies . . . of affliction." Carrier's will be one of twenty lives lost to America's most famous witch-hunt.

Alice Glasscock. Ursula Götz. Elizabeth Godman. Martha Carrier. All were caught in the snare of real events; all were players in a vast drama spanning key centuries in the history of what we now call "Western civilization." The idea of witchcraft has been part of that history as far back as the records allow us to see. Thousands of people like Götz, Glasscock, Godman, and Carrier have been pursued, harassed, injured, and killed because of it.

The reality behind the idea is another matter. That some attempts were made to practice witchcraft, and that certain individuals (at least a few) were willing to cast themselves as witches, seems beyond doubt. Where the idea was so prevalent and powerful, a portion of those it touched would, almost inevitably, decide to embrace it. There is great difficulty, however, in identifying such "actual" witches and their specific doings now. For the evidence we have is heavily filtered, coming (as it invariably does) from those who sought to oppose and suppress witchcraft: judges, inquisitors of various types, clergymen and theologians, or simply the countless ordinary folk who feared its use against them.

These distinctions frame a book—any book—on witchcraft history. The focus in what follows is the idea *of* witchcraft, as it melded with emotions *about* witchcraft, to prompt actions *against* witchcraft. Again: it is the idea, the emotions, the actions—not the actual practice—that we, from several centuries later on, can directly scrutinize. As a result, this is—first and last—a history of witch-*hunting*.

But witch-hunting is itself a large subject, hardly confined to any single part of the world. In fact, it rises virtually to the level of a cross-cultural universal; witches of one sort or another are, or previously have been, "hunted" just about everywhere—in Asia, in Africa, in Australia, and among native peoples all across the Americas. This book cannot, and does not, reach so far; its boundaries are those of the pre-modern, and modern, West.

There are other boundaries to flag, and additional subject areas that lie beyond reach. Witch-hunting, large as it is, belongs to a still more capacious terrain that also includes racism, sexism, and anti-Semitism, as well as pogroms, lynchings, genocide, and ethnic cleansing. To such patently downside matters, witch-hunting bears an obvious similarity—and even perhaps some dynamic connection. But one crucial element divides them. While the goal for all is separation from a despised "other," witch-hunting alone finds the other within its own ranks. The Jew, the black, and the ethnic opposite exist, in some fundamental sense, "on the outside"; the point of actions against them is to enforce difference and distance, and sometimes to eliminate them altogether. The witch, by contrast, is discovered (and "discovery" is key to the process) inside the host community; typically he or she is a former member in good standing of that community who has chosen not only to reject but also to subvert it. Thus, the idea of witchcraft holds at its center the theme of betrayal. Thus, too, witch-hunting has an intensely countersubversive, anti-conspiratorial tone. Always and everywhere, its goal is to root out the hidden enemy within.

Most of this book addresses witch-hunting in a quite straightforward sense: through a wide array of experience pertaining to witchcraft, as an explicit presence in Western society during the medieval and early modern eras (roughly A.D. 500–1700). However, its concluding section moves to the modern period, and broaches something more: what might be called witch-hunts without witches. This design reflects the widespread usage nowadays of the *term*—as a metaphor, a figure, for events that, while lacking witchcraft in the literal sense, seem in other respects remarkably similar to the old pattern. Presumably, the key link between literal and figurative witch-hunts is the search for enemies within. But that proposition needs testing against specific cases. In short, how fully is the witch-hunt metaphor justified? Can the modern, figurative witch-hunts be understood as "functional equivalents" of the pre-modern ones?

A final note: the book follows a kind of zoom-lens principle, combining long, broadly topographical views with others that are sharp

and close-up. Its four major parts move roughly in chronological order, from European witch-hunting, especially during the "craze"
years of the 16th and 17th centuries (Part One), to witch-hunting in
the early "colonial period" of American history (Part Two), to the notorious Salem trials of the late 17th century (Part Three), to the figurative witch-hunts of modern times (Part Four). Each part includes a
lengthy central chapter presenting the topic, from start to finish, in
summary form. And each is bordered, fore and aft, by "vignettes"
keyed to some particular episode, person, artifact, or career. The
aim is to balance the general against the particular, to juxtapose
structure and texture, to mix interpretation and analysis with narrative flow and human detail. History, *all* history, requires no less.

PART ONE

EUROPE

Though witchcraft is a very old presence in Europe, its origins were diffuse and scattered. Throughout the first millennium there were no witch-hunts as such. Still, the suffering of the early Christian martyrs can be seen as prefiguring the persecutions that would come later on; thus the vignette presented in chapter I.

With the passage of time, conditions would ripen for a full-blown "witch-craze" at the end of the Middle Ages. The ripening process, and the craze itself—a sequence without parallel in the history of the Western world—are the focus of chapter II.

As anxiety over witchcraft rose, and large-scale persecution began, a single book—the notorious *Malleus Maleficarum*—served to orient, and galvanize, those most directly involved. For more than two centuries it served as a virtual bible of witch-hunting; witness the tale of its "travels" recounted in chapter III.

CHAPTER I

Martyrs of Lyons:
A Story from the Beginning

A.D. 177; Lyons, France. (Its Roman name is Lugdunum, its province Gaul.) *Alarm spreads throughout this bustling city on the margins of the empire. The Christians, it is rumored, are once again engaged in their infamous rituals, and the entire community is thereby imperiled.*

"Thyestian feasts" form part of the rumor: lavish banquets, prepared in secret and held in the predawn hours while others sleep, with a great excess of food and drink. The main fare, the choicest delicacy, is human flesh. This, indeed, is the purpose of the entire event: drinking the blood and consuming the inner organs (especially the heart) of a fellow being—preferably a newborn child. Infanticide and cannibalism, nothing less.

"Oedipodean intercourse" makes a second part of the rumor: sexual orgies in which parents and children or brothers and sisters become partners. Incest, blatant and vile.

Finally, suffusing the rest, "black magic": the use of charms, spells, and invocations to wound, to spoil, to deform, to coerce. This is among the most familiar and notorious accusations against Christians; Lyons is but one of its many venues. As tension mounts, the municipal authorities take action. The city's governor is temporarily absent, but his tribunes (local magistrates) meet in their offices beside the Forum and announce a new policy. From now on the Christians must be confined and carefully watched. No longer will they be admitted to the public baths and markets. They are not to walk the streets and thoroughfares, except under close supervision.

But this is only a prelude. In the days to come, known Christians are dragged from their homes by mobs of irate citizens. Some are simply denounced and ridiculed. Others are beaten with whips and clubs, still others taken to the city walls and stoned. Their property is looted, their servants set free. Eventually, a large number are hauled to the central marketplace for a formal inquisition. The questions pour out in a torrent: Are you not among the accursed band of Christ-idolators? Have you joined in their forbidden feasts and orgies? Do you, like the rest of them, spurn the authority of the imperial state?

In the face of such extreme pressures, some yield, others stand fast. To confess is to risk the full wrath of the mob. To deny is to play the coward. To recant is to escape, at least for a time. In the end, most will be charged with treason and blasphemy, and cast into prison. Their fate will be decided upon the return of the governor.

These details reach us now by way of a long letter written after the fact by survivors of the Lyons "martyrdom." The letter begins with an address, "From the servants sojourning in Vienne and Lyons in Gaul, to the brethren in Asia and Phrygia, who have the same hope of redemption." It was meant, in short, for another band of Christians, residing far off in what today we call the Middle East.

At this point the Christian movement was just over a hundred years old. From ragged and uncertain beginnings in the aftermath of Jesus' death around A.D. 30, it had achieved strong gains. Its growth was especially marked during the early part of the second century, in the cities and villages between the Mediterranean and the Black seas, in Syria, in Egypt (around the ancient metropolis Alexandria), and (to a lesser extent) in Palestine. It had then begun to spread north and west into Roman Gaul. Lyons would quickly become the front line in this latest expansion, along with its sister city, Vienne.

Lyons had grown impressively during the previous decades. Originally just a small settlement of fishermen and boatmen near the point where the Rhône and the Saône rivers meet, it was colonized in the name of Rome as early as A.D. 43. There, a military garrison overlooking the river confluence would enable farther advance to the north. There, too, a nucleus of trade would rapidly develop. Soon the emperor Augustus would make Lyons the provincial capital. And his successor (and son-in-law), Agrippa, would create a network of roads reaching out in several directions from the town center—over and around the Alps, off toward the Pyrénées and beyond.

By the mid-2nd century, the city's population of perhaps 50,000 was divided into three districts. To the north lay the chief Roman settlement, with villas and barracks grouped around a large forum. To the west, on the back of a steep ridge, was the heart of the Gallic community; in its midst stood important public buildings, an amphitheater, and a terraced altar for worship of the emperor. Toward the south, straggling out on a narrow peninsula and along the opposite riverbank, was the lower city, home to numerous ship carpenters, sailors, porters, and tradesmen.

The people of early Lyons were remarkably cosmopolitan in spirit and diverse in origin. In addition to a large contingent of Romans (officials, soldiers, merchants), there were many immigrants from the Orient, especially the Greek cities of Asia Minor. Even the Gallic majority was a checkerboard of regional and local difference: peasants from the countryside both near and far, boatmen and traders from upstream sites beside the two major rivers. Latin was the language of state, and south Gallic dialects the main vernacular. Greek and Aramaic were also frequently spoken.

The city's economy was centered on trade; in virtually all sectors a market atmosphere prevailed. Grains, meat, and dairy products flowed in from the surrounding villages, and out again down the rivers. Craft production focused on ceramics and ironwares. There was wealth among the local aristocracy; there was poverty and vagrancy, too, within the ranks of the maritime workforce.

The culture of the city was no less variegated. Religious worship stretched across a remarkably wide range. The Roman gods came first: Jupiter, Juno, Minerva, and many others. State-run festivals, including veneration of emperors past and present, filled the calendar. But dozens of richly developed cults also clamored for attention. Among the various cult figures, some loomed especially large: Cybele, the Mother of Gods, of Phrygian origin but found in different guises all around the Mediterranean; Mithra, the Sun God; Isis, Osiris, and Serapis, brought by migrants from Egypt and now joined to Roman tradition; Bacchus and the Olympian gods of Greece. There were probably (though not certainly) some Jews at Lyons, as well.

And, finally, there were the Christians. These included many foreigners, recent arrivals from the much larger Christian communities across the Mediterranean. A few had attained some prosperity and local distinction—a physician, a public advocate—but most were of modest social position; some were slaves.

Regarded at first as members of a minor Jewish sect and thus as targets for traditional anti-Semitism, Roman Christians had gradually forged a separate identity. But precisely for that reason, they seemed worrying, and threatening, to their neighbors. More than Jews and devotees of the foreign cults, Christians set themselves apart. Living in what they thought of as the Last Times, and thus in full expectation of an approaching apocalypse, they declined to conform with common standards. On the contrary, they viewed the world around them with a hostile eye. Rome itself was for them a seat of idolatry, the new "Babylon." Throughout the empire, they saw ominous signs of Satan's influence growing apace, just as forecast by their Scriptures for the premillennial years.

In the eyes of the public at large, such attitudes seemed deeply subversive. Christian disdain, Christian clannishness, Christian proselytizing all bespoke a "conspiracy" gnawing at the entrails of the empire. Moreover, the details of Christian worship were uniformly horrifying. At regular intervals their members would gather for a rite called the Eucharist, which included deliberate acts of flesheating. Another of their ceremonies was the Agape—the "bond of love"—performed at night, in private homes, in order to achieve a mutual state of spiritual ecstasy. But not only spiritual—physical, sensual, sexual, too! And openly promiscuous, setting aside even Nature's ancient prohibition against intimacy within families.

Given all these elements—conspiracy, revolution, sacrilege, cannibalism, black magic, incest—the Christian movement posed a grave and gathering danger. The great gods, on whose protection the empire and all its citizens relied, would surely be angered; this, in turn, might bring catastrophe. According to one observer (writing some years later), it was widely assumed that "Christians are the cause of . . . every disaster that afflicts the populace. If the Tiber floods, or the Nile fails to, if there is a drought or an earthquake, a famine or a plague, the cries go up at once: 'Throw the Christians to the lions!'"

In the middle decades of the 2nd century, fears for the future of the empire began to merge with actual events. "Barbarian assaults" were launched at several points along the frontier: in the east, by the Parthians (in what is present-day Iran), and, to the north, by Germanic forces crossing the Danube and pressing down toward the Alps. Most were thrown back during the decade of the 160s, but at severe cost to the victors. Plague, carried by returning soldiers, would soon ravage entire populations in and around Rome itself. Military struggle bred political conflict; the new emperor, Marcus Aurelius, was forced to repel direct challenges from his own generals. Moreover, the prosperity of the early 2nd century would gradually erode. Trade slowed, debt rose, the ranks of the poor increased.

These darkening conditions obtained, to a greater or lesser degree, throughout the empire. And they helped build a rising tide of persecution that was directed mainly against Christians. In 166, there was a brutal killing, of the bishop of the church at Smyrna. Similar violence occurred at Gortyna (on Crete), in Athens, and in Philadelphia (today Amman, the capital of Jordan) at the eastern end of the Mediterranean. Other sites of martyrdom included Christian communities in the Anatolian Pontus, and perhaps Rome itself.

After some months, the imperial governor returns to Lyons from his journeying. Now he will hear the charges against the city's Christians. A crowd gathers at the amphitheater; the prisoners are brought in. As the hearing goes forward, a local dignitary named Vettus Epagathus can stand it no longer and asks to speak on their behalf. They are innocent, he says; there is nothing "atheistic" or "impious" about them. But he is shouted down by the onlookers. The governor demands to know if Vettus is himself a Christian; he admits to at least a sympathetic interest, and is immediately condemned. The crowd mocks him as "the comforter of the Christians."

Witnesses are summoned, including some who have been slaves in the households of the accused. Threatened with physical harm, they confirm the reports about their masters: again, the focus is "Thyestian feasts" and "Oedipodean intercourse." At this, the crowd turns furious. Several among the accused, in their terror, deny their faith. But others are ready to confess, and suffer the consequences: a deacon from Vienne named Sanctus, a Roman named Maturus, an immigrant from Pergamon named Attalus, a local slave woman named Blandina. All are subjected to grievous torture: burning with heated brass, stretching on the rack, beating and choking. Presently the bishop of their church—one Pothinus, said to be "over ninety years old and very weak physically"—is dragged before the governor. Refusing to recant or yield in any way, he is savagely clubbed to death.

The proceedings continue for many days before an increasingly maddened public. And a new element is added: forced combat with wild beasts. Maturus and Sanctus are badly injured this way. Attalus is paraded through the amphitheater behind a placard on which is written HERE IS ATTALUS THE CHRISTIAN; *later he will be torn apart by lions. The slave Blandina's steadfast faith serves only to goad the crowd to ever greater ferocity; after hours of excruciating torment, she is "thrown to a bull" and gored to death.*

Eventually the governor, armed with new instructions from Rome, orders the beheading of "all who appear to possess Roman citizenship," and sends the rest "to the beasts." But even this is not the end of it. The corpses of the victims are devoured by dogs or cast into the fire. And whatever yet remains is "for many days watched with a military guard . . . all unburied." Again the mob gathers; some "rage and gnash their teeth," others "laugh and jeer . . . saying 'where is their god, and what good to them was their worship?' " When six more days have passed, there is one final burning, with the ashes "swept into the river Rhône"—to foreclose the chance that "they might ever rise again."

◆ ◆ ◆

To repeat, all of this comes to us from a remnant of Lyons Christians who somehow survived. Thus it reflects their viewpoint, their feelings—their sorrow, horror, outrage, pride. But how would it be remembered by the large majority of citizens who were pagan? The latter left no direct record, but one can easily imagine . . .

The Christians have gotten what they deserve. Their shameful beliefs and practices place them wholly beyond the bounds of human community. They are atheists—devils—saboteurs—scum. And they must be destroyed.

CHAPTER II

Witch-hunting Panorama, 150–1750

Perhaps it seems ironic that a history of witch-hunting should begin with the persecution and martyrdom of the early Christians, for the later parts of this history will feature Christians on the opposite side—as themselves the persecutors and martyr-*makers*. There may, however, be some dynamic linkage here. Done-to becomes done-by: such reversals are not uncommon in groups as well as individuals.

Admittedly, the parallels are inexact and incomplete. The early Christians were an actual, easily identifiable community, whereas the "witches" of late medieval and early modern times were no such thing. Still, in both cases, the element of scapegoating loomed very large. In both, highly stereotyped images rooted in fantasy served to energize a horrific chain of events. Both expressed a strong anti-conspiratorial bent, a conviction of dark doings hatched in secret places with deeply subversive intent. And both, finally, drew upon a similar reservoir of feeling: terror, rage, revulsion, hatred.

Of course, it took many centuries to accomplish the change from victims to victimizers. Christianity had to move from its initially be-leaguered position—move, that is, in two directions, both *in* toward the center of the empire and *out* toward the margins of what was then called the civilized world. The conversion of the Emperor Con-stantine, and his founding of the city of Constantinople in 330 as a new Christian nucleus; the decrees of another emperor, Theodosius, which in effect equated orthodox Christian practice with good citi-zenship; the gathering momentum, from the 4th century onward, of missionary work among "pagan" peoples both within and beyond the imperial borders; the piecemeal assimilation during the 5th, 6th, and 7th centuries of "barbarian" conquerors (Goths, Franks, Visigoths) to Christian faith and culture; thus the leading milestones enroute to eventual hegemony.

There were also deep challenges to confront and setbacks to overcome. Some reflected internal strains: for example, the proliferation of "heresies" (Gnosticism, Manichaeism, Pelagianism, Arianism) and the great schism that gradually divided East and West (Byzantium and Rome). Others came from outside, especially the steadily encroaching presence of Islam. The overall range of Church authority would contract significantly between the 6th and 13th centuries, as the Holy Land (Palestine) and adjacent parts of the Mediterranean east, Asia Minor, North Africa, and southern Spain passed into Muslim hands. Still, throughout its European heartland, Catholic Christianity gained and held the role of a state religion.

This was, in most regions anyway, a patchy landscape. Bishops, priests, and other clerics shaped doctrine, maintained Church properties, and sought to control worship practice, usually with some official backing from secular princes and potentates. Popular religion was another matter: Among the vast ranks of the pre-modern peasantry, Christian faith remained relatively shallow, and was variously interwoven with many still-lively vestiges of paganism. For most it was chiefly about "works" and ritual observance: attending Mass, genuflecting to religious authorities, going on pilgrimage, venerating the saints (or living "holy men"), and so on. Thus, as one historian has written, "it could complement rather than compete with animist beliefs and practices."

Local cult activities, passed down from pre-Christian times, survived more or less intact in many areas. Typically, they focused on a host of immediate and practical concerns: crop fertility and weather; love, sex, and reproduction; protection of health and property; and all the vagaries of human relations. In some cases they included the worship of pagan deities; the Greco-Roman goddesses Hecate and Diana seem to have been particular favorites. These two were associated in popular belief with nocturnal rites—especially for women who might be magically transported over long distances through the use of special unguents or powders (or simple broomsticks). Indeed, this was a world in which magic of all sorts proliferated and flourished: philtres, potions, charms and incantations, the use of "sympathetic" imagery, fortune-telling, conjuring, and countless other practices so humble and obscure they left no traceable record. The substances used to arouse love, for example, included herbal potions and powders, pulverized bones, ashes, bathing water, menstrual blood, hair (especially pubic hair), and human feces. There were, moreover, specialists in such matters, known in everyday parlance as "cunning folk." In centuries to come these would become targets of increasingly dark suspicion; but throughout the Middle Ages they operated quite openly and, at times, with genuine public appreciation. To consult them, to follow their prescriptions, was simply part of everyday survival.

In the same milieu flourished sorcery, though this was always harder to see and to specify. *Maleficium,* the performance of harmful acts by supernatural means, was perforce a secret thing; we can glimpse it now only indirectly, through the manifest fears of those who wished to suppress it (for example, religious authorities) or to counteract it (the many ordinary people who considered themselves its victims). Often enough when misfortune struck—when the harvest failed, when hailstorms hit, when people or livestock mysteriously sickened—neighbors would turn on one another with accusations of dabbling in "the black arts." We cannot tell, from the distance of a dozen centuries and more, where the truth lay in any specific case. We can, however, be sure that the idea of sorcery had wide currency. We can also infer that in such a climate of belief and opinion, some individuals must have tried their hand at it: must have fashioned the charms, cast the spells, uttered the curses, conjured the spirits against all manner of rivals and antagonists.

We can assume, finally, that one person or another within a local context would over time have gained a reputation for the practice of sorcery. Such a person would be feared, would be despised and condemned (at least in private), yet would also be treated with a certain respect. He—or, more often, she—might upon occasion become the focus of intense suspicion. The most likely stimulus was a particular experience of loss and suffering among the people who lived nearby. At such times the suspect might be forced to undergo rigorous efforts of scrutiny—perhaps leading to some official penalty (fines, incarceration, flogging—even, in rare cases, execution) or else to personal assault (up to and occasionally including a lynching, as we might call it). A lesser, and presumably more common, response would be the deployment of counter-magic: spells, charms, and the like, used in a protective manner. In some cases there need not have been anything "counter" at all; the supposed victim would simply approach the alleged perpetrator with a direct plea for redress. The result would be a kind of negotiation, ending, if all went well, with comity restored.

People of this reputation could be found in every corner of Europe from the 5th through the 15th centuries. Variously called *striga* or *masca* or *vala,* they can all be covered well enough by our own term "witch." Usually, they were thought to cluster in families: a mother, a daughter, a granddaughter. Their powers and status would, in effect, be hereditarily transmitted. The danger they seemed to pose was considerable; yet it was not limitless. For long periods it could be managed, or at least mitigated. Witches and witchcraft belonged, then, to the regular business of life in pre-modern times.

Christianity's relation to all this was ambivalent; tolerance, not to say complicity, was frequently the norm. Individual priests might even double as conjurors, dispensing what were essentially magical remedies alongside their regular parish ministrations. It is also clear that some of the Church's own devotional practices closely resembled traditional magic: for example, prayers for saintly intercession; the veneration of sacred relics for the purpose of cure or other personal benefit; the hallowing of particular landscape sites; the use of outright charms like the widely-found *agnus dei* (a wax medallion made from paschal candles). Individual worshipers could move with

relative ease back and forth between such ostensibly Christian maneuvers and the nostrums and devices of the "cunning folk."

If this were the entire story of religion, magic, and sorcery during
the early Middle Ages, there would be no particular denouement
looming several centuries ahead—no point at which concern for
witches would shoot upward and outward with such explosive force
as to create a veritable "witch-craze." But, in fact, there is more to
the story, quite a lot more. And most of it involves the further evolu-
tion of the Christian Church.

Above and beyond its local operations, the Church was involved
in a lengthy struggle for self-definition that would increasingly engage popular culture around witchcraft, diabolism, and the foundations of faith itself. Its core was nothing less than the problem of evil:
how to account for the myriad, often surprising, always unsettling
adversities that attend every human life. Its beginnings predated the
Christian era. The Old Testament and related rabbinical texts had
presented Satan (a Hebrew word meaning "obstructor") as a lively,
sometimes menacing, presence. Here, indeed, lay the origins of the
idea that the Devil was a fallen angel—once a leader among God's
deputies and princelings, but now His most determined enemy. Also
in the pre-Christian era, and also directly foreshadowing some elements of Christian belief, classical Greek culture had posited the existence of *daimones* (demons), a category of supernatural beings that,
in effect, mixed evil with good in roughly equal proportions. In fact,
the chief gods of Greece on the their Olympian heights were similarly mixed—as much inclined to selfish wrongdoing as earthbound
humans.

It fell to Christianity to move these traditional understandings in
a drastically different direction, toward a far more basic dualism.
The Christian God was conceived from the outset as the essence of
perfection; how, then, to connect Him with any manifestation of
evil? Yet the pervasiveness of evil, the *power* of evil, seemed undeniable; hence the necessity of a separate force, an opposite cosmic prin-

ciple, to explain it. The all-good God, with His all-good Son and "host" of ministering angels, *versus* the all-bad Devil and his own demonic "legions": around this vast dichotomy would centuries of Christian thought and feeling revolve. Inevitably, there were logical difficulties at its center. A substantially empowered Devil meant, to just the same extent, a *dis*empowered God. The concept of divine omnipotence clashed directly with that of divine beneficence; church-based groups (and individuals) would be obliged somehow to split the difference. The orthodox position was generally a middle one, a partial or "modified" dualism that affirmed God's absolute power, while also (and in some contradiction) acknowledging wide scope for Satan to work his worst in human affairs. But again and again during the first millennium, this formulation would be challenged, usually by way of a more radical and complete dualism. In branch movements like Gnosticism (of the late 2nd and 3rd centuries) and Manichaeaism (3rd, 4th, and 5th centuries) God's perfection, purity, and power were fully counterbalanced by the forces of evil. Moreover, the same tendency would reemerge in numerous other "heresies" later on.

It was, then, within the frame of a modified dualism that mainstream Christianity would continue to grow. And along the way it would continue to confront enemies, both within and without. There was the ancient city and culture of Rome itself, that "seat of Babylon." There were the Jews, initially coreligionists but quickly recast as bitter antagonists. There were pagans of every sort. Such persistent adversarial conditions meant that the dualist viewpoint was continually reinforced; the other side, whatever its particular coloration, could easily be linked to Satan—or at least to Satan's "influence." Moreover, the sufferings of the early Christian martyrs, an essential ingredient of Church history, sharpened the issue by personalizing it; the stakes were literally life-and-death. Monasticism was another significant ingredient. Monkish "fathers," in their desert retreats, launched a long train of patristic literature in which stark confrontation with Satan—temptation by Satan—assault by

Satan—was fundamental. The writings of St. Augustine, especially his *Confessions* (composed circa A.D. 400), and later his masterpiece, *The City of God* (413–26), epitomized this theme. God and Satan; angels and devils; this world and the next; heaven and hell; the sacred and the profane; the spirit and the flesh; the saved and the damned: thus a whole panorama of dualisms, amongst which lowly human believers, caught in the midst of a cosmic battle, must somehow find their way.

Pagan gods and pagan ceremony could be fitted right into this overarching paradigm. And frequently they were. So were Gnostics, Manichaeans, and other "apostates" from orthodoxy. So, too, were sorcerers and "magicians" of various types. Magic had occupied a prominent, if ambiguous, niche in classical Greece and Rome. So-called low magic, performed by expert practitioners at the behest of clients seeking direct assistance from gods or demons (usually for morally dubious purposes), was roundly condemned by philosophers such as Plato. Yet "high magic" was something very different—was itself a branch of philosophy, embracing astrology, alchemy, and other forms of arcane knowledge, and affirming as its ultimate goal union with the divine. Early Christianity would, in any case, reject *all* forms of magic, and equate all with sorcery and paganism. The cumulative result was a lumping together of non-Christian beliefs— pagan, magical, heterodox, whatever—and a channeling of the whole into a rhetoric of highly ritualized invective. Solidified by the end of the 6th century, this rhetoric would be widely reinvoked, and repeatedly reinvigorated, for at least another 1,000 years. And within it, the figure of the witch would come to occupy an ever larger, more central, more menacing place.

Throughout the rest of the early Middle Ages, from roughly the 7th through the 10th centuries, organized Christianity seems to have held God and Satan in a kind of balance. Schismatic movements were, on the whole, less problematic than before. And witchcraft did not evoke the highest levels of concern. Still, it retained enough pres-

ence to prompt occasional sharp rejoinders from secular and ecclesiastical authorities alike. A pair of documents, separated by roughly
100 years in time, can serve to represent the overall range. The first,
carrying the imprimatur of Charlemagne, the greatest of the medieval Frankish emperors, was part of a "capitulary" (set of ordinances) issued to the Saxons following conquest of their territory in
786. In it, Charlemagne inveighed severely against "pretended sorcerers" and fortune-tellers; such persons, he said, deserved to be enslaved. He ordered the death penalty for anyone offering sacrifices to
the Devil (which might well be taken to mean one or another of the
traditional Saxon gods). He also prescribed execution for those who,
being "deceived by the Devil, shall believe, as is customary among
the pagans, that any man or woman is a striga . . . and shall on
that account burn that person to death." In short, it was the *idea*
of witchcraft, the belief *in* witchcraft, that mainly sparked the emperor's indignation. He himself refused to credit such belief, and
tried to suppress it in others. Indeed, he sought to halt the persecution of suspected witches by ordering dire punishment for their
persecutors.

A second such document, entitled the *Canon Episcopi*, comes from
the beginning of the 10th century. This was also a capitulary, anony-
mously authored in the name of the Church and addressed particularly to "bishops and their officials." Its opening part denounced "the
pernicious art of sorcery," and urged that "followers of this wickedness" be "ejected" from their home communities. Another section
turned to a more specific problem: the "illusion . . . [of] some wicked
women, perverted by the Devil," that they rode at night with
Diana, "the goddess of the pagans," and her "demon" followers—
supposedly for the sake of performing "her service." The *Canon* ex-
horted parish priests to "preach . . . to the people that this . . . [is] in
every way false," not to say a mere "phantasm . . . imposed . . . [by]
Satan." All who believed it showed blatant "infidelity," and, in effect,
rejected "the one true [Christian] God."

The *Canon Episcopi*, like Charlemagne's edict to the Saxons, can be seen as a kind of way station along the route to the full-blown witch-craze. It suggested, first of all, that paganism remained a considerable presence in 9th-century Europe, and that a fertility goddess like Diana might still command a large following (indeed, as the document said, an "innumerable multitude"). It made Satan responsible for "deluding" and "seducing" those followers. And it equated their situation with apostasy. At the same time, however, it scorned the specific beliefs involved—especially night-riding and ceremonial "service" to Diana—as "phantasms." Finally, it proposed as punishment for "pretended sorcerers" not death, not physical torture, not incarceration, but simple banishment. It seems, therefore, a relatively moderate response, at least when compared with what came later on. Indeed, as the first millennium ended, a far-seeing observer could scarcely have imagined that witchcraft might one day become an overwhelming, society-wide preoccupation. But perhaps the same observer could have identified certain predisposing tendencies, most especially a readiness among many of his contemporaries to link witchcraft and magic with apostasy and heresy—and all of these with the work of the Devil.

The belief in magic, including *maleficium,* was a continuous presence in pre-modern Europe; but it did wax and wane over time. The 11th and 12th centuries were a period in which it waxed. This was when Europeans began to recover the philosophy, science, and other "classical" learning of ancient Greece and Rome (largely by way of Arabic texts), including a considerable infusion of high magic. Once again such "mystic arts" as alchemy and astrology would gain a wide following, especially among the educated elite. And once again ecclesiastical authorities would rally on behalf of their faith against what they viewed as a deeply pernicious challenge.

The fundamental issue, as before, was that of divine power, since magic presented its own claims to contact with, and control over, supernatural forces. And the result was decades of highly agitated controversy, as proponents of high magic sought to reconcile their viewpoint with Christian tradition while at the same time disavowing connections to low magic (everyday sorcery and its accoutrements). Church leaders, for their part, rejected any such distinction and fervently reasserted the "diabolical" grounding of magic in all forms. The entire tradition of patristic writing—from its distant progenitor, Augustine, through its chief medieval exemplar, Thomas Aquinas—was united around this theme: magic as superstition, magic as subversion, magic as sacrilege.

The same disputes would be periodically renewed and reenacted, especially in the 15th and 16th centuries, as the appeal of high magic was itself renewed. Indeed, magic would find important new venues with the gradual development of a monarchical "court culture" in many parts of Europe. Wherever kings, princes, their families and retinues, plus assorted factotums and hangers-on, competed for influence, magicians of various types—high, low, and in-between—would find a welcoming niche. Within this steadily growing demimonde, conjurors, necromancers, fortune-tellers, alchemists, and soothsayers might be expected to offer just the sort of advantage needed to push one or another courtier ahead.

Seen in very broad perspective, the late medieval Church had entered a new terrain of heightened vulnerability. For even as it struggled to fend off magic on one side, it faced a rising tide of heresy on the other. The small and scattered "Reformist" movements of the 10th and 11th centuries yielded in the 12th to the far more severe challenge of Catharism. This amounted to virtually a separate religion, with its own institutional structure (including a dozen different bishoprics) and a geographical reach across much of France and Italy. Its doctrinal basis was a deep-seated dualism, with good and evil principles radically counterposed. (In some versions Satan was cast as a fully independent deity.) For the Catholic establishment, Catharism could only seem Devil-inspired; yet its own dualist tendency drove the Church at least partway in the same direction.

Another large heretical movement, Waldensianism, would form near the end of the 12th century; it, too, had a dualist slant. And there were numerous lesser deviations as well. (To name just a few: Amalricians, Joachites, Luciferans, the Brethren of the Free Spirit, the French pastoureaux, organized groups of ritual flagellants, and adherents of the so-called dance manias). The struggle around and against heresy would continue, at least intermittently, throughout the 13th and 14th centuries. Within mainstream Catholicism, its cumulative effect was to create an especially vivid and pejorative set of stereotypes. Heretics were increasingly viewed as outright Devil-worshipers, acting in secret, given to ritual "orgies" and "abominations" (abortion, infanticide), conspiring all the while to undermine true faith. Moreover, in many of the same times and places, other stereotypes also strengthened—of Jews as kidnappers and ritual murderers of infants, of lepers as willful contaminators of entire communities—with savage pogroms as the direct result. Taken together, these trends have led some to characterize late medieval Europe as a "persecuting society."

Finally, the ancient stereotype of the Devil was itself in constant process of enhancement and embellishment, so that by the close of the Middle Ages an elaborate diabology was in full view. For one thing, the nomenclature proliferated enormously: Satan, Lucifer, Beelzebub, Leviathan, Mephistopheles, the Prince of Darkness. For another, the physical imagery became elaborate, vivid, grotesque, and shocking. Traditionally represented in animal form—a serpent, a goat, a dog, a wolf—the Devil would henceforth be portrayed as a monstrous hybrid, combining elements of both human and animal appearance with the darkest, most twisted fantasy. Horns, hoofs, tail, body hair, wildly contorted limbs, piercing eyes, ravenous mouth, pointed ears: thus the makings of a kind of inverse iconography, in painting and sculpture no less than in words. As a result the figure of the Devil would come to seem not only larger and more hideous, but also more immediate and personal. And because Romanesque art forms spread to all parts of medieval Europe, especially its cathedrals and churches, this impression was popularized as never before.

In sum, three highly charged images converged here: the magician, the heretic, the Devil. Each was a focal point of both popular and learned belief; each was distinct in some respects, yet was tightly linked to the others. And alongside them stood the witch: also focal, also distinct, also linked, and so positioned as to draw both shape and substance from all the rest. Indeed, many of the same elements appeared almost indiscriminately across this entire spectrum: secrecy, conspiracy, blasphemy, monstrosity, inspiration by the forces of evil.

As time passed, the picture of witchcraft would gain strength from a growing emphasis on its *collective* aspects: shared rites, nocturnal meetings (the so-called *sabbat*) to renounce God and Christ, particular strategies of witch-to-witch recruitment, the making of an explicit "pact" with Satan. Indeed, without the *sabbat* and without pact, witch-hunting on a grand scale would hardly have been conceivable. The former was, for the most part, a creation of medieval Catholic culture; its roots are obscure, but may well have included at least the distorted memory of pre-Christian fertility cults (like those attributed to Hecate and Diana). Pact, for its part, was perhaps the single most energizing notion of all. Endlessly elaborated by learned theologians from the 12th century onward, it would in most versions include a formal rejection of the Christian God, a corresponding pledge of allegiance to the Devil, and a transfer of maleficent powers to the witch—variously sealed by a kiss (on the Devil's backside), by the affixing of a special "mark" (on one or another significant part of the witch's own anatomy), or by sexual intercourse. It was pact that transformed witchcraft from a matter of simple *maleficium* into apostasy and heresy, from individualized and localized sorcery into a massively generalized "plot" to destroy God's plan for the universe.

Taken as a whole, the concept of witchcraft joined popular tradition with the most elevated religious doctrine of its age. A long
spectrum of attitude and belief stretched from the witch in one's
midst—personal, domestic, all too familiar—to the broad philosophical problem of evil and the Devil's unending war against God.
It was, finally, witch-*hunting* that fused these different elements and
rooted them in particular times and places.

That some proceedings against witches occurred well back in the
Middle Ages there can be no doubt: witness the concerns expressed
in Charlemagne's capitulary and the *Canon Episcopi*. But, with rare
exceptions, records of these have not survived. What has survived,
from the early and middle decades of the 14th century, is evidence of
rising alarm over witchcraft, magic, and heresy—directed at (and
by) leadership groups in both church and state. For example, in 1317 a
French bishop was burnt at the stake for allegedly using witchcraft
in a plot against the life of Pope John XXII. In subsequent years the
same pope brought similar charges against others among his Church
adversaries. (Moreover, on two occasions he aided investigations of
sorcery thought to have been aimed at French kings.) Meanwhile, in
England, the Bishop of Coventry was tried for having made a pact
with the Devil (and was barely acquitted); and King Edward II repeatedly accused his political opponents of practicing witchcraft
against him. In Ireland, as well, political feuds led straight to witch
trials—most famously in the case of a noblewoman named Lady
Alice Kyteler. Caught in the midst of long-standing animosities
among several prominent Irish families, Lady Alice was charged
with murdering three successive husbands by witchcraft and in-
capacitating a fourth; in addition, she was thought to have led a
Devil-worshiping cabal and to have consorted frequently with an
"incubus" (copulating demon). Her trial took place at Kilkenny in
1324–25, under the general supervision of the local bishop. Though
she herself made a timely escape to England, many of her alleged associates were seized, convicted, and variously burnt alive, whipped,

imprisoned, or banished. Her considerable wealth wound up mainly in the hands of her accusers.

The list of individuals brought to trial in roughly the same time period includes others of high rank: a French abbot (1308), an English earl (1330), an Italian viscount (1320). Even a pope, Boniface VIII, was accused of being a sorcerer and entertaining a "familiar" spirit (1303). But most sensational of all was the state-sponsored, Church-abetted assault upon the so-called Knights Templar, spanning nearly a decade (1306–15) and touching many different parts of the continent. In the early 12th century, the papacy had constituted the Templars a military order under monastic rule; their mission was to protect the gains of the several medieval Crusades to the Holy Land. As time passed and the Crusader realm fell to Islam, the order was no longer linked to its original goals. Instead, it grew into a large, virtually free-standing, institutional edifice of extraordinary power and riches; in France especially, its activities supported (and profited from) key elements of the state. Inevitably, it aroused envy and acquired enemies in both the ecclesiastical and the secular establishments. Then, as the 14th century began, the French king, Philip VI (known as "the Fair"), set his eye on the Templars' wealth. With the off-and-on collusion of Church leaders and some direct assistance from the papal inquisition, Philip used the courts to bring the order down. The charges lodged against it ran a broad gamut from heresy to Devil-worship, from magic to witchcraft. By 1320 the Templars were finished as an organized body, with dozens of their leaders executed and their vast properties confiscated to shore up the monarchy.

This 30-year spate of politically motivated trials at the highest levels of society was unique; never again would the searchlight of persecution point so steadily and distinctly at monarchs, nobles, popes, bishops, and their ilk. It was, to be sure, somewhat blurred in its focus. Witchcraft was invariably a part of it, and was sometimes at its center; but heresy and magic were also frequently in the mix. Moreover, the specifically diabolical aspects, while present, did not overshadow the rest; pact, for example, appeared only to a limited

extent. In the meantime, witchcraft among the common people remained a small and scattered affair. Occasional trial proceedings,
amounting to an average of barely one per year for all of Europe,
around isolated suspects, and with little impact beyond a single village locality: such was the pattern throughout most of the 14th
century.

But with the century's last decades came the beginnings of
change. Trials increased in both quantity and scope; by the 1430s the
continent-wide average had virtually tripled. The reasons for this are
at best a matter of speculation, yet certain possibilities seem obvious.
The Black Death, a massive outbreak of plague, spread across Europe
starting around 1350; periodically recurring thereafter, it brought suffering and death on an unparalleled scale. (Overall depopulation
reached at least 30 percent.) Meanwhile, too, France and England
plunged into what became known as the Hundred Years' War, a series of on-and-off conflicts that took its own massive toll in blood and
property. With so much of life in disarray, authorities of all sorts
stood open to questioning by those to whom they had traditionally
offered protection. Thus it was hardly coincidence that this period
brought chronic rebellion among peasants and other marginalized
groups in many parts of the continent; their superiors responded,
not surprisingly, with fear and sometimes with brutal acts of repression. The immediate reverberations of such large trends need not
necessarily have centered on witchcraft; Jews, for example, were the
first group to be scapegoated in the Black Death. Still, disease, warfare, and rebellion would inevitably sour the climate of life almost
everywhere. And this, in turn, might set a stage for witch-hunting as
well as pogroms. (Moreover, in some specific cases, witches were
depicted first and foremost as rebels, reflecting the widespread fear
of social uprising.)

There were other contributing factors as well. Heresy seems, on
the whole, to have declined after the mid-14th century. The Cathars
and the Waldensians steadily shrank in both numbers and influence;

their remnants survived chiefly along the mountainous margins. Alarm about heretics, together with much associated imagery, was then refocused on witches. Central to this process, now as before, were the linked notions of pact and *sabbat*. As pact rose in importance, so, too, was its character changed. Instead of being a bargain between equals, it was increasingly construed as an act of submission in which witch-recruits acknowledged the fundamental supremacy of Satan. By the same route, Satan's role and power were substantially elevated; previously taken as a foil to Christ the Son, he now became a match for (and opposite to) God the Father—and thus a plausible object of full-fledged idolatry. The *sabbat,* for its part, was reframed as an elaborate worship performance, with traditional Catholic elements directly inverted (the Black Mass, and its "devilish" accompaniments). Witchcraft as an organized, Satan-centered antithesis to Christianity—here was heresy indeed!

Changing legal practice also played in. The main trend was a gradual shift from an "accusatorial" and "interpersonal" system, in which court proceedings were initiated and carried through by private parties, to an "inquisitorial" and "bureaucratic" one, with public authority at the center. The earlier pattern had left the chief responsibility for prosecuting crime, including witchcraft, to its supposed victims; the later one took crime as a matter of generalized civic concern. Specifically, this meant that judges and prosecutors (or "inquisitors") would take the lead by gathering up informal suspicions, conducting investigations, bringing charges, evaluating proof, and—not least—imposing penal sentence. (A prime example was the Inquisition itself.) The result was a significant widening of the door to witch-hunts.

A further widening came from the increased use of torture as a means to gain evidence, especially confessions. Because witchcraft could be viewed as a *crimen exceptum* (extraordinary crime) that threatened the very foundations of community, physical coercion seemed allowable, even (under some circumstances) necessary. And proof was so elusive that, as a contemporary theorist explained, "not one out of a million witches would be accused or punished if regular legal procedure were followed."

As these changes went forward, witchcraft cases moved from being the exclusive concern of the Church toward shared jurisdiction with the state; indeed, secular courts would sometimes take the lead. Finally, in most parts of Europe before the 17th century, such courts operated locally or regionally, without much oversight from central authority; in effect, they could do as they pleased. This, too, went in the direction of widening.

During the period between 1450 and 1500, the numbers of the accused continued to rise; a careful accounting of recorded trials shows a tenfold increase as compared with the previous century. By now, too, the conceptual picture of witchcraft had largely filled out while spreading continent-wide. Its main vehicle was the new print literature. Learned treatises on its theological and philosophical context, as well as practical "handbooks" for local inquisitors bent on actual prosecutions, proliferated widely—and constituted, indeed, a publishing genre virtually unto itself. The most famous of all witch-centered works, the *Malleus Maleficarum*, appeared in 1487. But there were others scarcely less important; taken together, they served to codify and publicize witchcraft on a grand scale. Their authors were, in nearly every case, drawn from the ranks of the educated elite: clerics especially, but also lawyers, scientists, philosophers, and other "humanist" intellectuals. To read these works was to enter some of the most learned discourse of the time. Moreover, they were used more and more in actual trial proceedings; thus they helped forge a crucial link between local, everyday witchcraft and witchcraft as highly elaborated demonology.

However, their impact was felt more in the long than in the short run. The *Malleus*, for example, would be read and cited as much as two centuries later—and by Protestants as much as by Catholics. Yet the years immediately following its publication saw relatively modest levels of witch-hunting. Indeed, the period from about 1500 to

1560 represented a kind of pause in this long and turbulent history. Witch trials were a continuing occurrence, with significant outbreaks in northern Italy and the Basque country. But in France and Germany, their past and future center-points, they hardly appeared at all. For Europe as a whole, the sum of prosecutions leveled off—and may actually have fallen somewhat.

Perhaps not coincidentally, the same period brought an eruption of religious conflict of completely unprecedented scope, as the Protestant Reformation (usually dated to Martin Luther's 1517 posting of his *Ninety-five Theses*) evoked the Catholic Counter-Reformation and an ensuing, intense competition in both the spiritual and the secular realms. The connection of all this to witchcraft was important but uneven; essentially, it followed a two-stage sequence. For several decades after the start of the Reformation, the energy previously devoted to witch-hunting seems to have lessened—drawn off, as it were, into the bitterness of sectarian struggle. It is striking, for example, that wherever such struggle resulted in open warfare, witch trials would decline dramatically, or even (temporarily) disappear. Conversely, the return of peace was likely to bring renewed attention to witchcraft. These correlations are not perfect, but do seem strong enough to imply some form of underlying, and dynamic, linkage.

This history has reached one of its most critical turnings, the start of the "craze" phenomenon in the second half of the 16th century. For roughly the next hundred years—albeit with considerable variance between different geographical regions—Europe and the British Isles were preoccupied with witches, witchcraft, and witch-hunting as never before or since. The following pages treat the *period* essentially as a unit. At the same time, however, they divide the *subject* into a number of descriptive and interpretive sections, each framed by a leading question.

Sequence. **What was the typical progression
of events in witchcraft cases?**

Always and everywhere, charges of witchcraft were grounded in
a web of local, intensely personal relations. Even episodes that
would ultimately grow very large started small. A quarrel between
neighbors—about cattle, about crops, about the terms of trade or the
payment of debts, about the boundaries of fields or social space,
about more bits and pieces of everyday experience than could possibly be enumerated here—thus was a seed sown, a process begun.
One quarrel would probably not be enough; but here and there, one
became two, or three, or several. Resentments built, angers festered;
these, in turn, might lead to an exchange of threats and cursing.

Then a new factor entered: misfortune and suffering for one or
the other party. A sudden, inexplicable illness in the family (most often a child); the death of a cow (also sudden, also inexplicable); the
disappearance of valued property; a surprise failure in work or human relations: another innumerable range. Now there would be
worry, doubt (including self-doubt), and a vexing, perhaps obses-
sively held, question: *Why? Why me? Why this?* The previous quarrels
were remembered, and configured in a new way: *Might she have . . . ?*
And yet it took time to make a witch—time, and many quarrels, and
a growing cluster of suspicion-laden victims. The end result was the
forming of a reputation: *Beware of her; she has a wicked spirit—"malice
and envy" in her heart—and she has "powers."*

Sooner or later would come a tipping point. The quarrels would
become so frequent and bitter, the misfortunes so troubling, that an
actual accusation would be voiced: aloud (previously it was muffled),
in public, in a local court. From here on, events would follow a legal
track. The basic charge would be *maleficium,* injurious action performed by supernatural means; sometimes, not always, there would
be additional reference to compacting with the Devil. Testimony
would be taken from a large group of witnesses. The suspect would

be formally charged, arrested, committed to prison. There she would be examined, both physically (for the so-called marks of a witch) and verbally (for evidence of ill will, unbelief, or "evil connection"). A trial would follow, with all the evidence presented anew. At the end, a verdict would be rendered: guilty or innocent. There might, or might not, be an appeal. The suspect, if convicted, might try to flee, might commit suicide, might effect some form of plea bargain by confessing and implicating confederates. But, far more likely, she would suffer the official penalty prescribed in such cases: possibly imprisonment, probably execution by hanging or burning at the stake.

Thus the bare bones of witchcraft's "smaller" cases, in which there was little or no need for follow-up. When the trial ended, a balance was restored, and life in the local community could proceed as before. Yet this did not mean that witchcraft would entirely drop from view. For there would be other suspects—who might or might not prompt other trials, depending on the circumstances. Virtually all pre-modern communities held a little pool of possible or probable "witches"; indeed, a village or town would hardly have seemed complete without them.

The bare bones' version is exactly that; actual cases would add a wealth of place- and person-specific detail. There might be other participants beyond the principals—in effect, a supporting cast. Sometimes "cunning folk" would receive and respond to a direct appeal from the victim(s); this might involve confirming the witch's identity or suggesting a remedy for particular forms of "affliction." Sometimes physicians would be needed to rule out natural causes. In certain contexts, clergy would come to the home of those most centrally involved to offer prayers for divine guidance and intervention. And a corps of associates and neighbors might enlist on one side or the other—to support, or rebut, the charges against the accused. In this way an entire community could be galvanized, and mesmerized, by the supposed operations of witchcraft, for weeks or months at a stretch.

At the other end of the witch-trial spectrum stood the full-fledged "panic" outbreak. This meant witch-*hunting* in a much more concentrated form. Sometimes it would grow out of an initially limited case, with a single suspect then joined to others in a steadily widening spiral. But sometimes it depended on the organized effort of inquisitors or "witch finders." Most often, the latter were clergy; yet secular authorities would usually run close behind and act in direct collaboration. The mood in such cases was most definitely one of panic, as accusations piled rapidly on one another. A central element was confession by the accused, for this would nearly always bring forth the names of fellow witches. And crucial to obtaining confession was the purposeful use of torture (or at least the threat). Common methods included various forms of physical distension—stretching on a rack, for example, or being strung up in midair by a device called the "strappado," a pulley system roped to the arms—or else of compression, by means of clamps or screws attached to head, legs, thumbs, and other sensitive body parts.

Episodes of panic witchcraft raised the stakes at every level. The emphasis would shift from *maleficium* to diabolism—from specific moments of personal injury and distress in a particular victim, to broad-gauge, Devil-inspired conspiracy against all of Christendom. Just here, the idea of *sabbat* would prove especially powerful. What the inquisitors most wished to hear, and what the accused did frequently provide, was detailed information about this utterly blasphemous nighttime proceeding—with the Devil himself in full charge—and including not only a parodied version of the traditional Christian sacraments but also naked dancing, sexual orgy, ritual infanticide, and gluttonous feasting on human flesh.

The process of concluding a panic outbreak, with its invariably high toll in lives taken or radically disrupted, is hard to discern from several centuries later on. It must often have involved some form of retreat, with the details left unrecorded. Perhaps there came a point of sheer exhaustion. And probably there was a sense among some in positions of authority that events had gone far enough, if not already too far. Occasionally the spiral of accusation might seem to have overreached itself by touching certain quite unlikely targets (persons of high social rank or previously unquestioned moral character). Then, one way or another, those at the center would decide to stand down.

Time and Space. **How was witch-hunting distributed, chronologically and geographically?**

The great European witch-hunt, as it has occasionally been called, was not a single, sustained continent-wide event. To the contrary, it was actually a series of events, an assortment of somewhat smaller hunts, loosely linked and raggedly distributed through time and space. Meanwhile, village witchcraft in the old sense, locally sited and modestly scaled, continued basically as before, though its specific occurrence would be increasingly obscured by all the new and spectacular "panic" outbreaks.

There was, throughout, a heartland of persecution in north-central Europe, including much of what was then the Holy Roman Empire and is today Germany, Switzerland, northeastern France, and the southern part of the Netherlands. This region, with somewhat less than half the continent's population, seems to have produced roughly three-quarters of its witchcraft prosecutions. Additional centers of major witch-hunting were spotted farther to the north and west, in Scotland and Denmark, and to the east, in Poland, Hungary, and Transylvania. More moderate levels of involvement could be found in England, Sweden and adjacent Finland, central and southern France, Spain, and northern Italy.

There was also a peak period of witch-hunting as measured simply in quantitative terms, lasting from approximately 1580 to 1650. And, within that stretch, the years 1610–30 produced an especially massive bulge. But, again, there were other peaks both earlier and later. Some parts of southwestern Germany experienced panic witch-craft as early as the 1560s. On the other hand, Sweden's peak did not come until the late 1660s and early '70s. Poland had barely started with witch trials in 1650, but then maintained a high rate through the end of the century and even beyond. And in the Bavarian region of southern Germany, trials continued, sometimes with considerable intensity, until at least 1750.

As this brief summary immediately suggests, it is only when space and time are brought together that witch-hunting begins to look at all patterned. On the one hand, political fragmentation and the coexistence of small, chronically struggling state entities seem to have been especially conducive to panic witch-hunting. The Holy Roman Empire itself was vulnerable this way, with its inherent institutional weakness and its messy internal patchwork of quasi-independent units (duchies, principalities, counties, bishoprics). On the other hand, political integration and strong centralized gov-ernment seem to have worked in the opposite direction—that is, largely to restrain witch-hunting. In France, seat of the continent's most advanced monarchy, witch trials occurred only to a moderate degree—with the significant exception of certain borderland regions (Normandy, Lorraine) where the hand of royal government was weakly felt. In short, the presence or absence of broadly effective state authority does suggest one element of patterning.

On the temporal side, it seems clear that the 1580–1650 period brought extraordinary forms, and levels, of hardship to much of Eu-rope: a persistent inflationary spiral and periodic depression in trade; the start of a wrenching transition to commercial agriculture, with much resultant dislocation and dispossession for large elements of the peasantry; recurrent political turmoil, including local revolts, re-ligious and civil wars, and even national revolution; harsh climato-logical change; and epidemics of plague with accompanying famine. These broad tendencies, while impossible to correlate with particular bursts of witch-hunting, helped create an atmosphere of anxiety and suffering within which such events might more readily occur.

A narrowing of focus to smaller territorial units brings a sharper, more differentiated image into view. In Scotland, for example, there were major peaks in the early 1590s, again at the end of that decade, and also in the late 1620s, the late 1640s, and the early 1660s. None of these lasted for more than a couple of years, and the long intervals between them were virtually devoid of witch trials outside the most limited, local context. The Scottish peaks can be more or less directly linked to political upheaval; the first two, indeed, seem to have been instigated by the monarch himself (James VI), while the later ones reflected struggles within the governing elites. In southwestern Germany, a particular hotbed for witch-hunting, peaks occurred in 1594, in 1611, and, most extensively, between 1627 and 1632. However, what the German situation especially reveals is the importance of single-community venues; only in such connection can clear patterns be established. Thus Wiesensteig experienced a witchcraft panic in 1562 and again in 1583, Ellwagen in 1611–13, Baden in 1627–31, Esslingen in 1662, and so on. Here the causal chains run more to specifically local events: outbreaks of disease, periods of famine, internal factionalism in the aftermath of warfare. Occasionally, witch-hunts would spread from one place to another, as if by a kind of contagion. But most places within the same general region produced a quite distinctive profile of witch prosecutions over time; this was true even of close neighbors.

Scope. **How many people were prosecuted— and how many lives were taken—in witch-hunting?**

There is no way now to reach exact conclusions about the number of individuals directly involved in the "craze." Records from the time have been lost, and were imperfectly kept to begin with. Any broad total is perforce a composite of figures for numerous different places and regions, some of which have not yet been carefully studied. At best, therefore, the available numbers are estimates.

But such numbers have been a source of much interest and speculation for a very long time—indeed, for as far back as the craze period itself. Inquisitors were eager to gauge the size of the enemy's forces, and confessing witches would frequently try to assist them. In 1570 one such confessor warned the French king of 300,000 Devil-followers mustering around his realm. Several years later Henri Boguet, a respected judge and demonologist, used that figure to project a total of 1,800,000 witches for Europe as a whole; moreover, Boguet commented, witches "are everywhere, multiplying upon the earth as worms in a garden." *Sabbat* attendance was often a special focus here: witch-hunters wanted to know, *how big a crowd?* The answers varied widely, between a few hundred and many tens of thousands per gathering.

The point is that for people of the time witchcraft seemed *huge*—quantitatively huge. And historians followed their lead. Thus, until not so long ago, a figure of 9,000,000 was widely accepted as the total of executions from witch trials. Recent studies have, however, drastically scaled this down; now most estimates fall in a range of 50,000 to 100,000. The most reliable regional subtotals come from the British Isles (about 1,000, with at least half of those in Scotland), Switzerland (about 5,000), and France (about 4,000). The various German territories would, presumably, account for much the largest number of all—probably in excess of 20,000.

Note that the overall range is meant to cover the entirety of Europe before, during, and after the craze period. And remember, too, that it includes executions only. In fact, executions represent only a rock-bottom minimum of witchcraft involvement. People arraigned and tried—in short, all the defendants—would make a separate, much larger category. The best modern scholarship suggests a ratio for tried to executed of approximately two to one. But this is just an average; one must assume great variation around it. In many German communities gripped by "panic" outbreaks, a summons to trial would be a virtual sentence of death. By contrast, a substantial majority of English cases resulted in outright acquittal.

The sum of actual trials was, then, probably between 100,000 and 200,000. And most trials engaged a large roster of participants: defendants, first of all, but also prosecutors, judges, bailiffs, jailers, and witnesses—plus an unrecorded host of keenly interested spectators. (There were special subcategories as well: for example, "witch-prickers" and "searchers," experts called in to test mysteriously insensitive spots on a suspect's body or simply to find the Devil's "mark.") Take all such groups into account, and the total of those involved increases by some exponential amount. Consider, finally, that many who were never officially brought to trial lived nonetheless "under suspicion" and likely were subject to periodic harassment or even to informal, unsanctioned attack. Under such conditions people might think about witchcraft, talk about witchcraft, worry about witchcraft, and act against witchcraft at almost any time.

Hence the field of experience *around* witchcraft was, to repeat, huge. The threat itself seemed huge. And the response would, necessarily, be of matching dimensions.

Participants: the accused. **What sorts of people did witch trials especially target, in such terms as sex, age, marital status, economic and social position, and personal character? In short, who *were* the witches anyway? Did they, taken as a group, present a coherent profile?**

Few questions in witchcraft study have seemed as obvious, important, and controversial as the one about gender. The bare facts are thunderously clear. The vast majority of accused witches were female; the Europe-wide proportion was approximately 80 percent. To be sure, a not-insignificant minority—and a group that included some very striking individuals—was male. (In at least a few particular

venues, accused men approached or actually reached a majority.)
Moreover, the prevalent pattern of demonological thinking did not
ostensibly single out women; a witch might, in theory at least, as
easily be male as female. And the Devil himself was certainly male,
as were many of his attendant "demons." Still, in practice—and practice does count most of all here—a witch was typically a woman.
Put differently: suspicion of witchcraft was sex-related, if not fully
sex-determined. Was this perhaps the result of patriarchal social
structure?

It is clear enough that pre-modern Europeans took male dominance as a given, at least in a formal sense. Men were the leaders in
many key sectors of routine experience: in community life (especially as "governors" of one sort or another), in family life (as "heads"
of households), in law (where men alone could initiate judicial proceedings), in religion (as clergy), in cultural life (as authors, philosophers, artists, and poets). The prevalent modes of Christian belief
furnished direct validation here; as the playwright John Milton famously put it in *Paradise Lost*, "he for God only, she for God in him."
Yet there were definite countertendencies. Women exerted their
own forms of influence—for example, in their homes (as caregivers),
neighborhoods (as overseers of moral standards), and local market-
places (as purveyors of essential goods). Moreover, women's lives
overlapped men's at many points; a wife might serve, in almost any
arena, as her husband's deputy. At the same time, women would
everywhere form social groups (and work groups) limited to their
own sex; these, too, carried influence. Indeed, clusters of neighbor-
women would often appear at the center of witch trials—as accusers
of other women.

But if social structure does not help very much to explain the
woman-witch equivalence (again, equivalence *on the whole* and *in
practice*), ideation gets somewhat closer. From time out of mind,
European cultural tradition had affirmed a broad-gauge principle
of masculine superiority. Men were, according to this tradition, simply stronger and better than women: in physique, in powers of

"reason," in moral instinct. The difference was a matter of degree rather than kind; men had *more* of the key attributes that defined and elevated humans above the animal world. This was the essential point in speaking, as pre-modern folk endlessly did speak, of women's inherent "weakness," of their being "the weaker sex." And, for certain, it had much to do with witchcraft. Women's weakness made them vulnerable to the Devil's attentions; in effect, they lacked the mental and moral strength to resist him. In this connection the biblical story of Eve, tempted by the serpent and thus made "first in sin," was seen throughout European Christendom as paradigmatic.

However, the explanatory power of European cultural tradition carries only so far. For witch-hunting was, and is, a *cross*-cultural, *trans*historical phenomenon—an attacker, a killer, of women almost everywhere. In present-day Africa as well as the Far East, among pre-modern Native Americans no less than pre-modern Europeans, witches have been "found" mainly among women—sometimes overwhelmingly so. There must be a reason that goes beyond the cultural and the historical.

And there is: enter the psychological. Witchcraft embodies, in each and every one of its otherwise disparate settings, a basic impulse of misogyny—a fear, and a hatred, of women so generalized that it crosses virtually all boundaries. This includes the boundaries of gender itself, for women are misogynous, too. According to current developmental theory, the roots of such feeling lie buried deep in our psychic bedrock; they reach back, indeed, to our first experiences of life. Because in every known society women are primary caregivers to infants, those first experiences and the unconscious traces they leave behind put female presence squarely at the center. A mother—a woman—is the primal Other, the nonself from which self is progressively distinguished; further, she disposes a kind of absolute power to meet, or reject, infantile need. As such, she retains forever afterward an "aura" of what a discerning psychologist has called "magically formidable" qualities. Moreover, much of this weighs inevitably on the downside: the Bad Mother, who denies and displeases, alongside the Good Mother, who nourishes. The link to misogyny, and from there to witchcraft, is obvious; what more apt modifier for a witch than "magically formidable"?

At the same time, another part of these inner-life foundations seems clearly sex-defined. Male anxieties about woman-power— as expressed in sexuality, menstruation, and, most especially, childbearing—are patent through much of the old demonological writing. The evident disconnect between such power, on the one hand, and the formal structures that affirmed male dominance, on the other, might readily generate worry and tension, and a sense of weakness—specifically in men.

This tableau is perhaps too brief to be more than suggestive— and needs, in any case, a few modifiers. First, the woman-accusing-woman aspect of witch trials is worth underscoring; for this, more than anything else, undercuts arguments centered on simple patriarchy. Second, the woman-witch equivalence was very clear in the small, fully localized cases, but had some tendency to break down whenever "panic" attitudes took over; then the trendline of accusation might shift somewhat to encompass increasing numbers of men. Third, those men who did find themselves accused, in whatever context, were often linked to women who had previously fallen under suspicion. They were the husbands or sons of supposed witches, and thus could be seen as contaminated by close contact. Indeed, they were subject to a quite literal process of guilt by association.

From sex we turn to age. There is, of course, a hoary stereotype to reckon with here: the figure of the *elderly* witch, the "old hag." The stereotype is accurate only in part. True, a disproportionate number of convicted witches were on the "old" side; quite a few were age 60, 70, or more. Still, many others belonged to what we would call the midlife cohort. Moreover, when the focus is shifted from court trials and convictions to suspicions and accusations, the age median drops substantially. Most of the accused seem to have acquired a reputation for witchcraft—an important benchmark—as early as their 40s and 50s. From such beginnings a chain of events might then unwind, until time and accumulated suspicion brought official charges—and a summons to trial.

The pattern here reflected deep discontinuities in the life-cycle experience of early modern European women. A good many would be widowed during or after the middle years, and thus left in an impoverished situation; henceforth they would constitute a burden on their families and communities. At the same time, and somewhat paradoxically, a smaller subgroup—the widows of well-to-do men— might suddenly assume independent control of property, in direct contrast to prevailing norms. Either way, such women might become targets of resentment and suspicion. And either way, they lacked the protective influence afforded by male next-of-kin. In fact, the extant records do suggest that widows were disproportionately represented among accused witches. But even without being widowed, women in midlife were obliged to absorb a profound loss of status, as menopause brought an end to their childbearing years. The same cultural traditions that had hitherto affirmed—even celebrated— their role in "replenishing the earth" (the biblical phrasing) would now declare them "barren." As such, they could be presumed to harbor feelings of dispossession, not to say raw envy.

Other attributes of the accused can be presented more simply and categorically. Most were poor, many quite wretchedly so. And most were drawn from well below the "middling ranks" in the traditional social hierarchy. (There were also, as previously noted, important exceptions.) Finally, many, if not most, were regarded as being of unpleasant, abrasive character: too self-centered, too quick to anger, too "meddling," too "covetous," and so on. These descriptors proved especially telling when applied—as they were applied, again and again—to women. To be sure, they came largely from the testimony of accusers; but where there was so much shared opinion, there may also have been some reality behind it. Clearly, the wisest course in early modern community life—especially for a woman—was to blend in and *not* to seem too openly self-assertive. To be, or to behave, otherwise was to open oneself to suspicion of witchcraft.

Participants: accusers and victims. **What sorts of people would
typically take the lead in accusing others of witchcraft?
And who were most often the victims?**

In a sense, almost anyone was potentially an accuser of witches.
For belief in, and fear of, witchcraft was virtually universal in pre-
modern Europe. Given so many different venues, spanning such a
long period, individuals of every stripe would somewhere, sometime, be cast as accusers.

Most conspicuous of all were those who led the way in full-
fledged "panic" witch-hunts. They could be clerics, including popes
(such as John XXII), bishops, and priests of lesser rank (or ministers,
in the case of the Protestants). They could also be secular authorities, ranging from crowned monarchs (James I of Scotland, Philip
the Fair of France) to zealous bureaucrats (Nicholas Remy, a publisher and prosecutor in French Lorraine, and Wolfgang Kolb, a frequent "interrogator" in southern Germany, among many others).
Some were self-appointed "witch-finders"; two such, Matthew Hopkins and John Stearne, orchestrated virtually by themselves the big-
gest single panic outbreak ever to occur in England (during the early
years of the Puritan *interregnum,* roughly 1645–47).

Behind the leaders in the process of accusation marched many
followers, ordinary folk whose interest and anxiety was easily mobilized. They were the ones to provide personal testimony on particular suspects and the details of *maleficium.* For the most part, they
seem an indistinct mass of frightened, beleaguered souls, revealed
to us now through a screen of heavily doctored legal and ecclesiastical writings. Generalizations about them can only be suggestive,
nothing more. Still, the special importance of female accusers is,
as previously noted, quite beyond doubt; to repeat here, a women-
against-women dynamic was fundamental to many witchcraft cases,
especially those playing out at the village level. However, men were
also everywhere involved, and not just as leaders but also as part of

an accusing chorus. Strikingly, in certain contexts children might play the critical role. A Swedish witch panic of the 1670s that claimed some 200 lives featured accusers as young as seven or eight. And lesser panics in the Basque country, in Poland, and in some parts of southern Germany also appear to have included children at, or near, the center of things.

It goes almost without saying that many accusers were also victims of witchcraft (or so they believed), and vice versa. Yet the match was less than total. Some victims were not in a position to speak for themselves: infants and the very youngest children especially. In such cases a parent, or another adult, would have to bring charges on their behalf. (Of course, parents might well feel personally attacked by the witch-induced "affliction" of a beloved child.) Other supposed victims included some who had already died, some who were too sick or injured to come forward, and some who were perhaps too frightened. Conversely, certain groups of accusers were not usually victims themselves: for example, many of the official prosecutors, inquisitors, and "witch-finders."

Victimhood invariably spanned a broad range of experience, and its emphasis might differ greatly from one setting to the next. Yet the importance nearly everywhere of youthful victims is impossible to miss. Injury, illness, and death among the young appeared again and again, along with moments of interference in the care of such victims (difficulties in breast-feeding, for instance). Add to this the matter of reproductive failure—an inability to conceive, miscarriage, still-birth—which might be, and often was, attributed to witchcraft. Add, furthermore, another kind of productive (not reproductive) mischance: crops that withered on the vine, cows that wouldn't give milk, fields that didn't yield as expected. Roll them together, and the common denominator throughout was nothing less than human, and environmental, fertility. Witches were thought to target fertility above all else.

Today we can mostly take fertility for granted. We use our knowledge of reproductive biology and the mechanics of contraception to control procreation. And we manage environmental productivity through a parallel combination of science and technology. How different the lives of our pre-modern forebears! For them procreation was always a matter of deep randomness and mystery—the work of "providence," nothing less. The connection between sex and pregnancy was but partially understood, if not *mis*understood; for example, widely prevalent opinion rated the menses as the most likely time for a woman to conceive. Individual families and whole communities struggled constantly to maintain a delicate reproductive balance. A dearth of newborn children, or an epidemic that struck at the young with particular force, could threaten group survival into the future. And so could an excess—by creating too many mouths to feed, from too-scarce resources. On the environmental side, much depended on the success of the annual harvest. In some years there was plenty, in others want; and whatever made for the difference was largely beyond the reach of human contrivance.

Thus, in one life sector after another, fertility was all—with uncertainty, anxiety, a fear of failure, as its regular accompaniments. No wonder the links from fertility to witchcraft ran so deep and spread so wide. And no wonder the witch-craze years coincided with the climatic period of the so-called Little Ice Age and with what historians of northern Europe now describe as both a severe demographic squeeze and a widespread "crisis of subsistence."

Community. **How did witchcraft reflect the shapes and structures of community life?**

The most common venue for European witchcraft was a rural village of perhaps 100 households, covering a territorial expanse of a dozen square miles—with a traditional peasant economy and largely self-sustaining, but also in some regular contact with its nearby surroundings. The single, most striking aspect of everyday experience in such a place was sheer social density. All families and all individuals were directly known to one another; life proceeded at every point on an up-close, face-to-face basis. Witchcraft, too, was up close and face-to-face. Accusations were almost never directed toward strangers; instead, the culprit would likely be a neighbor, would certainly be an acquaintance, and might even be an erstwhile friend. Where so much else was personal, suffering and victimhood would logically have a personal cause: *she* did it, *he* made it happen— not fate, or environmental mischance, or vast social and economic forces.

"Panic" outbreaks, in attaining a much larger scale, followed a different pattern. The setting for many of these was not a peasant village, but rather a town or a small city. Such was true during the craze period in southern and central Germany, where most of the major witch-hunting centers were places of considerable size (perhaps 1,000 households, plus or minus) and at least partially urban character (including some involvement with commerce as well as agriculture). There accusations would begin to spiral by outgrowing the level of personal animosity. Strangers were often accused; indeed, this was key to the spiraling. Whereas the social density of village life might breed an initial round of suspicions but then limit their spread, the somewhat looser structures of the town could actually encourage panic episodes. Accusations would multiply where, and because, the element of personal connection was less likely to serve (sooner or later) as a source of restraint.

Meanwhile, still further out along the same spectrum, the truly large cities of the period—London and Paris, for example—saw relatively few witch trials of either the ordinary or the panic type. In their case, experience was so impersonal and diffuse that the old forms of *ad hominem* suspicion could hardly take hold. Rapid population turnover, the differentiated and complex urban economy, the growth of bureaucracy, the general atmosphere of life *en masse:* such factors, individually and together, served as antidotes to witchcraft.

These points lead to another important and controversial question, that of "functionalism." The term, and the concept, belong to modern anthropological study, from which witchcraft historians have borrowed quite liberally. The question is whether witchcraft was to some extent advantageous—hence "functional"—for the communities in which it lay embedded. And the answer is decidedly mixed: yes, maybe, no, and sometimes quite the contrary.

Witchcraft served, first of all, to line out crucial boundaries of behavior. The figure of the witch epitomized and personified evil. To trace that figure in detail was to identify the particular qualities deemed most negative by the community at large; hence, in a very basic sense, witchcraft belonged to the realm of moral philosophy. But this element extended beyond simple boundary marking, to embrace boundary *maintenance* as well. The fear of being labeled a witch undoubtedly influenced individual conduct, for persistent wrongdoing would invite such labeling. Even victims of witchcraft could come under suspicion; neighbors might ask, why have these particular persons been singled out for attack? Thus did moral philosophy mutate into a potent instrument of social control.

And it went further still. The presence in a village community of a suspected witch worked both to deflect hostility from other targets and to concentrate blame, like a boil on the body that pulls in toxic fluids. To bring the suspect eventually to trial was, in effect, to lance the boil and release its toxicity. Court proceedings were in most instances a highly collaborative affair; neighbors took action as a group, and so reaffirmed their common bonds. The action was shared, the goals were shared, the feelings (fear, excitement, relief) were shared. And when the proceedings were over—especially if the witch and her wickedness had been fully excised—the community felt a sharper, more unified sense of itself. Put differently: it was cleansed.

This is admittedly a too-simple and schematic view; the reality of particular cases could easily become much more complex. Communities were not always of one mind about a suspect; if she had determined defenders, a trial might leave deep residues of bitterness or outright division. Furthermore, with panic witch-hunts it is hard to see any positive social function at all. Beyond the toll in lives lost, there would be massive disruption of familiar routines: work stopped, trade frozen, governance bent out of shape. In large-scale cases, witchcraft might tear a community apart and leave such devastation in its wake that full recovery would take decades or generations.

The picture, then, is truly ambiguous: sometimes gain (for the group, obviously not for the accused and her kin), sometimes severe, even catastrophic, loss. That witchcraft was deeply, elaborately threaded into the fabric of community life can hardly be doubted. But no single "functionalist" formula will stretch to cover the entire range.

Class. **To what extent, and in what ways, did class difference contribute to the development of witchcraft cases?**

Witchcraft could mean remarkably different things to different people. And class (or "rank," as people of the time would have said) was indeed a major divider. Peasants and all those who made a living with their hands approached witchcraft in an immediate, specific, fundamentally practical way—as a potential threat to everyday security. Particular forms of *maleficium* were their chief point of concern. Gentlefolk—in short, all who were *not* obliged to work with their hands—shared this concern but added to it a strong interest in the more broadly "diabolical" aspects, Satan's relentless machinations and the cosmic struggle between the forces of Good and Evil. And among the "gentle," a subgroup of the most literate and educated people, especially the clergy, placed the greatest emphasis on the diabolical; for them, *maleficium* was but a subordinate part of a much larger whole.

In the small-scale witchcraft cases, as noted already, the usual starting point was an accusation by one villager or several against another. However, in order to reach the point of an actual trial, and then perhaps a conviction, it helped greatly if prominent local leaders decided to add the weight of their own influence. It was, in many instances, a combination of interest from different social levels that proved decisive against the accused. Or it could go another way: an accusatory process might shut down at a certain point because community leaders withheld their support. At least occasionally, magistrates would directly refuse to validate some particular charge; then a verdict might be set aside and a defendant released. Throughout these oft-repeated dramas one feels a certain tension between the viewpoints of "common" and "gentle" folk. Sometimes they were fully aligned; sometimes they were at odds; often enough they mixed, and jostled, and eventually found their way to a middle ground.

Even among the ranks of the "common" there were finely graded distinctions between some who had a bit more and others with a bit less. A good many witchcraft accusations followed a pattern that some historians now refer to as "the refusal-guilt syndrome." One villager, in a state of evident need, would approach another to request assistance: some food perhaps, or drink, or wood for the fire, or simply a chance to perform paid work. Then the request was refused, for whatever reason: *We have not enough for ourselves; we've already promised someone else; we need to save for the future.* And this led to personal recrimination, including—so the refuser might later claim—threats by the refused: *I shall be even with you.* As a further step, the refuser would experience some "loss" or difficulty of a seemingly mysterious nature. From all of which he would draw the inevitable conclusion: *Witchcraft! She was angry, and spiteful, after I turned her away. And this is her revenge.*

In peasant communities across Europe an ethic of neighborly cooperation, and of charity toward those "in want," had governed daily life for centuries. So the refusal at the heart of this little scene constituted a breach; the refuser was left feeling guilty, and vulnerable, and perhaps (at some level) anticipating punishment. In fact, versions of the same sequence might appear in all sorts of contentious exchange, whenever the reasons for a person-to-person rebuff seemed questionable. But the refusal-guilt element, in particular, suggests a close link to traditional neighborly values—at a moment in history when those values had begun to erode. Especially in a place like Britain, as the first serious stirrings of market capitalism became evident, "individualism" was a growing cultural presence. And witchcraft cases took shape on the cusp of that momentous development.

The refusal-guilt pattern produced accusations that aimed down the ladder of social and economic status, from those a rung or two higher up toward others underneath. But there were also situations in which the aim went up. Perhaps a market-minded producer seemed overly self-regarding and "individualist"; he might then open himself, or members of his family, to charges of witchcraft "from below." This reminds us that witchcraft accusation was an extremely flexible and adaptable weapon: useful in some contexts for defending established positions and in others for launching a tradition-subverting attack.

Religion. **How did religious thought, religious commitment, and religious conflict intermix with witchcraft?**

Much of the energy behind the great witch-hunts during the "craze" period derived from a supercharged intensity about religion. As the Protestant Reformation proceeded past its initial stage and engaged head-on with the Catholic Counter-Reformation, ideas clashed, attitudes hardened, emotions strengthened on every side. Taken together, the two great movements served to Christianize and spiritualize European culture in ways both broad and deep. Their goals became fully evangelical; vernacular preaching exposed ordinary folk to religious and moral exhortation as never before. Gone was the old sense that religion belonged chiefly to specialists (priests and monks); henceforth, each individual soul must take direct responsibility for his or her spiritual condition. This was, of course, the doctrinal heart of Protestantism, but it was also evident in practice among newly energized Catholics.

In such a context, witchcraft loomed larger than ever. The appalling menace it presented would certainly extend to all branches of "true religion"; hence the need for vigilance was constant. Unbelief, apostasy, and sin in every conceivable guise were rolled together in the figure of the witch. And behind her, towering over her, stood the Devil himself; he, too, seemed more immediate, more personal, more dangerous than before. It was also important that the Bible be taken in increasingly literal ways. This included a famous line from the Book of Exodus: "Thou shalt not suffer a witch to live." The word itself was suffused with Satanic implication; "a witch" meant, first and last, a person sworn to do the Devil's bidding.

Both Catholics and Protestants contributed hugely to witch-hunting. Much of the supportive ideology, as well as strategy and tactics, was shared between them. The idea of diabolic pact, for example, held central importance on both sides. And torture was a prime instrument of persecution almost everywhere, with England as a notable exception. Still, it does seem that the quantitative profiles of witch-hunting—Catholic versus Protestant—diverged over time. Whereas in the 16th century their victim totals were roughly similar, in the 17th Catholics forged ahead while Protestants gradually fell back; the 10 largest witch-hunts at the height of the craze in southern Germany (1600–1630) were all based in Catholic communities. There were also significant differences of emphasis: Protestantism made much of the witch's individual relationship to the Devil, while Catholicism stressed its collective aspect, as exemplified by the *sabbat.* Catholic views were loaded with sexual preoccupation: *incubi* and *succubi* as "copulating demons"; promiscuous orgy as a feature of the *sabbat;* witchcraft as a cause of both impotence in men and infertility in women. The equivalent Protestant imagery downplayed sexuality but elevated the theme of sheer aggression: the "blasting" of crops and fields; injury to personal property and competence, and to lives.

Yet, once again, such differences fade when seen in any truly comprehensive perspective. For the most part, Protestant and Catholic witch-hunters—clergy and laity alike—worked in a competitive (if unacknowledged) tandem. Furthermore, differences *within* their respective ranks were sometimes much greater than those between. In fact, it would be wrong to see either Catholic or Protestant opinion on witchcraft as a monolith. Variable shadings of belief, and even quite basic structural contradictions, were present in both systems. Witchcraft theory was always a matter of debate and dispute; its leading parts could be, and often were, subject to shifting forms of interpretation. There were well-known, widely read skeptics and doubters: for example, the German physician Johann Weyer and the British country philosopher Reginald Scot. Weyer spoke for a considerable group of Continental thinkers, all of whom in one way or another rejected the usual claims made for witchcraft. The Devil, said Weyer, was even more powerful than generally realized and had no need whatsoever for assistance from human followers. Scot, on the other hand, argued that witchcraft belief implicitly slighted God's own stature, by attributing "to a creature the power of the creator." Both writers, and others too, decried the way hapless old women— in Scot's words, "lame, blear-eyed, pale, foul, and . . . poor . . . wretches"—were such frequent targets of witch-hunting. Most of the accused, they argued, had little means of defense, and some who confessed were simply deluded or deranged. Such strands of belief extended into the "craze" years the old, moderate *Episcopi* tradition, according to which diabolism was dwarfed by the reach and powers of Providence.

Governance. How did the predominant structures of civil authority engage with witchcraft—and vice versa?

The 16th and 17th centuries witnessed the birth of the modern nation-state. Within that era, a traditional and very medieval jumble of geopolitical arrangements—autonomous cities and towns, principalities, fiefdoms, duchies, baronies, bishoprics, kingdoms, and so on, right up to the vast but nebulous entity of the Holy Roman

Empire—began gradually to realign into a somewhat more orderly checkerboard of "states." Meanwhile, the powers of rule became concentrated in national or regional centers, where newly-expanded bureaucracies would exercise them on an increasingly regular basis.

Religious belief in general, and witchcraft belief in particular, helped fuel this evolutionary process. In most of the emergent states, ruling elites were eager to harness the influence of the church, whether Catholic or Protestant, to their own ultimately secular purposes; there was no easier way to acquire legitimacy. In Scotland, for example, a revised and refurbished monarchy used the arrival of Calvinism as the means to extend control over a previously fragmented citizenry. In England, too, monarchy was greatly strengthened by the establishment of a nationally based Anglican church. In Germany a raft of smaller state-units solidified themselves on the principle of *cuius regio, eius religio* (whoever rules, his religion): some were strongly Catholic, others just as strongly Protestant. Thus did Christianity, in one guise or another, serve as political ideology, redefining orthodoxy and helping to make state power felt at ground level.

Often enough, witchcraft would appear right at the center of this trend, alongside energetic programs of social reform. The drive for religious and political conformity imposed a kind of moral cleansing on the populace as a whole, with the figure of the witch held up as the quintessential subversive—the enemy incarnate—plotting against both God and the state. Put differently: the ideal of political order seemed virtually to require an antithesis of *dis*order; and witchcraft might conveniently serve that purpose. It was no coincidence that witch-hunting peaked in Scotland in the 1590s, when King James I (himself the author of a fervid demonological tract) was beginning his reign. And the same factors were at work in several of the major German witch-hunts of the early 17th century. Indeed, it seems reasonable to describe most of the latter as state sponsored, since secular authorities were usually at their forefront (albeit in close co-operation with church leaders).

Taking a very long view here, one can see the key role of privileged and powerful groups in large-scale witch-hunting. Whereas village witchcraft in the traditional mode would mostly involve persons of lower rank (who at least occasionally aimed accusations up, at their social betters), the great outbursts of the "craze" period were generally aimed down, from the rulers against the ruled. As such, they served to build and to reinforce enduring patterns of hierarchy.

Mentality. **How did witchcraft reflect, and contribute to, the prevailing worldview of its time?**

Of course, in some respects this question is answered by way of religion: witches as minions of Satan, as enemies of God. But behind and beneath such consciously articulated doctrine lay another level of popular belief—this one at least partly *unconscious* and *unarticulated*, yet deeply influential nonetheless. There, too, witchcraft played a central role.

Wherever found, witchcraft served as a favorite mode of *explanation* for painful and baffling experiences. Disappointment and failure could be conveniently attributed to witchcraft: failure in work (crops that didn't grow, cattle that didn't thrive, butter that wouldn't churn, beer that went sour in the basement barrel); failure, too, in human relations (unrequited love, broken friendships, not to mention the various neighborhood enmities that might lead directly to witchcraft charges). In short, here was a way to avoid, or divert, the burden of responsibility. To be sure, playing the part of witchcraft victim was itself a vexed, even risky, business, but owning up to one's personal shortcomings might feel much worse.

All such experiences belonged to what another historian has called "a world of wonders" filled with the manifestations of supernatural influence. In such a world little happened by chance; to the contrary, events of every sort were seen as caused, and motivated, in highly specific ways. Misfortune and failure—to consider that important problem once again—evoked a broad range of potential "reasons." Besides witchcraft, the chief possibilities included: God's punishment for sin, or some other, perhaps inscrutable, aim of "Providence"; the movement of the stars, the alignment of the sun and moon; human plotting, or some similar expression of malign intent; and various kinds of "natural"—or, as we would say, mechanical—forces. (To be sure, personal incompetence might also figure in.)

In confronting such a daunting array, the plain folk of Europe had long deployed a variety of countermeasures, including many designed specifically for protection against witchcraft. Traditional charms and invocations might serve, at the least, to hold anxiety in check: a horseshoe hung over a doorway, a bottle of urine thrown into the fire, a mysterious rhyme said aloud three times (possibly suggested by direct consultation with local "cunning folk"). However, the two great 16th-century reformations, Protestant and Catholic, sought to suppress the use of all such "remedies" as being themselves a form of magic. For many among the clergy, prayer and prayer alone, became the recommended response to witchery. But this, in turn, could seem disarming to some who received the recommendation. From then on they would have to face the onslaught of witch-enemies without their accustomed means of defense, and might turn instead to the courts. Thus did religious reform work, in yet another way, to stoke the fires of panic witch-hunting.

Emotion. **What was the range, and role, of emotional experience in relation to witchcraft?**

Emotions, those "primary motives of man," served everywhere to energize witch-hunting. Take emotions out while leaving the rest intact, and you have no craze certainly, and perhaps not much in the way even of small-scale episodes.

Always, to begin with, there was interest and excitement of extraordinary intensity. Mere talk of witchcraft sharpened the senses and elevated the pulse. Rumor and gossip about witches passed person to person, and neighborhood to neighborhood, in typ breathless tones. *Have you heard? Did you see? Be sure to look out for . . .* Then, as matters proceeded, with charges made and evidence heard, the level of feeling rose higher still. *Would you believe? Can you imagine? At last we understand. . . .* Finally came the verdict; if it was *guilty as charged,* death would usually be the prescribed punishment. The resultant execution scenes were nothing less than high drama, replete with confessions (sometimes), further accusations (occasionally), fires rising, bodies burning or hanging, lives ending, as large and fascinated crowds looked on. *How shocking! How uplifting! How terrible! How just! . . . God's will be done. Amen.*

As to the witch herself, the predominant imagery expressed a range of deeply-rooted, intensely negative feeling. She was motivated—so people thought—by a special kind of jealous anger, what (in British cases) was formulaically called "malice and envy"; here, indeed, was her emotional wellspring. She would act as she did because she resented—no, *hated*—her victims, and coveted their "goods." Moreover, the Devil himself, her patron and leader, was invariably depicted as a fount of "infernal wrath."

Perhaps accused witches were, in actual fact, unusually angry folk; the record suggests as much, but scarcely proves it. What seems more clear is the way they drew out anger from their accusers and victims. To bring a suspect to trial was, of course, a hostile, and potentially murderous, act. The process can be reconstructed, in psychological terms, as follows. A quarrel with a suspected witch leaves her supposed victim feeling angry and wishing to attack. But the victim cannot easily own up to such feelings, and so unconsciously assigns them to his or her adversary. She or he then proceeds to a formal accusation against the intolerably "angry" witch. This maneuver allows the victim to have it both ways: the unwelcome affect and the inadmissable wish are indulged and disowned at the same time.

But anger was far from the whole of it. No less important was fear—or, to use a stronger, more apposite term, outright terror. Witches and their works were nothing if not terrifying. The threat they posed was enormous: to health and safety, to livelihood, to the very preservation of life. Moreover, in psychological terms they endangered the foundations of the self. By targeting fertility and the whole realm of human generativity, they stirred deep concerns about personal adequacy and efficacy (and its obverse, helplessness). The threat was cosmic too; the Devil and his legions would, if they could, destroy all that gave life meaning. Hence those who cast themselves as witchcraft's victims presented, in their various testimonies, a virtual catalogue of fear-filled hours, days, years—much of it reflecting the very substantial ways in which emotion might distend and distort their experience. Victims gripped by terror would blunder into all sorts of difficulty: would injure themselves or their property, would forget, would misjudge, would lose track. Sometimes their actual powers of perception might be compromised. Bewitchment might make them blind, or deaf, or mute (at least for a time); alternatively, they might see, hear, and feel things that weren't "really there." Moreover, at the extreme outer edge, even their ability to sustain life might be imperiled. Modern medical science recognizes a phenomenon, sometimes called "voodoo death," where extreme affective stress brings dire physiological change—in heart rate, in adrenal production, in the nervous, circulatory, and other key bodily systems. The eventual result can be a severe decline in blood pressure, leading finally to death from an acute state of shock. This process has been observed in present-day cultures where witchcraft belief remains strong. And it presumably explains at least a portion of the cases, from earlier times, in which people were seen as "bewitched to death." Thus would witchcraft prove, in a sense, directly efficacious; intense emotion, especially fear, created the means of its own confirmation. Moreover, the process was circular. Fear of injury by witchcraft led to actual injury—which, in turn, led to more fear—and so on.

Anger and fear, fear and anger: thus the two great emotional engines of witch-hunting. Without them this entire history would be different.

By the mid-17th century, the great witch-hunt had peaked. England endured a considerable panic in the 1640s, when Hopkins and Stearne prowled the countryside in search of "those who follow Satan." And (as previously noted) there would be similar episodic outbreaks across several parts of Europe in the decades to follow. But, as a whole, witch-hunting was set on a course of decline.

A current of skepticism about all such matters had been gradually building—first and foremost among the educated elite, for whom a "rational" religion (and way of life) would soon become *de rigueur*. Theologians were carefully refining their notions of God, so as to make His "superintendency" of the universe more orderly, more regular, more amenable to human understanding. Within this revised framework of belief, sudden and mysterious interventions caused by the Devil or witchcraft seemed less and less plausible. Nature itself was yielding its secrets to a new "mechanical philosophy" personified by the likes of Francis Bacon, René Descartes, Isaac Newton, Robert Boyle, and Pierre Bayle. Boyle's chemical experiments, for example, sapped the underpinnings of traditional alchemy. And the work of various other investigators served to recast understanding of magnetism and electricity, which had long been associated with occult influence, as the movement of microscopic particles.

Through all this intellectual and scientific advance coursed a new spirit of questioning, of what we now call empiricism. Demonstration, replication, proof: thus the hallmarks of a dawning "Age of Reason." The middle and later decades of the eighteenth century would carry the process several stages further. Then, in "Enlightened" circles such as those of the French *philosophes,* organized religion itself came under direct attack. Catholicism, in particular, was identified with the forces of reaction, and the witch-hunts of the preceding centuries were reinterpreted as both a cruel delusion and an instrument of Church-inspired oppression.

Inevitably, the law—and the entire panoply of judicial process—would reflect these elite-culture trends. In England, for example, a Parliamentary Act of 1736 repealed all previous statutes on witchcraft. It would be illegal henceforth to call another person a witch, or to harm him or her in that connection. Moreover, an open claim to possess magical powers might also lead to prosecution and imprisonment. In short, belief in witchcraft, rather than harmful *maleficium* itself, became the focus of concern; the act presumed that such belief was illusory, and pernicious in its public effects. Another statute, passed in 1824 and commonly known as the Vagrancy Act, further proscribed "pretending or professing . . . to tell fortunes, or using any other subtle craft, means, or device . . . to deceive and impose"; again it was "professing," not practice, that concerned the Parliament.

With these laws on the books, and with a generally skeptical attitude now well established among the ruling groups, formal prosecution of witchcraft became impossible. However, among country people in both Britain and continental Europe, old ways and old beliefs survived. "Cunning folk" would remain a strong village-level presence well into the nineteenth century. As before, their activities encompassed a broad range of folkloric and magical ministrations (including some expressly designed to counter witchcraft); at least occasionally they might be viewed as witches themselves. Moreover, where legal recourse was denied, putative victims and accusers could resort instead to informal modes of response: counter-magic, threats, petty harassment, shunning, and personal violence up to and including outright lynching. There were at least occasional "witch mobbings" in England throughout the 19th century, with one reported as late as 1945.

Even later, the idea of witchcraft hung on, and with it a propensity to "hunt" for perpetrators. This was true especially of small communities on the margins of modernity, where cultural developments, including education, did not much penetrate. Indeed, in such places vestigial remnants of the old belief system can be found right to the present: versions of the Evil Eye, for example, ritual cursing to achieve some malignant effect, and such seemingly bizarre notions as the "riding" of unfortunate victims at night, during sleep. Under certain conditions, village folk may yet feel inclined to personalize the source of their difficulties, and may then band together to punish individual suspects in their midst, through isolation and gossip (if nothing more).

Thus does the long arc of witch-hunting stretch from the 2nd century to the 21st, from Roman proconsuls to scattered groups of our own contemporaries. Though trending further and further downward over many successive generations, it has not quite reached its end point even today.

CHAPTER III

The Malleus Maleficarum:
A Book and Its Travels

1484; the town of Ravensburg (in what today is southwestern Germany, near the Swiss border). A team of Catholic priests, members of the Dominican order, presses forward with an investigation of witchcraft. Their leader is a dedicated and experienced inquisitor named Heinrich Kramer (sometimes Latinized to Institoris). Eight women are put on trial for causing injury to people and animals, and for raising "tempests" to destroy the harvest. This is, in fact, the culmination of a four-year campaign within the town and its satellite villages; the roster of the accused will eventually total 48. At least half this number, perhaps more, will be convicted and burnt at the stake.

From Ravensburg the witch-hunters move on to Innsbruck, a large Tyrolean community farther east. But here their reception is different. The resident bishop declines to support the charges they bring against several local women and derides Kramer as a "senile old man." After some weeks the accused are set free, and the inquisitors are forced to depart.

In fact, Kramer's efforts against witches have achieved only mixed results—success here, resistance there—in the dozen or so years since the papacy named him chief inquisitor for southern Germany. Thus, at some point in the early 1480s, he and his Dominican colleague Jakob Sprenger decide to seek a stronger mandate. They appeal to the newly installed pope, Innocent VIII, who quickly obliges them with a "bull" (official statement) that amounts to a license for unlimited witch-hunting.

"It has come to our ears," the pope writes, "that in some parts of upper [i.e. southern] Germany . . . many persons of both sexes . . . forsaking the Catholic faith, give themselves over to devils." These miscreants then use "incantations, charms, and conjurings" in causing all sorts of harm to

"men and women, cattle and flocks and herds . . . vineyards also and orchards, meadows, pastures, harvests, grains, and other fruits of the earth. . . . Moreover, they deny with sacreligious lips the faith they received in holy baptism." (The list of their "abominable offenses and crimes" goes on and on. And it seems strangely reminiscent, in at least some details, of the crimes attributed to the early Christians more than a millennium before.) To make matters worse, "certain of the clergy and laity" impede the work of "our beloved sons" (Kramer and Sprenger) in bringing such persons to account; hence "the aforesaid offenses . . . go unpunished." This situation cannot be permitted to continue; from now on the inquisitors will have free and full scope for "correcting, imprisoning, punishing, and chastising, according to their deserts, those whom they shall find guilty."

At about the same point, Kramer embarks on a further, and closely related, project: to prepare a book about his inquisitorial activities. Written in Latin, entitled the Malleus Maleficarum *(English translation:* The Hammer of Witches), *and published at Strasbourg in 1486, this work will come to be seen as an epitome of witch-hunting.*

The *Malleus* was not the first work of its kind—a list of witchcraft treatises from the preceding half century runs to more than three dozen—but it would become far and away the most famous. Read today, it seems very much a hybrid: part bible, part encyclopedia, part operational guide. It is long: some 400 pages in a mid–20th century reprinting. It is densely written, with lots of heavy scholastic verbiage: "Here is set forth" . . . "With reference to these words it is to be noted that" . . . "Firstly . . . secondly . . . thirdly . . . fourthly." Its expository method is basically that of a catechism, with questions raised (and answered), objections posed (and resolved), principles stated, "admonitions" tendered, conclusions declared. Its goal is to describe and analyze the entire panoply of witch-related phenomena, and to offer judges and fellow inquisitors a comprehensive model of response.

The book has three main parts. (Its preface is the pope's recent bull, republished entire.) The first part lays some theoretical groundwork—by establishing that disbelief in witches is rank heresy, by showing the irrevocable connection between witches and the Devil, by canvassing the numerous harms *(maleficia)* they bring, and by tracing their usual biographical profile (with special emphasis on their female gender). The second part describes the leading forms of witchcraft—its causal ways and means—and declares certain general principles of investigation. And the third part provides an exhaustive account of the legal steps to be taken against witches: details of charging, examining (including the use of torture), sentencing, and executing.

The argument builds and builds, through abundant reference to "authorities": to the Scriptures, most of all, but also to patristic sources (especially St. Augustine and St. Thomas Aquinas) and other demonologists from around the same time period, as well as to classical writers and philosophers with something valuable to say on the subject (Aristotle, Cicero, Seneca, Terence, Cato, and many more). It also invokes the "credible experience" of the authors themselves in pursuing their targets. As such, the *Malleus* is, from first to last, a compendium of stories: here are a few representative examples.

A young girl in the village of Breisach (near Basel, Switzerland) was "converted" to witchcraft by her aunt who "had [subsequently] been burned in the diocese of Strasbourg." This aunt "one day . . . ordered her to go upstairs . . . where she found fifteen young men clothed in green garments after the manner of German knights." She was then "sorely beaten" and forced to have sex with one (or more) of the men, and afterward was "initiated" into the Devil's ranks. During the following weeks and months she "was often transported by night . . . over vast distances" in order to meet other witches "in conclave." There she observed the ritual killing of infants; among other horrors, she recalled a time when "she had opened a secret pot and found the heads of a great many children."

A confessed witch "in the state of Berne" (Switzerland) also spoke of child-murder, and added to it the element of cannibalism. "We set our snares chiefly for unbaptized children, . . . and with our spells we kill them in their cradles or even when they are sleeping by their parents' sides. . . . Then we secretly take them from their graves and cook them in a cauldron, until the whole flesh comes away from the bones to make a soup which may easily be drunk. Of the more solid matter we make an unguent which is to help us in our arts and pleasures and our transportations; and with the liquids we fill a flask or skin—whoever drinks from which, with the addition of a few other ceremonies, immediately acquires much knowledge and becomes a leader in our sect."

A third story, from the German town of Regensburg, where Kramer's inquisition had just recently been active, expressed another theme very prominent in the *Malleus:* sexual dysfunction, supposedly caused by witchcraft. A young man, having broken off "an intrigue with a girl," suddenly "lost his member . . . so that he could see or touch nothing but his smooth body." During a visit to a local tavern, he lamented his loss to a fellow patron, who urged that he confront his former sweetheart and demand her to "restore to you your health." He did just that, but the girl protested her innocence; whereupon "he fell upon her, and . . . choked her," threatening her very life. At this, "She . . . with her face already swelling and growing black, said 'Let me go, and I will heal you.'" And she "touched him with her hand between the thighs, saying 'Now you have what you desire.' And the young man . . . plainly felt . . . that his member had been restored to him by the mere touch of this witch."

This last belonged to a much larger discussion—of witches, devils, and sex. The key questions included: "How in Modern Times Witches perform the Carnal Act with Incubus Devils"; "How, as it were, they Deprive Man of his Virile Member"; and "Whether the Relations of an Incubus Devil with a Witch are always accompanied by the Injection of Semen." Some of the answers were ingenious and mystifying (as perhaps befits such a literally Satanic subject). For instance: in order to effect their "abominable coitus," devils would assume bodily form "through condensation by means of gross vapors raised from the earth." Devils, and witches too, might then create "an illusion of glamor . . . to collect male organs in great numbers, as many as twenty or thirty members together, and put them in a bird's nest, or shut them up in a box, where they move themselves like living members . . . as has been seen by many and is a matter of common report." Indeed, the questions went on and on. Where did the semen used on these occasions come from? (Perhaps the Devil would collect what he needed from "nocturnal pollutions in sleep." Or possibly he got it by taking the form of a woman and seducing concupiscent men.) Did intercourse between devils and witches afford "venereal pleasure"? (In some cases, yes; but a devil's penis was often uncomfortably cold.) And might such connection lead to pregnancy—and thus to devil-spawned children? (When certain necessary "causes concur," the result could well be "progeny that are . . . [uncommonly] powerful and big in body.") In one way or another, the sex act was crucial to the spread of witchcraft, not only because of its "natural nastiness," but also because it had "caused the corruption of our first parents and, by its contagion, brought the inheritance of original sin on the whole human race."

Child-murder and sex are recurrent preoccupations in the *Malleus*. But what seems most striking of all, as viewed from half a millennium later, is something else again: the flat-out, unblinking misogyny in which the entire work is drenched. Right at the start, the authors asked: "Why it is that women are chiefly addicted to evil superstitions?" Then, at great length and with fervent conviction, they offered their answer. Women, they declared—invoking long-familiar stereotypes—are "more credulous" and "more impressionable" and "feebler in mind and body" than men; these qualities, separately and together, naturally invite the attentions of the Devil. But this is just the beginning. A woman has a "slippery tongue," and is "a liar by nature." Thus she inclines always to "deceit"; moreover, "her gait, posture, and habit [betray her] vanity of vanities." A further "natural reason" for her basic "perfidy" is that "she is more carnal than a man, as is clear from her many carnal abominations"; indeed, her "carnal lust . . . is insatiable." Finally, "it should be noted that there was a defect in the formation of the first woman, since she was formed from a bent rib . . . in a contrary direction to a man. [Thus] she is an imperfect animal." To repeat: credulous, impressionable, feeble in mind and body; lying, deceitful, vain; insatiably carnal; and defectively formed in the first place. Put the whole together, and "it is no matter for wonder that there are many more women [than men] found infected with the heresy of witchcraft."

Perhaps it seems unsurprising that two aging male priests, sworn to lifelong celibacy, would spew such pointedly woman-hating invective. But, in fact, Kramer and Sprenger were as careful here as throughout the *Malleus* to cite numerous other writings in support of their views. Again and again they invoked the Bible: for example, "There is no wrath above the wrath of a woman" (Ecclesiastes 25). And also the saints: "What else is a woman but a foe to friendship, an inescapable punishment, a necessary evil, a natural temptation, a desirable calamity, a domestic danger, a delectable detriment, an evil of nature painted with fair colors" (St. John Chrysostom). And, not least, the sages of antiquity: "The many lusts of men lead them into one sin; but the one lust of women leads them into all sins; for the root of all woman's vices is avarice" (Cicero). Indeed, this aspect of the *Malleus* is best understood as a pulling together of misogynous attitudes from many different sources and centuries. As such, it exemplifies a virtual mother lode of feeling (especially, but not exclusively, in men) that fueled witch-hunting everywhere.

In its final section, the *Malleus* turns from theory to practice— from witchcraft as a social, cultural, and cosmological presence to the specific requirements of inquisition. Witch-hunting was then in the early stages of a highly consequential shift; formerly the special province of the church, it would soon become a prime focus for the state, as papal inquisitors yielded more and more responsibility to secular courts and judges. The *Malleus* was a major instigator, both in furnishing overall warrant and as a source of particular strategies and tactics. The chief arguments favoring secular prosecution were: "First, because . . . the crime of witches is not purely ecclesiastical, being rather civil on account of the temporal injuries they commit"; second, "because special laws are provided for dealing with witches"; and, "finally, because it seems that in this way it is easiest to proceed with the extermination of witches." The *Malleus* did, at every point, emphasize *maleficia* ("temporal injuries") over broadly theological issues. Governments had recently begun to write witchcraft into statute law. And, for certain, there was no quicker, more efficient way to achieve the ultimate goal of witch "extermination."

The specifics, reflecting as they did the authors' direct experience, ran the gamut from basic principles of law to elaborate counter-magical tips. Thus, on the one hand: "The judge is not bound to publish the names of deponents"; or, "an Advocate shall be allotted to the accused"; or, "while she is being questioned about each point, let her be often and frequently exposed to torture"; or, "take note whether she is able to shed tears . . . [for] if she be a witch, she will not be able to weep." Yet, on the other hand, there are certain detailed "precautions" to be taken by judges and their assistants: "They must not allow themselves to be touched physically by the witch . . . [and] they must always carry about them some salt consecrated on Palm Sunday or other Blessed Herbs . . . [as] remedies against illnesses and diseases caused by witchcraft." Moreover: "The witch should be led backward into the presence of the Judge [to prevent her from casting an evil eye]. And "the hair should be shaved from every part of her body . . . [since witches] are in the habit of hiding some superstitious object . . . in their hair, or even in the most secret parts of their bodies, which must not be named." Follow such procedures, the *Malleus* concluded, and judges would be safe, witches would be punished (or "eliminated"), justice would be served.

The Malleus *will have a place in the history of printing as well as the history of witchcraft. The invention of movable type by a German goldsmith named Johannes Gutenberg, just a few decades earlier, has already begun to reshape the contours of European culture. Books are pouring from presses in many different countries, and the* Malleus *will move quickly into the van-*

guard of period "bestsellers." By 1523 it has appeared in no fewer than 13 different Latin editions. Then come several decades during which it is not republished, as witch-hunting in general seems to stall. However, near the end of the 16th century, it inspires a new burst of printings—29 of them before all is said and done. Considered as a whole, this first century of its publication history seems to embody not only the technology but also the mind-set of a new age—when witch-hunting, like so much else, follows an increasingly secularized track.

Meanwhile, new "handbooks" come along as well. Perhaps the most influential are by the French philosopher Jean Bodin (De la demonomanie des sorciers, 1580), a French judge and prosecutor, Nicholas Remy (Daemonolatreiae, 1595), and a Belgian Jesuit priest, Martin Del Rio (Disquisitionum magicarum libri sex, 1599). All credit the precedence, and importance, of the Malleus. Even skeptical authors, most notably the German physician Johann Weyer, whose De praestigiis daemonum appears in 1563, make similar acknowledgment, though in their case the Malleus is more a target than a source of inspiration.

This pattern continues into and throughout, the 17th century. Trial records from the peak craze years are sprinkled with explicit or implicit reference to the Malleus. And writers on witchcraft as far away as New England's Increase Mather give it mention. When parts of the book appear in Polish translation, it helps open a new front for witch-hunting in northeastern Europe. Finally, in the 18th century, and more especially in the 19th, the Malleus begins to fade from sight. But then, against all odds, it undergoes something of a revival in the 20th century, when an eccentric Catholic intellectual named Montague Summers steps forward to defend witch-hunting. Indeed Summers vigorously champions the entire project in which Kramer and Sprenger played such an important part: he affirms the existence, and powers, of the Devil as traditionally conceived, and affirms, too, the menacing reality of witchcraft. In 1928 he puts the Malleus back into general circulation and 20 years later publishes yet another "modern" edition. Summers describes it, rather grandly, as "one of the world's few books written sub specie aeternitatis [of eternal significance]."

Still in print and widely available, the Malleus remains a lightning rod *for passionate debate even today. A favorite online bookseller lists no fewer than 71 "reviews" by current readers. Their opinions stretch across a wide range, from complete disapproval and disgust to equally fervent appreciation. A clear majority take one or another negative position: the* Malleus *as "a pack of myths and bigotries"; "a compendium of fifteenth-century paranoias"; or "a detestably cold and calculated book of horrors." Some detect close parallels to "totalitarian modernity," especially Nazism (with the* Malleus *cast as "the* Mein Kampf *of the Middle Ages"). Several seize the chance to belabor "traditional Catholicism," for having initially sponsored "the best example of Christian sadism." Additional commentators mix revulsion with a feeling of interest. One finds it "both special and vile." Another gains from it "a fascinating insight . . . into the fearful mind." A third regards it as "a history lesson . . . and a way to weed out false beliefs." A fourth offers this extravagant encomium: "The magnificent* Malleus Maleficarum *is one of the greatest works of psychology and sociology ever written."*

Like witch-hunting as a whole, the Malleus *has traveled a long journey. And it travels still.*

PART TWO

EARLY AMERICA

Inevitably, the idea of witchcraft crossed the ocean with the first European colonists coming to America. And so, too, did witch-*hunting* cross over. Chapter IV presents a specific case from 17th-century Connecticut: specific, local, small-scale, altogether ordinary in its particulars, and for these very reasons a good example of the general type.

Chapter V zooms out and up to survey the entire landscape of Colonial-era witch-hunting, as if from a historical mountaintop. Virginia and its southern neighbors; the so-called middle colonies of New York and Pennsylvania; New England most especially (up to, but not including, the Salem trials of 1692–93): thus the scope of the view. Concern with witchcraft can be seen everywhere, albeit in widely differing proportions.

Chapter VI returns to ground level, and to the earliest phase of New England history, in order to follow the course of a single life, in which suspicions of witchcraft involvement played a recurrent role. As the folk themselves might have said, once a witch, always a witch—so, on both sides, *be careful*.

CHAPTER IV

Windsor, Connecticut, 1654:
A Town Entertaining Satan

An autumn afternoon in the year 1651; the town of Windsor, in the colony of Connecticut. Several dozen men have gathered on the local "training field" for militia drill. They march in formation, with officers at the front. Drums beat; colors fly from a long, hand-hewn staff; muskets are raised and lowered on command. Presently the group divides in two, so as to engage in mock battle. Each side moves back from the center, turns, crouches, and fires over the heads of the other. This exercise is repeated a number of times.

As the trainees resume their original positions and prepare to break ranks, there comes a sudden, sharp report from somewhere in their midst. Seconds later, one of them staggers out of line and falls heavily to the ground; he has been hit by an errant bullet fired from close-up. Blood flows from a deep wound in his neck. Other men run toward him and attempt to help. Presently they carry him on a makeshift bier to a nearby house, where the town physician can attend to him. But he is beyond saving; he dies later that night.

His name was Henry Stiles, his age about 58. The source of the shot that killed him is a musket belonging to another man named Thomas Allen; the two were marching side by side. Allen is young (not yet 20), carefree, and self-absorbed. Eyewitnesses to the afternoon's events will later recall Allen's blatant mishandling of his gun. He failed to secure its firing cock and lowered it virtually to Stiles's head. Then he swung it heedlessly back and forth. And then, somehow, it discharged.

There is a funeral the next day, at which the people of Windsor grieve their loss. Stiles, though a bachelor, has many relatives living nearby; their sorrow and anger run deep. A week or two later, Stiles's will is read, his estate tallied and taken to probate. He was not without means; his personal inventory includes several parcels of land, a few cattle, some carpentry tools, a musket and two swords, "2 pair of silk garters" and one "silk girdle," six loads of hay, 90 bushels of corn, 200 pumpkins, "half a canoe," and both "money and wampum." But he also stands liable for a long list of debts, some of them quite substantial, most owed to a man named Thomas Gilbert. Within days, his property is dispersed, his accounts settled. Slowly, and very incompletely, the town tries to heal.

Another month passes. In the meantime, the magistrates who make up Connecticut's General Court, the colony's highest governing body, appoint a jury to conduct a "grand inquest" into Stiles's death. In early December the Court convenes in regular session, and receives the jury's report. Its conclusion is straightforward: "This jury finds that the piece [firearm] that was in the hands of Thomas Allen, going off was the cause of . . . death." The court then hands down a formal indictment: "that thou, Thomas Allen . . . didst suddenly, negligently, carelessly cock thy piece, and carry the piece just behind thy neighbor, which piece being charged and going off . . . slew thy neighbor, to the great dishonor of God, breach of the peace, and loss of a member of this commnonwealth." Allen confesses the facts as presented, and is found guilty of "homicide by misadventure." (We would say: accidental murder, or manslaughter.) For his "sinful neglect and careless carriages" the court orders him to pay a fine of 20 pounds, a large sum in that time and setting. In addition, his father must submit a bond to guarantee the young man's "good behavior" throughout the following twelve months, with the special proviso "that he shall not bear arms for the same term."

This sudden, shattering "misadventure" in their midst has unsettled the people of Windsor very deeply. Talk of it does not abate. Questions linger and multiply. To be sure, the surface details are clear enough: Allen's carelessness, his proximity to Stiles, all the mechanics of poorly carried gun, cocked trigger, inadvertent firing, speeding bullet, torn and bleeding body. Yet how much does this finally explain? After all, the two men might not have been positioned exactly so. And Allen, neglectful though he was, might still have held his gun in such a manner as to preclude its lethal discharge. And the men might have trained in a different place, on a different day; indeed, Stiles might have been sick, or traveling, or otherwise removed from the scene. Moreover—and here perhaps is the single most tormenting piece—even if everything else had been just as it was, the bullet might have gone in a thousand different directions; only one would yield such an awful result. Henry Stiles's death was the product of innumerable small and highly specific contingencies. Why—why—why had they all converged this way? Surely, such an extraordinary, and tragic, outcome cannot be ascribed to mere chance.

How best, then, to understand it? God's will, they wonder? Or, perhaps more likely, the Devil's? Does it not, in fact, bear some clear marks of maleficium? The good people of Windsor will ponder all this, for months—indeed, years—to come.

Windsor had been founded more than a decade before by a little band of settlers from Massachusetts in search of good land on which to build a new community. Most had lived for a few years in the Bay Colony town of Dorchester (adjacent to Boston). They traveled to Connecticut largely as a group. Their leader in every sense, spiritual and otherwise, was a clergyman named John Warham. They were farmers and craftsmen, wives and children and servants; for the most part, they were arrayed in families. Their surnames bespoke their solid English stock: Stebbins, Drake, Gibbons, Moore, Hawkins, Tilton, Bissell, White, Grant, Torrey, Young, Stiles (the unlucky Henry's family line), Allen (including young Thomas), and Gilbert (with Thomas as family head, and Lydia, his wife).

The fertile lands on the west side of the Connecticut River provided the opportunity they were seeking; after some negotiation with the local Indians, they staked their claim and settled in. Their village plan conformed to what would become the New England pattern: house lots arrayed from north to south along a main street, fields and pastures farther out. They grew corn, some wheat, and garden crops; later their yield would include hops and tobacco. They also raised livestock, scattering herds of cows and sheep from one end of town to the other.

Most of all, these early Windsorites were what their English peers called "Puritans." That is, they were religious radicals of a particular kind. In a broad sense, they were heirs to the Protestant Reformation; the starting point for many of their beliefs was the 16th-century Swiss theologian John Calvin. Their English mother church had not—so they contended—sufficiently rid itself of "papist" corruptions; reform must proceed much further. Their concerns embraced doctrine, worship, and church governance, in roughly equal measure. A more direct and personal relation to God, a deepened sense of human sinfulness, simplified ritual, and a decentralized system of ecclesiastical administration: such were the goals they held in view.

Their cosmology, their picture of the universe, was a distilled version of ideas held throughout the Christianized world. Human history, they believed, unfolds in the shadow of overarching warfare: between God and the forces of righteousness on the one hand, and Satan and his own "infernal legions" on the other. At some point the struggle must end in God's complete triumph, with an all-decisive Day of Judgment immediately to follow. Many Puritans thought that point was close at hand; hence they spoke of theirs as an "End Time," and looked eagerly for signs of its actual arrival. In such a climate of opinion, all of life was intensified; all was potentially meaningful. God's purposes, and Satan's too, informed each and every fragment of experience.

As the seasons pass, the people of Windsor continue to brood on Henry Stiles's death—its causes and meaning for their own lives. In so doing, they carefully evaluate key parts of the dead man's personal history. For example: during most of the previous two years, he had lived as a lodger in the home of Thomas Gilbert; he slept there in a room of his own, took his "diet" (meals) there, kept his "goods" there. This was, in itself, unusual: few, if any, other local men were similarly circumstanced. But so, too, was his bachelorhood unusual; few if any other men did not have wives and households of their own. Might this have made him—in some way hard to understand later on—also unusually vulnerable?

But there are other, more ominous, questions to raise here. As his inventory clearly showed, Henry Stiles, the lodger, had borrowed significant sums of cash and property from the Gilberts, his landlords; he is, to his dying moment, deeply in their debt. Did they perhaps press him to repay? And was he unable or unwilling to respond? Was there not, in fact, some open bitterness between the two parties? Had they not been heard, from time to time, shouting in anger across the Gilberts' dining table? And were they not observed to "slight" one another when seated on adjacent benches in the meetinghouse? Indeed, was it not a threat—maybe even a curse—that Goody Gilbert had flung at Stiles when they arrived together for Sabbath service one day last summer? And what of Goodwife Gilbert as a person—her qualities, her "carriages"? Didn't she sometimes seem too querulous, too "forward," too quick to anger, too slow to sympathize? Hadn't her neighbors suffered strange "losses" and difficulties, now and then, after dealing with her? Didn't one or two of them even suggest darkly that she might have been in league with . . . ? The questions, the suspicions, the bits and pieces of gossip will go on and on. And eventually they will all come out in the same place.

November 28, 1654; again the court is convened at Hartford. But this is not a regular session; instead it is announced as "special." Three years have passed since the first hearing on Stiles's death; now there will be another. A new jury is sworn "by the ever living God . . . [to] faithfully present . . . what criminal offense you shall judge meet." The room is crowded with anxious spectators, including many who have made the ten-mile trip down from Windsor. The magistrates preside at the front, from heavily-framed armchairs set on a raised platform. Below them stands a middle-aged woman, her legs in ball and chain—evidently a defendant. Today there is one matter, and one only, on the court's agenda. The clerk reads aloud: "Lydia Gilbert, thou art here indicted . . . that, not having the fear of God before thy eyes, thou hast of late years, or still dost, give entertainment to Satan, the great enemy of God and mankind; and by his help hast killed the body of Henry Stiles, besides other witchcrafts, for which, according to the law of God and the established law of this commonwealth, thou deservest to die."

The jury has been taking evidence in support of these charges for weeks;
many Windsor townsfolk have come forward to testify. The damage and
danger attributed to Goodwife Gilbert spans a broad range: spoiled food,
the loss of cattle, illness and injury in several of her neighbors. But Henry
Stiles's death is the clincher; that is what brings her to the present moment.
Clearly, she had a motive to attack him, even kill him. (Remember all he
owed her, and the angry words that passed between them.) Likely, too, she
had the means; her prior "witchcrafts" are proof enough. Yes, she might
well have agreed to "give entertainment to Satan"; and Satan, for his part,
must have given in return—the extraordinary power to perform malefi-
cium. Now, at last, a deeper cause of Stiles's death can be openly acknowl-
edged. The bullet that took his life was not simply a random mischance; to
the contrary, its course was carefully and purposefully guided. Here, then,
is the sum of it: a spiteful witch has used a young man's carelessness to mur-
der another whom she hated. The jury declares: "The party abovementioned
is found guilty of witchcraft." Therefore, Lydia Gilbert, "thou deservest
to die."

And a few days later, she does. On the gallows, with a rope pulled tight
around her neck.

Postscript: Many of the records from the Gilbert witchcraft case
have not survived; historians can never reconstruct the full story.
But we may at least imagine a further piece or two. . . .

Even with the question of cause—motivated cause—resolved, another
remains: Why had God allowed this awful tragedy to happen, in the first
place? Witchcraft, like all else in the universe, needs God's permission.
So . . . why now? And why here, in Windsor? The person best able to an-
swer is, of course, the minister, John Warham. And he makes it the topic of
a sermon soon after Lydia Gilbert's execution.

On the day appointed, the meetinghouse is filled with local parish-
ioners, deeply shaken by all they have been through. What will Reverend
Warham say to them? His message is neither surprising nor pleasant to
hear, but it does carry a purgative force. The gist is that the Windsor towns-
folk must themselves bear part of the blame. More and more, in recent

months, they have strayed from the paths of virtue: overvaluing secular interests while neglecting spiritual ones, "tippling" in alehouses, "nightwalking," and, worst of all, engaging one another in repeated "controversy." In such circumstances Satan always finds an opening; on such communities God necessarily brings retribution. The recent witchcraft episode is His warning to the people of Windsor to mend their ways, and a reminder that He still watches over them.

The questions that so troubled them have finally received a complete response; its several parts stretch out before them, links in a long chain. From Henry Stiles's violent death, to Thomas Allen's careless mishandling of his gun, to Lydia Gilbert's spite and powers as a witch, to Satan's eager, and evil, intervention, to God's permission, oversight, and ultimate justice. Most of them feel calmer now, and reassured. Time to resume the routines of everyday, their faith in the cosmic balance at last restored.

CHAPTER V

Witch-hunting in the American Colonies, 1607–92

Much of the early "settlement" phase of American history is shrouded in obscurity. Records are few, and historians' access correspondingly limited. We do know a good deal about the leaders, their broad goals and strategies, but we have little that illuminates the lives of the rank and file.

Still, we can visualize, infer, imagine—starting with the process of migration itself. Tiny (by our standards) sailing ships, crammed with people, animals, "goods." Sickness, including near-constant nausea for the many who had never previously been to sea; sometimes death. Intense feelings of anticipation, hope, puzzlement, worry, and (for at least a few) suicidal despair. No doubt individual settlers were fortified, to some extent, by the Old World heritage they carried with them—in their heads and hearts as well as their shipping trunks and boxes. They were Europeans, through and through: English (by far the largest number), French, Dutch, Swedish, Finnish, Spanish, and a small scattering of others. They were Protestants (again, the largest number), Catholics (most of those headed to one place in particular, the colony of Maryland), and Jews (just a handful). In a great many ways, they reflected the traditional stock from which they were sprung. To be sure, they did not constitute an entirely representative sample: "Puritans," for instance, were disproportionately included, and "gentlefolk" (persons of high rank and privilege) were scarcely to be found at all. Still, when considered from the broadest possible perspective, their values and opinions, their habits of thinking and doing, fell within the usual range for European folk of their era.

The first of several migration bursts coincided in time (the early 17th century) with the peak of the great European witch craze. Hence the migrants themselves would surely have known witchcraft— and feared witchcraft, and maybe experienced, or even practiced, witchcraft—firsthand. As well, they would have carried it with them to their new homes overseas. Indeed, the Devil troubled them, both literally and figuratively. An elderly New Englander, reflecting late in life on his decision to migrate some 50 years before, remembered the hope "that I should be more free here than there [i.e. Old England] from temptations"; in fact, however, "I found here a devil to tempt, and a corrupt heart to deceive." Were there individual passengers, aboard the first transatlantic ships, suspected of performing witchcraft? That does seem a reasonable presumption. Evidence from a generation or two later suggests that ocean travel may actually have primed witchcraft suspicion in special ways. In 1654, on a ship traveling from London to Maryland, sailors spread a "rumor . . . [that] one Mary Lee, then aboard the said ship, was a witch." At first the captain rebuffed their urging "that a trial might be had of her"; but then, as "cross winds" rose to impede the voyage and "the ship grew daily more leaky—almost to desperation," his attitude changed. The sailors were permitted to "search her body," and quickly discovered "the mark of a witch upon her . . . [whereupon] they importuned the Master [Captain] to put her to death." He replied that "they might do what they would, and went into his cabin." And so, "laying all their hands to the execution of her," they proceeded finally to "hang her as a witch." A similar scene was enacted a few years later on a boat sailing to Virginia. Details of this one have not come down to us but, according to a later summary filed in a local court, "An old woman named Katherine Grady . . . [was] accused of witchcraft . . . [and] hung from a yard's arm," supposedly at the "clamorous demand of . . . passengers during the progress of a violent storm."

In sum: bad weather, sickness, confining conditions, uncertainty about the future, and real danger in the present must together have served to heighten anxiety and suspicion during sea journeys. Always there were shipboard prayers, fervent pleadings for divine mercy (especially in the face of ocean storms). And, alongside such outward, openly voiced entreaties, there would have been— there had to be—inward, perhaps unvoiced, imprecations against the Devil and his human confederates. God and Satan; angels and demons; pious folk and "foresworn" witches; the saved and the damned; righteousness and sin: these pairings were omnipresent and indivisible.

Such matters must have preoccupied settlers of every ethnic and religious group, no matter what their specific New World destination. If we had some way to peel back the years, and to visit wherever we liked in 17th-century North America, we would find many signs of witchcraft belief. We might land, say, in a Massachusetts village, and accost one or another inhabitant as he walked along the rutted street: *What can you tell us, Goodman Jones, of witchcraft in your town?* And he would have stories to offer, perhaps about his own experiences or (at a minimum) those of his neighbors. *'Twas Whitsuntide when my cow fell a-roaring, and her belly swelled strangely, and she died after a fortnight, and I could never tell the reason of it, but thoughts of witches kept running in my mind.* We could stop at an "ordinary" (tavern) by a crossroads in the tidewater region of Virginia and eavesdrop from a seat near the back wall. And, sooner or later, the conversation would turn to whatever had recently gone bump in the night. *Last Sabbath eve Mr. Watson was kept up to all hours with great noises like stones flung upon the roof of the house, and looked out and saw nobody; and he said there was a Devil abroad.* We could linger at a public well in Albany (then a thriving little *entrepôt* up the Hudson River from New York) where local women gathered to draw water; their chat, too, might move in the same direction. *Goodwife Gerritsen's daughter is fallen into fits and complains of Mistress Sanders for afflicting her.* Again, most of this lies beyond the reach of any surviving records, and may never have been written down in the first place. But some of it does turn up, at least indirectly, in witchcraft cases from later on. And all of it belonged to the prevalent popular mentality on both sides of the Anglo-Atlantic world.

The same mentality conditioned the response of colonists to the native people they would encounter upon coming ashore. Indeed, it had framed expectation throughout Europe even before such encounters began. From well back in the 16th century, a large and constantly expanding literature of New World travel had cast American Indians as "Devil worshipers." The notorious English explorer-pirate Francis Drake, for example, reported seeing a native group dance in "hellish" costumes on a beach with the aim (so he believed) of destroying his ships. Similarly, Captian John Smith—he of the legendary "rescue" by the Indian princess Pocahontas—regarded Virginia's Powhatan tribe as being very much "in league with Satan." And Reverend Alexander Whitaker, an early visitor to the same region, wrote at length to a colleague at home about the strange "antics" of Indians. "All these things," he concluded, "make me think that there be great witches among them, and that they are very familiar with the Devil." Farther to the north, Governor William Bradford remembered, in his history *Of Plymouth Plantation*, how Indian "powwaws" had greeted the little settler band he led by gathering "in a horrid and devilish manner . . . to curse and execrate them with their conjurations." Even Roger Williams, long regarded as uncommonly sympathetic to native cultural ways, declared flatly that Indian "priests [are] . . . no other than our English witches."

The same refrain continued to be heard in all regions long after the initial period of colonization: Indians as "minions of Satan," as "sorcerers" and "conjurors," as consorters with "Evil Angels." However, there is a notable gap in such depictions: Indians do not appear as perpetrators of *maleficium*. This element, the infliction of injury by diabolical means, was everywhere key to the image of homegrown witches; hence, its absence in portrayals of native culture is striking.

In fact, the activity that the colonists were identifying as Indian witchcraft was what we would now call shamanism. The powwaws were, for the most part, practitioners of traditional medicine: witch *doctors* perhaps, but not witches in the full and classic European sense. One early colonist noted that their main "office and duty" was "curing diseases of the sick and wounded." Another described them as "partly wizards and witches . . . [and] partly physicians"; in the latter capacity, moreover, "they seem to do wonders." What made them objectionable, in European eyes, was their apparent "familiarity with Satan," their propensity to "cure by the help of the devil"— in short, their methods rather than their intended and actual results. Close-up observation brought their "Satanism" into sharp focus; a typical account of an Indian powwaw emphasized his "hideous bellowing and groaning . . . sometimes roaring like a bear . . . foaming at the mouth like a chased boar, smiting his naked breast and thighs with such violence as if he were mad," all of which "will he continue sometimes half the day." Such "fiendish rites" could only be inspired by the Archfiend himself. And they were bizarre, awesome, terrifying.

Still, none of this is quite the same as *maleficium*. So, again: Did individual Indians, and especially the powwaws themselves, attempt to effect their own forms of harmful witchcraft? And did Indians at large believe in such possibilities? Certainly this was true of native groups well inland—the Sioux of the Great Plains, the Navajo in the Southwest. However, for eastern Indians, those living closest to the early colonies, evidence of such belief (and practice) is virtually nil. If the colonists had seen signs of native *maleficium,* they surely would have said as much.

It seems significant, moreover, that native people (including their powwaws) were never prosecuted in colonial courts on charges of witchcraft. They could be, and sometimes were, prosecuted on other charges—violating English laws against public drunkenness or theft or murder, for example—but not on this one. Moreover, the colonists, while harboring a deep revulsion against native powwawing, appear to have felt that it held no power to affect them, either for good or for ill. Nor, for that matter, could it much affect native converts to Christianity; they, too, had a kind of cultural immunity. Thus the overall picture was sharply mixed. Europeans were predisposed to associate Indians with Satanism and witchcraft, and were deeply troubled by the connection. Yet absent *maleficium*, Indian witchcraft seemed a different, and distinctly lesser, thing. As time and experience would repeatedly confirm, for colonists everywhere the most dangerous witches were those found within their own fold.

As the years passed, a third major cultural stream would intersect those of native people and European settlers: the African, and African American. Small groups of Africans began arriving in the British colonies as early as 1619. (Of course, they were migrants of a very different sort: kidnapped from their homelands and transported entirely against their will.) Their numbers grew at a gradual pace through the rest of the 17th century, and then quite explosively in the century that followed. The single most important element in their lives was, of course, enslavement; especially after about 1660, almost all Africans and their American-born progeny were held in perpetual bondage by white colonists. But perhaps the second most important element was the persistence, in various forms, of their own indigenous traditions.

In their homelands, magical practice, including witchcraft and sorcery, had been central to a rich and enormously variegated pattern of engagement with the supernatural. When transferred to America it became, necessarily, truncated and in many ways distorted. In broad terms, it encompassed a host of "spirits" whose influence on the quotidian details of life had always seemed large and now grew even more powerful. At the same time, its point and purview would gradually shift away from the ostensibly beneficent (fertility, healing, and the like), toward the more directly harmful (loss, injury, and death). This, one imagines, reflected the darkened—not to say desperate—circumstances in which such cruelly transplanted people found themselves.

Much of the evidence we have here flowed initially from the pens

of white colonists. Time after time their writings referred to "conjurors" and "poison doctors" among the slave population. They made
frequent reference, also, to specific episodes of magical practice, and
even to the particulars of method and technique: charms, invocations, and substances such as "powders, roots, herbs, and simples."
A different, literally more solid sort of evidence comes from under
the ground. Archaeologists have been able to recover some of the
paraphernalia of African American magic: amulets, beads, carefully-
shaped objects in glass, ceramic, and wood—even, in one striking
instance, a stringed penis bone from a raccoon (perhaps to promote
fertility). There are linguistic markers as well: words found in both
African and American venues, such as *juju* (for evil spirit), *moco* (for
witchcraft or magic), *ubio* (for charm), and, most famously, *wudu* or
vodun (for what we now call voodoo, or "black magic"). Taken together, these materials reveal a distinctive African-American spiritual presence in the colonies—especially the southern and Caribbean
colonies where slavery would greatly proliferate after 1700.

As a matter of actual usage, most of this was confined within the
black population itself. But slaveowners, and other white folk too,
repeatedly expressed fears of harm from the "sorceries" of their
bondsmen; most of all, they feared "poisoning." This term seems
notably elastic wherever it shows up in written documents. In some
cases it described a straightforward physical process (the ingestion of
a lethal substance), but in others it apparently referred to supernatural power (poisoning by way of spirits or malefic magic). Dozens, if
not hundreds, of slaves would eventually be suspected, accused, convicted, and put to death—burnt at the stake, drawn and quartered,
or simply hanged—for alleged acts of poisoning.

Slave sorceries, real or imagined, directed against masters and other
white people were an exception. The largest source of "diabolical"
danger, or so most colonists believed, remained with and among
their own kind. And, to repeat: such belief was prevalent throughout
the entirety of British America during the colonial years.

But prevalence was one thing, intensity another. In some regions—the "middle colonies," for example—concern with witchcraft was thinly maintained, and rarely led on to official action. In others, especially New England, it was a deeply rooted, activating presence; there, formal accusation, involving whole communities and generating full-blown legal proceedings, remained plausible, even (at intervals) likely. This distinction may structure our further inquiry. Indeed, it is itself a subject for inquiry: New England as compared with all the rest. Let us start with the rest.

Virginia holds the site of the first colonial settlement in British America. And Virginia is also the source of the earliest surviving (and unambiguous) traces of witchcraft in British America. In 1626, its General Court heard charges against a certain Goodwife Joan Wright. During several years at the Kickotan plantation, Wright had earned the reputation of "a very bad woman" by telling fortunes (usually about impending death), "railing" at neighbors, and, most ominously, uttering mysterious threats of harm to any who "crossed" her. Her targets included two men who had subsequently failed in hunting despite "coming to good game and very fair to shoot at," another whose "plants were . . . all . . . drowned," and an entire family made sick and "dangerously sore." (The exact circumstances and final disposition of this case are not known. Indeed, the volume in which the testimony survives would have perished, together with most other records from Virginia's earliest years, in a fire during the Civil War, had not Thomas Jefferson carried it off long before; it is found in the Jefferson Papers today.) In 1641 another court adjudicated a dispute between two women, Jane Rookins and the wife of George Busher (her given name is not recorded). They had fallen into a loud quarrel, at the height of which Rookins denounced Busher as a witch. Busher's husband then brought suit for defamation on her behalf. Rookins claimed not to recall the alleged accusation, but apologized anyway. The court took this as a sufficient resolution of the matter, adding simply that the defendant must pay all the costs of prosecution.

Versions of the same story would be repeated many times in other small communities nearby. Indeed, most recorded references to witchcraft in early Virginia actually come from defamation cases. All told, there were approximately 20 of these, with a roughly even split between acquittals and convictions. Punishments, when ordered, typically involved the payment of fines. Often, as with Busher versus Rookins, a public apology was the most important element, since reputations were so obviously at stake; one plaintiff explicitly stated that, as a result of being labeled a witch, her neighbors refused to "keep company" with her. There is evidence, too, that some of the individuals thus defamed had been subject to physical assault and felt their lives to be in danger.

The records afford at least a glimpse of the particular suspicions aroused—of curses, for example, and of "spells." One woman, in the heat of "controversy," was said to have uttered "a kind of prayer" against her neighbor that "neither he nor any of his family might prosper"; shortly thereafter, sickness did in fact overtake the neighbor's household. Another man claimed "bewitchment" of his cow; another, injury to his horse; yet another, the sudden and mysterious death of some chickens. Several described experiences of being "ridden" like a beast of burden by supposed witches, over long distances and usually at night; one such left its victim "wearied nearly to death." There were occasional references to the Devil's "imps," and also to shape-shifting. (For example, a witch suspect allegedly "rode" her neighbor here and there, then changed into a black cat and slipped away through a crack in the door.) There were also elaborate accounts of counter-magical activity. In one particularly vivid instance, a woman who "thought herself to be bewitched" ordered a servant "to take a horseshoe and fling it into the oven, and when it was red-hot to fling it into her . . . urine." According to the servant, this tactic produced immediate, and telling, results: "So long as the horseshoe was hot, the witch [suspect] was sick at the heart, and when the iron was cold she was well again."

A much smaller group of cases involved the prosecution of witchcraft itself, not simply its link to defamation. There juries would be empaneled, witnesses deposed, defendants interrogated—all very much in line with traditional English legal practice. By the same token, a suspect's body might be carefully examined by "ancient and knowing women," in search of "teats, spots, and marks not usual on others." (If found, these would be attributed to the Devil, and understood as an apparatus for suckling his imps.) The result of one such examination was recorded in detail: "She is like no other woman, having two things like teats on her private parts of a black color." Moreover, a defendant's house might be searched "for all images [witch dolls] and such like things as may strengthen the suspicion." And at least a few suspected witches were ordered "to be tried in the water by ducking." This time-tested method of "discovery" meant that the accused would be immersed in a pool or stream "above a man's depth, to try how she swims therein." If she floated too easily, the Devil was presumed to be at work on her behalf; if she sank, she could be exonerated. (And if she drowned? The records do not mention this possibility.)

Just as Virginia was the first colonial site for court proceedings around witchcraft, so, too, was it among the last; trials occurred as late as 1706. Meanwhile, there were similar cases in adjacent Maryland. These, however, were fewer overall, and were entirely by way of slander. A typical instance involved a certain Peter Godson, when confronted by his neighbor Richard Manship as to "whether he would prove his [Manship's] wife a witch." According to testimony Godson then replied: " 'Take notice what I say. I came to your home, where your wife laid two straws [on the floor].' And the woman in a jesting way said, 'they say I am a witch; if I am a witch they say I have not the power to skip over these straws;' and [she] bade the said Peter to skip over them. And about a day after[ward] the said Godson was lame, and thereupon would maintain Manship's wife to be a witch." This little scene nicely conveys the flavor of folk belief in regard to witchcraft: the laying of straws, the skipping over (another means of "discovering" witchcraft), the supposed link to *maleficium*.

Godson would later retract his accusation, and the court case would be dismissed; but the residues of neighborhood animus may well have lingered.

New York, another of the oldest colonies, witnessed occasional witchcraft cases (though not, apparently, during its initial, Dutch incarnation as New Netherland). A lengthy trial in 1665 charged a Long Island couple named Ralph and Mary Hall with using certain "detestable and wicked arts, commonly called witchcraft and sorcery," to cause the illness and death of their neighbor George Wood and his infant child. In the end, however, there were no convictions. A jury found "some suspicions" of guilt in the woman, but not of sufficient "value to take away her life"; the man, for his part, was acquitted outright. Other, more casual imputations of witchcraft are scattered through New York records until the end of the 17th century, with a few rising to the level of legally actionable slander and one involving the banishment of a suspected witch who had moved in from nearby Connecticut.

Witchcraft also surfaced periodically in the early Swedish and Finnish settlements on Delaware Bay. The records here are especially meager, but we do find mention of figures like "Lasse the Finn" and "Karin the Finnish woman," both apparently imprisoned as witches in the Swedish fort at Christiana. Moreover, a Swedish "handbook" from the time, perhaps (though not provably) brought to the New World, beautifully suggests the manifold interactions between witchcraft, medicine, household routine, and folk culture. Here, in translation, are a few of its specific prescriptions:

—*A cross should be cut into a broom to prevent witches from riding on it.*
—*A psalm-book should be placed below the head of the newly-born child to prevent its being exchanged for a changeling (or elf-child) by the evil spirits.*
—*Bleeding is stopped by grasping around the sore with the hand and repeating the formula, "Thou shalt stand as firm as Jordan*

stood, when John baptized in the name of the Father, of the Son, and of the Holy Ghost."

—*When a cow is sold a bunch of hair should be taken from her and preserved to prevent the good luck from leaving the house with the cow.*

—*A little of each course from the Christmas table should be taken on Christmas morning and given to the cattle to preserve them against witchcraft.*

—*If milk is accidentally spilled into the fire, salt should always be thrown in to avoid misfortunes.*

—*If the spinning-wheel is kept going after 6 o'clock on Saturday evening, the sheep will not prosper.*

Pennsylvania's founding came in 1682, relatively late; thus it had a briefer, more attenuated involvement with witchcraft. The Quakers, who made up by far the largest part of its population, seem not to have yielded any principals in such proceedings. Still, in 1684 the "proprietor" William Penn and his council conducted a full-blown prosecution of charges that had come from within the ranks of the colony's Swedish minority. Two women, Margaret Mattson and Greta Hendrickson, stood accused of bewitching cows and practicing other "sorceries" over a span of at least 20 years. The jury returned an unusual sort of split verdict: "guilty of the common fame of a witch, but not guilty in manner and form as she stands indicted." In 1701 a Philadelphia butcher and his wife were charged with slander for identifying a neighboring couple as the cause of a "very sudden illness . . . [in] a certain strange woman lately arrived in this town"; the plaintiffs claimed as a result to be "suffering much in their reputation, and by that means in their trade." (The "strange woman," perhaps their lodger, had been found with "several pins . . . in her breasts," and other seeming indicators of witchcraft.) The case, however, "being inquired into, and found trifling, was dismissed."

The word "trifling" jumps off the page here; it does not appear in any similar proceeding from the previous century. And, by this point, concern with witchcraft—at least *official* concern with witchcraft—was beginning to fade out almost everywhere. Indeed, in all these places outside New England, it had never amounted to a great deal. Certainly, it was part of local culture. And certainly it could for brief intervals, around particular persons, intensify considerably. But the sum of its effects was modest: no executions, no clear-cut findings of guilt, occasional prosecutions (and the majority of those for slander only, with the roles of accused witch and accusing victim turned around). This was, in fact, a mere shadow of what had obtained—and to some degree still obtained—in the Old World settings where all these colonists had originated.

And so to the New England Puritans. This most familiar group of settlers—actually two groups, the Mayflower "pilgrims" who arrived at Plymouth in December 1620 and a much larger contingent coming to Boston and its environs beginning a decade later—have long been accorded special pride of place as a source of American character. Some of their cultural DNA lies deep in our national core, whether for good or ill. Moral or simply moralistic, single-minded or narrow-minded, upright or uptight: such opposite yet complementary descriptors have served to frame a centuries-long process of soul-searching around Puritans. On one point, and perhaps one only, all sides seem to agree: these folk were important—they left their mark—we live with their legacy still.

Defined from the outset as religious reformers of a radical and universalist bent, they nonetheless refracted the temper of their times. For they were *social* reformers as well. In both aspects, the social as well as the religious, they struck a fundamentally reactive—even backward-looking—pose. The English church as they knew it was "corrupt"; in response they would "purify" it by returning to the habits and principles of the early Christians. English society at large was no less compromised; they would restore it by recapturing the "brotherly" spirit of a previous and simpler age.

Their social critique is of special importance here. They saw themselves, not without reason, as born to an epoch of unprecedented change. Rapid population growth, runaway inflation in prices and rents, the fitful development of trade and industry, the swelling sprawl of towns and cities (spectacularly so in the case of London), the disruption of ancient manorial and parochial systems in the countryside: these trends were felt in many quarters as unmooring the stays of traditional culture. To Puritans most especially, the accompanying social costs seemed enormous—with vagabonds roaming the highways, beggars infesting the urban marketplace, disease, fire, and crime in rampant display—all appearing to presage an ultimate breakdown. Their writings formed a litany of outrage and sorrow on the evils surrounding them. "Why meet we so many wandering ghosts in shape of men, so many spectacles of misery in all our streets?" asked Governor John Winthrop upon exiting England to lead the new colony of Massachusetts Bay. Pride and the inherent "baselessness" of human nature provided one part of the answer here; but "society" constituted another. Hence, wrote Robert Cushman, a thoughtful pamphleteer on behalf of New England colonization, "the most wise, sober, and discreet men" were often reduced to penury.

Puritans lived, in short, with a pervasive fear of disorder—even, as one historian has put it, "on the brink of chaos." Yet they found in their religious faith a vital measure of reassurance—strength, hope, the promise of "a new life"—centered in precisely those values that history seemed bent on destroying. Puritanism enshrined, above all, the principle of *control,* both inner control of the individual person and outward control among the community of "saints." Intense and unrelenting discipline would be the appropriate answer to disorder.

Having crossed the ocean and fetched up at various points along the New England shore, Puritan leaders seized a unique opportunity to begin anew—to found communities where the law of God and the law of man would become the same. That they expressed their goals in theological terms should not mislead us; there were, after all, no other terms available to them. In contrast to the selfish spirit characteristic of their motherland, they would strive to re-create an organic connection among God-fearing folk. In contrast to disorder, they would establish harmony, peaceableness, the subordination of individual interest to "commonwealth." Countless New England sermons would later bear witness to the preeminence of these values; here, for Puritans, was the true meaning of Christian love. As Winthrop put it in a famous shipboard lecture en route to Massachusetts, "We must be knit together . . . as one man . . . and . . . must delight in each other, make others' condition our own, rejoice together, mourn together, labor and suffer together, always having before our eyes our commission and community in the work." This "commission" to be "knit together"—they also called it their "errand"—expressed the very heart of what they were about.

The pursuit of these goals involved Puritans in strenuous measures of self- and collective improvement. Individual striving for holiness was one important element here; an attitude of unflinching "watchfulness" toward one's family and neighbors was another; a community-wide commitment to consensual (not majoritarian) decision making yet another. But being and acting "knit together" proved to be a most difficult ideal, one they could never fully realize. Indeed, they often disappointed themselves as, all across their newly-created homeland, towns and villages fell into "controversy" and divided into "factions" around matters both large and small. To some extent Puritanism itself was to blame for this; for, in rejecting the established ecclesiastical hierarchy, it had also relinquished many traditional checks on the possibility that individuals might plot their own course (in religion and otherwise). Thus did various forms of sectarianism arise and flourish in early New England. Some of these were quite large-scale, with the potential to split entire communities. Others went right down to the level of lone believers moved by a personal "inner light." Moreover, New England's special brand of Puritanism was challenged from the outside as well: by regular Anglicans (members of the official "established church" of the realm), by Baptists, by Quakers.

A final sort of challenge came from a different quarter altogether. Here was no competing sect or church institution—and not even a religious (in the strict sense) belief system—but rather, ancient traditions of "folk magic." Interest and belief in magic had certainly crossed the ocean with the first cohort of New England settlers and had then taken firm root in the cultural soil of their nascent communities. Its traces are numerous and varied (if often somewhat sparse in detail). Ministers referred to it in their sermons and published writings; Cotton Mather, for instance, declared that "in some towns it has been *a usual thing* [emphasis added] for people to cure hurts with spells, or to use detestable conjurations, with sieves, keys, and peas, and nails, and horseshoes, and I know not what other implements." Courts inquired into it, most often as part of witchcraft prosecutions. Ordinary "inhabitants" mentioned its use, and sometimes its efficacy, in their diaries and letters to one another. Its pervasiveness, even in this most religiously oriented of colonial regions, is beyond doubt.

As in the Old World, the term magic covered a broad spectrum of belief and practice. So-called high magic, including alchemy, natural astrology, numerology, and other such arcane disciplines (with a pedigree stretching back to classical Greece and Rome) was the province of learned men; as such, it remained a respected, even admired, branch of "humane" knowledge. Some of New England's foremost magistrates and ministers were among its devotees and practitioners: for example, John Winthrop Jr., midcentury governor of Connecticut and New England's most sought-after "physician," and Reverend Gershom Bulkeley, a leader of the Connecticut clergy.

Folk magic, however, was a different and far more controversial matter. For this there were specialized adepts, "cunning men" (and women) prepared to assist those who came to them in times of need. The largest group of recorded cases involved divining, the use of occult methods to foretell the future, to find lost or stolen objects, to access private information. In fact, fortune-telling represented the single most prominent category here, much larger in New than in Old England; examples can be piled up very fast. In Connecticut, a diviner working as a servant in a merchant's household forecast to a fellow "maid" that she would not marry her current sweetheart but rather "one named Simon" (which proved to be exactly the case). In Maine, the white mother of an illegitimate, mixed-race child had once been told by a fortune-teller "that she should mix seed with another nation, and that was true." In Massachusetts, yet another woman received a prediction "that she should meet with great trouble, if she escaped with her life"; transfixed with "horror," she then flung out of her house and was found dead the following day. Moreover, the famous Salem witch-hunt was thought to have begun when a group of young girls gathered around a glass with an egg white suspended inside—in effect, a primitive crystal ball and thus a traditional method of divining.

In the Salem case, there seems to have been no intermediary, no specialist, involved: the girls were acting on their own. And so it was in many other cases as well, for "folk magic" was truly a matter of the folk—ordinary individuals who knew something of the traditional lore (the procedures, the prescriptions) and sought to apply it as best they could. Besides divining, their efforts would frequently embrace healing, in response to illness and injury. One man had "an effectual remedy against the toothache," another "a cure for the ague"(fever, perhaps malaria), still another a quick fix for a broken leg. Two elderly brothers quarreled over a medicinally powerful "piece of gold" inherited from their mother; she had said "it might be of some benefit if any of us got a bad sore."

A detailed picture of these ideas and practices in actual operation can be drawn from the testimonies given in a court case against a "doctor woman" named Ann Burt of Lynn, Massachusetts, by several of her erstwhile patients. According to one, Burt had prescribed potions from a certain "glass bottle . . . and when I had drunk of it I was

worse." The same man would go on to experience frightening encounters with "familiar" animals, and then with Burt herself "upon
a gray horse . . . or one in her shape." A second witness reported that
on being "taken . . . to be cured of her sore throat," Burt had proffered a pipe "and said 'Sarah, will you smoke it?' . . . [And] she
smoked it, and . . . fell into fits . . . and said that Goodwife Burt
brought the Devil to torment her." Still others described the woman
invoking a force they called "her god," apparently as part of a treatment procedure. For example: "She said that her husband did not believe in her god and could not be cured, and that her maid did
believe in her god and was cured." This suggestion of a distinct
supernatural being—apart from the orthodox Christian pantheon—
is rare, if not unique, in the annals of New England folk magic. It
may have appeared in other cases as well; but if so, the traces have
long since been lost.

Another example of folk magic gone wrong comes from a New
Hampshire witchcraft case in 1680. A little boy had been taken ill,
and a neighbor, thought to be adept at healing, offered to try a cure.
Coming to the child's bedside in strange garb, "her face daubed with
molasses," she proceeded to enact the following ritual: "She . . .
smote the back of her hands together sundry times, and spat in the
fire. Then . . . having herbs in her hands, [she] stood and rubbed
them . . . and strewed them about the hearth. . . . Then she sat down
and said 'Woman, the child will be well,' and then went out of the
door." Even outside her actions continued; according to the parents'
later remembrance, she turned back to face the house and stood
"beating herself with her arms, as men do in winter to heat their
hands, and this she did three times . . . [while also] stooping down
and gathering something off the ground in the interim." As events
turned out, the child did not get well, but died within a few days.
And the would-be healer was held responsible, with her supposed
"remedy" construed now as witchcraft.

In fact, the lines between beneficent magic (including healing)
and *maleficium* were tenuous at best. And their strategies might

directly intersect. Image magic was considered especially potent and
dangerous—for example, the use of "poppets" (another name for
witch dolls) to represent particular human targets. Pinch or prick or
twist the poppet, and the intended victim would fall ill, break into
fits, or (in extreme cases) suffer mortal injury. As noted above, local
courts might order that a suspect's house be searched for such paraphernalia, and, at least occasionally, would claim to have found what
they were seeking. In a Boston case, this procedure yielded "several
small images . . . made of rags, and stuffed with goat's hair and other
such ingredients." The same results attended similar efforts made in
the course of the Salem trials.

Closely related to image magic as practiced *by* the witch were
various forms of counter-magic directed *against* her. For example,
urine might be taken from the victim, poured into a special con-
tainer, infused with pins and nails, and heated over a fire; this was
supposed to bring an immediate reaction—scalding, burning, or
other painful sensation—in the suspected perpetrator, wherever she
was. The same maneuver might also compel her to approach the
scene of her crime. In one such case, a suspect was observed "walk-
ing to and fro" beside her victim's house; she did not leave for some
hours, until after a certain urine-filled bottle had been "unstopped."
Thus might revenge and identification be achieved in a single stroke.
The key element in every instance was a powerful line of influence
believed to connect the witch and her victim—a kind of invisible,
magical tether—with effects that could travel in either direction.

Most, if not all, such practices appeared on both sides of the Atlantic; in this, as in much else, the colonists were simply carrying on
age-old Anglo-Saxon traditions. So-called witch bottles—most of
them stoneware jugs embellished with the frightening image of a
bearded man—have been recovered from rivers and trash-pits in
England. Typically they contain hair, fingernails, and other human
traces; presumably these, like urine, served to effect counter-magic.
(In one remarkable case the contents included a cloth heart pierced
with pins.) No similar discoveries have as yet been made for the

American colonies, but written evidence confirms the use of witch bottles there as well.

To these methods of magic and counter-magic were added many more. Palmistry, for one: much could be learned about "persons' . . . future condition by looking into their hands." Indeed, this was something of a learned discipline (broaching high magic); New England palm-readers would occasionally claim to have consulted books in which "there were rules to know what should come to pass." One diviner was skilled not only at reading hands but also in scrutinizing "veins about the eyes," apparently as a way to predict length of life. Astrology was yet another such resource. A Connecticut fortune-teller boasted of "great familiarity" with the noted English astrologer William Lilly—perhaps from personal acquaintance, or else from having "read [his] book in England" (her listeners couldn't be sure which).

Palms, eyes, and the stars; crystal balls, and obscure manipulations of keys, nails, table silver, "sieve and scissors": the accoutrements of folk magic went on and on. Indeed, everyday objects of various sorts might, under suitable circumstances, be associated with occult power, though many of the particulars are irrecoverable today. There were charms, too, involving the use of mysterious words and letter combinations—sometimes in written, sometimes in spoken, form. For instance, a Boston man used a "secret" healing ritual, organized around "five letters, viz., x, a, etc . . . written successively on pieces of bread and given to the patient." Conversely, there were curses, "ill words" designed to injure. Thus a Massachusetts woman, angered by a neighbor's charge of countenancing theft, wished that her accuser "might never *mingere* [urinate] or *carcare* [defecate]"; soon thereafter the neighbor was "taken with the distemper of the dry bellyache."

Toward all this—the interest, the beliefs, the actual practices of magic—the orthodox clergy of New England maintained a resolute, vehement opposition. For them it was nothing less than sacrilege, an affront to their own authority and, most of all, to God's. If layfolk needed protection against the slings and arrows of everyday life, this must come from the Almighty—and none other. If particular individuals experienced privation and suffering of a "remarkable" sort, redress should be sought through "solemn prayer"—and that alone. The difference between folk magic and "true religion" lay precisely here: the one was manipulative and human-based, the other supplicative and divinely ordained. And wherever magic had apparently succeeded in achieving some intended effect, its motive source could only be the Devil himself.

Christian clergy all across Europe had long held folk magic in dim repute; this was true for Protestants and Catholics alike. But to the extent that Protestants, more than Catholics, stressed the absolute sovereignty of God and the utter inability of man—to that same extent magic became an even greater, more blasphemous challenge. In fact, Protestantism may have unwittingly *invited* such challenge. For Protestants were, relative to Catholics, effectively disarmed, with traditional "intercessory" means denied them. No more saying of rosaries, no use of holy water or holy relics, no recourse to elaborate and enveloping church ritual; no potentially comforting doctrine of salvation by works. Instead, inherent sin and irrefutable weakness in the face of an all-powerful, largely inscrutable Deity: for Protestants, the human situation was as stark and as desperate as that. Individual men and women could only wait, only pray, only hope, only fear. Is it any wonder that some found this predicament too great to bear, and the temptation to magic—for the same reason—too hard to resist?

Within the full complex of Protestant belief, nothing evoked more anxiety, more agonized searching and speculation, than "predestination," the idea that God had already ordained the salvation or damnation of every living being. One's destiny was certain, and beyond all possibility of change; yet one could never know its nature. Such belief seems to have fostered an attitude of particular concern with the future: first and foremost, with the afterlife, but also with more immediate matters of everyday, "earthly" existence. This, in

turn, may help to explain the very unusual prominc
and fortune-telling in 17th-century New England.

Hear, now, a sampling of Puritan invective aga
Reverend Cotton Mather (Boston): "Tis in the Devil's
things are done, and in God's name I do this day charge tnem as viic
impieties." *Reverend Increase Mather* (Boston): "God in his word doth
with the highest severity condemn all such practices . . . declaring . . . that all who do such things are an abomination to him." *Reverend John Hale* (Beverly, Massachusetts): "[Magic] serves the interest
of those that have a vain curiosity to pry into things God has forbidden, and concealed from discovery by lawful means." *A "consocia-
tion" of ministers* (Connecticut): "Those things, whether past, present,
or to come, which . . . cannot be known by human skill in arts or
strength of reason . . . nor are made known by divine revelation . . .
must needs be known (if at all) by information from the Devil." *Reverend Cotton Mather* (again): "They are a sort of witches who thus
employ themselves." Indeed, Puritan ministers particularly emphasized the matter of links to witchcraft and the Devil; thus counter-
magic was also fatally compromised. *Reverend Deodat Lawson* (Salem,
Massachusetts): "Unwarrantable projects . . . [such as] burning the
afflicted person's hair, or stopping up and boiling the urine . . .
[amount to] using the Devil's shield against the Devil's sword."

As this controversy—folk magic versus orthodox religion—
simmered along, ordinary New Englanders were frequently caught
in the middle. And the middle is where at least some of them preferred to remain. Resisting the clergy's pressure to choose, these
persons would remain Christians, remain churchgoers, remain adherents of Puritan doctrine—yet would also avail themselves of
magical "remedies" when need and opportunity coincided. In the
language of our own time, they were (perhaps unwittingly) eclectics
and syncretists, inclined to move back and forth between rival systems despite strong pressures to the contrary. Sometimes, to be sure,
they paid a price in local reputation or feelings of guilt. A case in
point was Reverend John Hale's experience in dealing with a woman

parishioner much given to fortune-telling. She admitted to consulting "a book of Palmistry," and professed her sorrow and "great repentance." Hale told her this was, most assuredly, "an evil book and an evil art," after which she appeared "to renounce and reject all such practices." But some years later she was found to have resumed her former interest, to the point of obtaining additional books on the same subject.

Moreover, certain forms of magical practice seemed in themselves to bridge the gap to religion. The charms used in healing rituals could include "Scripture words" alongside others; for example, "Nomine patris, Filii, et Spritus Sancti. Preserve thy servant, [and] such . . ." (The Latinate phrasings here may suggest a Catholic derivation, which for devout Puritans would create a special objection.) The Bible itself was subject to magical deployment, with its aura of sanctity harnessed to efforts of healing or divination or counter-magic. The touch of a Bible on the forehead of a sick child might serve to begin a cure. A key placed between its pages could help reveal the location of objects gone missing. In one extraordinary instance, a group of New Hampshire townsmen marched out to brawl with some local opponents, led by their minister, who carried a Bible raised aloft on a long pole. In another, a Rhode Island man sought to insure his personal safety by ostentatiously reading his Bible in the town square while an Indian attack raged fiercely around him. Such behaviors, amounting to a kind of totemism, came as much from the magical side of traditional culture as from the formally religious one.

It was against this cultural backdrop that New England's notorious part in witch-hunting would begin to unfold. Of course, the *most* notorious part—and for many today the only known part—is everything that happened at Salem, Massachusetts, in 1692–93. Thus it seems necessary to emphasize here the very considerable amount of thought, feeling, and motivated action that swirled around witchcraft during the four or five decades preceding the Salem trials.

There are intimations of witchcraft in the records of the important and intensely felt "Antinomian controversy," in Massachusetts, as early as 1637. Anne Hutchinson, who led the movement at the center of this struggle and whose doctrinal claims seemed to challenge the very foundations of the Puritan establishment, was a unique presence: deeply thoughtful, eloquent, visionary, and charismatic, qualities that seemed somehow enhanced by her being also a woman. Her large following, composed of the many Boston folk who attended her special worship meetings, was another attention-getting element. Governor John Winthrop, her chief antagonist, referred to her as a "prophetess," and the term does seem apt. But such a woman would invite suspicion as well as admiration; she was, in a sense, too strong, too "nimble" of wit, for her own good. Her prophesying, in particular, would be held against her; her gifts that way seemed to some "beyond Nature." For example, a fellow passenger on the ship that had carried her to New England recalled her commenting as Boston came in sight, "if she had not a sure word that England should be destroyed, her heart would shake." *A sure word?* From where? In what sense? It seemed "very strange and witchlike that she should say so." Two years later, when the authorities brought her to account in a full-dress ecclesiastical trial, Winthrop would write more pointedly that her doings "gave cause of suspicion of witchcraft."

In fact, she was never formally accused as a witch; her trial, conviction, and subsequent banishment focused instead on her "heretical opinions" and "traducing authority." But she was charged with having been, at the very least, "deluded by the Devil." Moreover, two of her "confederates," Jane Hawkins and Mary Dyer, were similarly accused. Hawkins, like Hutchinson, was a midwife, whose practice allegedly included the use of traditional fertility potions; as a result, according to Winthrop, she became "notorious for familiarity with the Devil." Dyer and Hutchinson both experienced problematic childbirth—in Dyer's case, a stillborn and obviously deformed infant (perhaps the condition known to modern medicine as anencephaly); in Hutchinson's, a more extreme anomaly (probably what

is today called a hydatidiform mole). Such "monstrous" outcomes—
for so they struck her contemporaries—seemed a clear sign of diabolical connection.

That these suspicions did not lead straight to witchcraft prosecution was probably owing to a pair of convergent factors. First, heresy
was itself an enormously compelling, and damning, charge (especially in New England). Second, the usual prelude to witchcraft
cases—the gradual, piece-by-piece buildup of worry and doubt, over
many years, fostered always by a vigorous climate of local gossip—
was lacking here. Hutchinson, Hawkins, and Dyer were relatively
recent arrivals in Boston; so, too, were their adversaries. In a sense,
neither side knew the other sufficiently well to support a full measure of witchcraft accusation. Indeed, there would be no actual witch
trials in New England during the entire decade and a half following
the initial settlement in 1630. This pot needed a lengthy period of
brewing and stirring before it would boil. But eventually its time
would come, and trials would begin. And, once begun, they would
go on almost to the end of the century.

The earliest firm documentation of a formal proceeding against
witchcraft comes from the town of Windsor, Connecticut, in 1647.
Sometime that spring a local diarist recorded the following:
"One _____ of Windsor arraigned and executed for a witch." The
blank is filled in the notes of the town clerk: "May 26, '47 Alse Young
was hanged." Thus it was Alice Young's unfortunate distinction to
have been New England's first legally certified witch—and the first
to have suffered the prescribed punishment. About this woman only
a very few, very bare facts can now be discovered. She was apparently the wife of a certain John Young (or Youngs, as the name is
sometimes written) and the mother of at least one daughter. She was
probably middle-aged, in her 40s, when charged and convicted. John
Young was a man of limited means, perhaps a carpenter. He, and
presumably his wife, had settled in Windsor by or before 1640. He
sold his land there, and moved away, soon after his wife's death. And
that is the extent of her, and his, known story.

Within barely a year of Alice Young's execution at Windsor, the nearby town of Wethersfield began its own involvement with witch-hunting. Again, the official record is sparse, saying only: "The jury finds the bill of indictment against Mary Johnson, that by her own confession she is guilty of familiarity with the Devil." Fortunately, a later writing by Cotton Mather offers more. Johnson was evidently a domestic servant; Mather refers to the Devil's readiness to play tricks on "her master" in her behalf. Indeed, "she said that her first familiarity with the Devil came through *discontent,* and wishing the Devil . . . to do that and t'other thing, whereupon a Devil appeared unto her, tendering what services might best content her." From this she progressed to "uncleanness [sexual contact] both with men and with devils"; somewhere along the way, she also "murdered a child." Such confessions, rare enough in the record of witch trials, left no room for doubt; a sentence of death was assured. Her minister preached at her execution, "taking great pains to promote her conversion from the Devil to God." She seemed in her last moments "very penitent. . . . And she died in a frame extremely to the satisfaction of them that were spectators of it."

From Connecticut the witch-hunt trail swings north and east, to the communities surrounding Massachusetts Bay. An obscure case in Cambridge, possibly as early as 1647 or 1648, resulted in the execution of a certain Goodwife Kendall. Another proceeding, in 1648 against Margaret Jones of Charlestown, brought a similar outcome, this one more fully recorded. Jones had been acting as a fortune-teller and healer; perhaps she was a regular cunning woman. In any case, it was the details of her "practicing physic" that first aroused suspicion. "Her medicines . . . though [seemingly] harmless . . . had extraordinarily violent effects." Moreover, she showed "such a malignant touch as many persons (men, women, and children) whom she stroked or touched with any affection or displeasure . . . were taken with deafness or vomiting or other pains or sickness." When searched for the Devil's mark, she was found to have "an apparent teat in her secret parts." And a witness to her nights in prison (while awaiting trial) noted the comings and goings of a "familiar" spirit in the shape of "a little child."

In sum: four different towns, four suspects, four trials, four convictions, four executions—all within the short span of two years. To be sure, in Europe at the same time these numbers would not have seemed large. The Hopkins-Stearne witch "panic" had just recently concluded in the English countryside, where the total of those accused reached more than 300 (perhaps a third of whom were executed); many more cases would be prosecuted there during the 1650s. In southern Germany the craze rolled on unabated, with a toll in convictions and in lives too high for ready calculation. Still, given New England's infant state—two dozen towns and a few thousand people as of midcentury—four witch trials was considerable. And the pace would continue through the years that followed.

In 1651 Wethersfield tried and convicted two more of its inhabitants, a married couple named Carrington, for "having entertained familiarity with Satan, and by his help . . . done works above the course of nature." Little else is known about this pair, and nothing at all about their trial. Around the same time there were slander cases in several communities (Watertown, Marblehead, and Springfield, Massachusetts; Windsor, Connecticut): lawsuits filed on behalf of women against neighbors who had defamed them by intimating, or openly charging, their involvement in witchcraft. (Example: "She said . . . that there were diverse strong lights seen of late in the meadow that were never seen before the widow Marshfield came to town." And again: "it was publicly known that the Devil had followed her house in Windsor.")

In 1652 a much more substantial and serious case took place in Springfield. As one correspondent would describe it for a London newspaper: "Sad frowns of the Lord are upon us in regard of fascinations [magic] and witchcrafts. . . . Four in Springfield were detected, whereof one was executed for murder of her own child, and was doubtless a witch, another is condemned, a third under trial, a fourth under suspicion." The author of an early treatise on New England noted that the same little cabal had, "as is supposed, bewitched not a few persons, among whom [are] two of the reverend elder's children." At the center of these events was another married couple, Hugh and Mary Parsons; it was Mary who had allegedly killed her infant son. And there was much else as well, all of it fully laid out in numerous depositions that have come down to the present. The list included mysterious "disappearances," strange illness and injury, "threatening speeches" (especially by Hugh Parsons), and, perhaps most important, "fits" in several apparent victims. Mary seems to have admitted her guilt; her own testimony recounted startling details of "a night when I was with my husband and Goodwife Merrick and Bessie Sewell in Goodman Stebbins' lot. . . . We were sometimes like cats and sometimes in our own shape, and we were a-plotting for some good cheer. . . ." Her conviction, and execution, followed in due course. Hugh, though denying everything, was also convicted and condemned; however, the verdict was later reversed, and he fled to Rhode Island. The disposition of the other suspects is not recorded. But it seems clear enough that Springfield was convulsed for many months by this unfolding sequence; participants in the Parsons trial came from over half the town's households.

Taken as a whole, the 1650s would prove to be the single most active period for witchcraft prosecutions in New England (if the very large count from the Salem trials of 1692–93 is excluded as a kind of anomaly). The decade-long totals are: 27 separate trial proceedings with witchcraft at the center (including a few for slander), involving accusations against 35 different people, yielding 8 convictions and 7 executions. The towns represented were 22 in all—12 in Massachusetts, 7 in Connecticut, 2 in New Hampshire, and 1 in Maine. Only little Rhode Island escaped, perhaps because its culture was uniquely heterodox (an amalgam of religious sectarians and "freethinkers").

Another striking case within this same subset occurred in Boston, in 1656. The defendant, Mrs. Ann Hibbens, was a person of unusually high social position; indeed, she stood right at the pinnacle of the local elite. Her husband, William Hibbens, was a merchant of substantial wealth; moreover, he was an admired and important civic leader, a magistrate and member of the Court of Assistants, the colony's highest governing body. Mrs. Hibbens doubtless shared in the prestige of her husband's position. However, her personal style and ways of acting would frequently bring her to grief. In 1640 she had engaged in a long and bitter dispute with a group of carpenters hired to refurbish her house; she accused them of overcharging and other "false dealing." A resultant lawsuit in civil court went in her favor. But the manner in which she had pursued her case was so abrasive that the Boston church soon called her to account in a widely noticed ecclesiastical inquest. When she refused to apologize for her "very turbulent . . . actions" toward the carpenters, the church first admonished, then excommunicated her. Her husband pleaded on her behalf, yet also implicitly acknowledged her "uncharitable . . . and unChristian-like" behavior. Church authorities accused her of wronging him, too; as one of them put it, she had "against nature usurped authority over him [whom] . . . God hath set to be your guide." And the congregation itself suffered "offense" when she "obstinately" resisted its efforts of censure. Thus were her original "miscarriages" in several ways compounded.

Apparently she experienced (or caused) still other difficulties with her fellow townspeople; a contemporaneous writing, William Hubbard's *A General History of New England*, mentions her widespread reputation for "natural crabbedness of temper." And when her husband died in 1654, it was as if she had lost a protective shield. At this point, in Hubbard's words, "the *vox populi* went sore against her"; within months she was accused, and arraigned, as a witch. The details of her final trial have been lost, but we do know its outcome—conviction and a sentence of death by hanging.

At about the same time suspicion was aroused toward several people whose career as supposed witches would last for decades. Mary Parsons of Northampton, Massachusetts, was one such. Eunice Cole (Hampton, New Hampshire) was another; also Elizabeth Godman (New Haven, Connecticut), Jane James (Marblehead, Mas-

sachusetts), and John Godfrey (Andover, Massachusetts). These individuals fit a classic pattern, in which a reputation for practicing
witchcraft might never be shaken off; hence, they were subject to repeated court prosecutions.

Godfrey's was an especially remarkable story. In one respect it
was unusual; he was male. Within the relatively small subgroup of
accused men, most were husbands of previously suspected women;
theirs was a form of guilt by association. But Godfrey was unique in
being unmarried; he had no wife nor, for that matter, any other identifiable kin. He had reached Massachusetts by or before 1642, and had
almost immediately plunged into a blizzard of legal proceedings. Before he was through, he would set a new standard for litigiousness in
a generally litigious society. Suits and countersuits piled up around
him by the dozens: for debt, for breach of promise, for defamation,
for "abusive carriages" and "contempt to authority," among others.
Often he appeared as the plaintiff—Godfrey versus, Godfrey going
after, one or another of his neighbors—with more cases won than
lost. However, he was also a frequent defendant, and the charges
against him sometimes involved criminal conduct. He was accused
of theft, of arson, of suborning witnesses, of physical assault. And
he was accused, again and again, of practicing witchcraft. The testimonies generated by his nonstop legal involvement are large in
quantity and consistent in quality. Taken together, they depict a man
continually at odds with his peers over a host of quite specific, personal, and mundane affairs. They reflect, too, his typical manner:
his roughness, his unpredictability, his "threats" and "provocations"
and "rages." In all this he directly epitomized the character New
Englanders expected of their "witches"; he served, in effect, as an
extreme example of a typical pattern.

It is notable, finally, that Godfrey remained in and around his
Essex County home for more than three decades until his death
in 1675. Five times he stood in court under formal indictment for
witchcraft—which was, after all, a capital crime. And five times
he (more or less narrowly) escaped conviction. At least once a jury

declared him "suspiciously guilty of witchcraft, but not legally guilty according to law and [the] evidence we have received." Put on notice again and again, he kept coming back for more. Why not move off, and try for a new start elsewhere? Why take the chance that sooner or later he might indeed be found "legally guilty," and die as a consequence? The answer is elusive; but it seems that, at some level, his life and the lives of his Essex neighbors were forever locked together. Perhaps Godfrey's baleful presence served to focus a good deal of community distress, and even to explain a variety of personal (and social) misadventures. Meanwhile, he may himself have derived some covert gratification from his special notoriety as a "witch." Thus he could not—or, at any rate, would not—go away.

Eunice Cole of Hampton was a female version of John Godfrey. She, too, was repeatedly accused and often prosecuted for witchcraft, but never convicted. She, too, was an uncommonly rough and abrasive presence, given to "unseemly speeches" and outright physical brawling. Her reputation, like Godfrey's, was widely known; indeed, it would long outlive her. Tales of her supposed witchcraft entered into local folklore; some were recounted (as one Hamptonite of the 19th century put it) "from generation to generation." In 1938, on the 300th anniversary of the town's founding, its people took official action to reconcile with her: "Resolved, that we, the citizens of Hampton . . . believe that Eunice (Goody) Cole was unjustly accused of witchcraft . . . in the 17th century, and we do hereby restore . . . her rightful place as a citizen of this town." Even today, children in Hampton know her name and reenact her supposed misdeeds, and shudder a bit when they pass near her old homesite.

Goodwife James, Goodwife Godman: their stories, too, were variations on the same theme. Suspicion that went on and on; occasional court trials; acquittals each time (but, in some cases, accompanied by a stern warning). Also: uninterrupted residence among the very people whose enmity and suspicion threatened their lives. With the passage of many years, such "witches" became fixtures of local culture, almost as familiar as Sabbath services and barn raisings.

The decade of the 1660s was nearly as prolific of witchcraft cases as the one preceding, with 25 trials all told, 32 people charged, 5 convictions, 4 executions, and 16 different towns represented. However, now a new element was added: the years 1662–64 brought New England's first experience of "panic witchcraft"—the sort that spreads and multiplies in contagious fashion, with one accusation feeding another and another and another. Its seat and source was Hartford, Connecticut. Its exact origins are obscure, but the "very strange fits" of a young woman in the town seem to have been central. As these developed, "her tongue was improved by a Demon to express things which she herself knew nothing of." Strangely, too, her "discourse passed into a Dutch-tone," and then revealed "mischievous designs . . . [by] such and such persons" against several neighbors.

"Such and such" included, first of all, a certain "lewd and ignorant woman . . . by the name of Greensmith," who was already imprisoned "on suspicion for witchcraft." (Those are the words of Boston's Reverend Increase Mather, writing about the Hartford trials some years later. Rebecca Greensmith appears, from other evidence, to have been a fairly ordinary New England goodwife, with no public record of lewdness or any similar misconduct.) In accordance with established procedures, the accused was examined by a group of magistrates and ministers, who gradually drew out of her an expansive confession. She described all sorts of "familiarity with the Devil . . . [including] carnal knowledge of her body," and witch meetings "at a place not far from her house . . . [where] some appeared in one shape, and others in another; and one came flying amongst them in the shape of a crow." Why did she admit to so much? Was she delusional? Had she yielded to intolerable social and legal pressures? (An apparent eyewitness to her interrogation described her feeling "as if her flesh had been pulled from her bones . . . and so [she] could not deny [her guilt] any longer.") Her statements were more than enough to bring about her conviction and a sentence of death. Moreover, they directly implicated her husband, and he, too, was executed, "though he did not acknowledge himself guilty."

With a victim whose Devil-fueled "discourse" had identified a variety of possible suspects, and a self-confessed witch whose statements did essentially the same, there was every reason to press for further inquiry. So now the net of accusation spread out across Hartford, and into neighboring towns such as Wethersfield and Farmington. The full sequence can no longer be recovered, but at least a few striking details are known. Suspicion fell on another couple, and a group of townspeople decided to try the notorious "ducking" test. Accordingly, both husband and wife "had their hands and feet tied, and were cast into the water." When they appeared to float "after the manner of a buoy," bystanders concluded that the Devil must be holding them up. The ministers, including Increase Mather, who reported on the use of this procedure, regarded it as ignorant superstition; perhaps they even tried to intervene. One way or another, the accused couple managed to escape; as Mather described it, "however doubting that a halter [i.e. for hanging] would choke them, though the water would not, they fairly took their flight, not having been seen in that part of the world since." Among the additional suspects—about a dozen were prosecuted over a period of nearly three years—four were acquitted, six convicted, and at least two (plus the Greensmith pair) executed. It made for a total unmatched in any other single episode, until the Salem trials.

There is another case from the 1660s that offers an especially clear view of the predicament to which a supposed witch might come. The principal was a Connecticut woman named Katherine Harrison. Wife of a well-to-do merchant, mother of three, and a longtime adept at fortune-telling and folk healing, she was also reputed to have been (in years previous) a "sabbath breaker," a "notorious liar," and "one who followed the army in England" (in short, a prostitute). In 1666 her husband died suddenly, and Katherine was exposed to a withering blast of local antagonism. Almost immediately she endured a flurry of lawsuits: three or four around questions of property, two more on charges of slander. She lost them all, and was ordered to pay large fines and damages. In pleading her side, she asked the court for special consideration, "being a distressed widow, a female, a weaker vessel meeting with overbearing experiences." The latter were detailed in a separate declaration under the heading of "many injuries which have happened since my husband's death"— chiefly, assaults on her property. They included: "A yoke of oxen . . . spoiled . . . before our door, with blows upon the back and side . . . A cow spoiled, her back broke and two of her ribs . . . 30 poles of hops cut and spoiled . . . A cow at the side of my yard, her jawbone broke . . . and a hole bored in her side . . . A three-year-old heifer . . . stuck with a knife . . ." The list continued through 13 separate incidents. Read today, it suggests the profound vulnerability of a woman struggling to carry on alone amidst a throng of bitterly hostile foes. (How could she sleep at night, knowing what threatened on every side? Maybe she couldn't. To whom might she turn for help? Apparently there was no one.)

Witchcraft charges followed soon enough. And Katherine was subjected to three separate court proceedings over a span of roughly 18 months. The first ended in her acquittal, the second in a hung jury, the third in a conviction that was, however, reversed by the magistrates. ("This court cannot concur . . . so as to sentence her to death.") By then she had apparently decided to pack up and leave, "having disposed of the great part of her estate." The court added a further nudge of its own, directing her "to mind the fulfillment of removing from Wethersfield, which is what will lend most to her own safety and the contentment of the people who are her neighbors"; this may have been a politely worded form of banishment. Several weeks later she appeared in Westchester, New York. But her reputation had preceded her, and her wish to resettle there was immediately opposed. New litigation began, and dragged on for months. This time she would eventually be vindicated—cleared of "suspicion," and allowed to "remain . . . where she now resides." Even so, there is a strong possibility that she was again deemed a witch by her neighbors. And here her trail peters out.

The 1670s began with no sign that the tempo of witch-hunting would slacken. There were new cases in Massachusetts, in Connecticut, and even in rarely affected Rhode Island. One, in particular, stands out, although it did not produce an actual court proceeding. Its focus was "diabolical possession," with the Devil apparently invading his victim's very person and taking control of her from the inside. This was always a possibility with witchcraft, and at least occasionally a key element. And when it happened, it could be sensational.

Such was the case at Groton, Massachusetts, toward the end of the year 1671. A teenage girl named Elizabeth Knapp had for some time been living and working as a maidservant in the home of the town's minister, Samuel Willard. There, as autumn came on, Elizabeth began to experience fits of steadily increasing intensity. Luckily for historians, Reverend Willard decided to keep a written account of her difficulties. (He did not, to be sure, have historians in mind; rather, he wished to create a record that would be useful to other clergy confronting similar situations.) He was meticulous to a fault in noting the many baffling and unsettling details. At one point, he described Elizabeth being "seized . . . in such ways that six persons could hardly hold her; but she leaped and skipped about the house perforce, roaring and yelling extremely and fetching deadly sighs as if her heartstrings would have broken, and looking with a frightful aspect, to the amazement and astonishment of all the beholders." At another, "she was . . . suddenly thrown down into the midst of the floor . . . and with much ado . . . kept out of the fire from destroying herself." At still another, "she was hurried into . . . striking those that held her [and] spitting in their faces." Willard noted, too, how "her tongue [would be] for many hours drawn into a semicircle up to the roof of her mouth, and not to be removed (for some tried with fingers to do it)." And he especially remarked the times when she "barked like a dog and bleated like a calf, in which her organs were visibly made use of." By the time he was done, descriptions like these filled dozens of pages.

As both her minister and her master, Willard had a special responsibility for Elizabeth; thus, he sought repeatedly to calm her, to converse with her, to pray over her. He, and many others who came to lend a hand or simply to gape at the spectacle, wished most of all to discover the source of Elizabeth's troubles. Near the start she "seemed to impeach one of the neighbors" as a witch (and thus as her presumed tormentor). But, for reasons the minister did not explain, this accusation was disregarded. Some time later she "cried out" against a second person, but that too failed to convince. Henceforth, suspicion would shift to the possibility of her own guilt. Pressed hard by Willard, she conceded to having met with the Devil, and "given of her blood . . . and made a covenant with him." She quickly regretted these admissions, and tried unsuccessfully to retract them. Her fits grew stronger and stronger. Bystanders crowded around in ever increasing numbers. Finally came the climax—on a Sabbath day, in front of a large, frightened, utterly fascinated audience of local townspeople. Her body assumed a succession of "amazing postures." Then a strange "grum" voice—nothing like her own— erupted from somewhere deep inside her, reviling the minister in terms such as the following: "Hold your tongue! Hold your tongue! Get you gone, you black rogue! What are you going to do! You have nothing to do with me! . . . I am a pretty black boy, and this is my pretty girl." It was blasphemy, all blasphemy, from start to finish.

In Willard's mind, this appalling scene resolved any doubt "whether she might properly be called a demoniac, or person possessed by the Devil"; there could be no other explanation. Elizabeth's troubles waxed and waned for several weeks longer, and "the same voice" produced at least one more bravura performance. "Thus she continues . . . to this instant . . . followed with fits," wrote the minister. But here his narrative abruptly broke off. Sooner or later she must have recovered. She remained a resident of Groton. Within a few years she married, and began to bear children. Supremely notorious at one point in her girlhood, she now settled back into the ranks of ordinary folk in her village community.

Reverend Willard, meanwhile, would soon leave Groton for a far more prestigious pastorate in Boston. There he became a leader of the ministry at large. And there, some two decades later, he again came face-to-face with "diabolical" forces as a riptide of terror rolled down from Salem. This time he would advocate on the side of caution. His sermons warned of the danger that innocent parties might be impersonated—their "shapes" unwittingly assumed, their identities simulated—by the Devil. Here was an implicit challenge to Salem's "afflicted" accusers, whose lethal charges rested mainly on "spectral" evidence. For such temerity he would himself be denounced as a witch by some of those same accusers; fortunately, his friends among the judges refused to listen. And through it all, one cannot help but wonder: Did he perhaps hear echoes, from years before at Groton, of his long and difficult struggles over poor, possessed Elizabeth?

The middle part of the same decade brought new forces and new preoccupations suddenly to the center. The largest of these was a truly horrific race war—"white versus red," colonists versus Indians—known to succeeding generations as King Philip's War. The human toll was unparalleled before or since in American history, with a casualty rate approaching 10 percent of total population on the side of the colonists, and even higher among the Indians. Warfare drew attention away from witchcraft: what there was of that remained mostly at the level of local suspicion. In the four years from 1675 through 1678, only one witchcraft accusation generated an actual indictment. But at war's end the pace picked up again, with nine indictments and six full-fledged trials (five resulting in acquittal, one in a conviction that was subsequently reversed) during the next four-year span (1679–82). There was additional activity in the half-dozen years after that, but without trial convictions. It is worth noting, and underscoring, that no one was executed for witchcraft anywhere in New England between 1663 and 1688.

Was this history, then, gradually playing itself out? At the time it might have seemed so. But in 1688 an especially strong prosecution developed in Boston against a supposed witch surnamed Glover.

(Her given name is not recorded.) She was Irish, Gaelic-speaking, and presumably Catholic—all of which would, from the start, have placed her in a dubious light for most New Englanders. Her leading accusers, and putative victims, were members of a neighboring family who had employed her as a laundress. The sequence was familiar enough: dispute, angry exchanges, fear of retaliation—and then, crucially, "fits" in several of the neighboring family's children. The upshot was a full-blown trial, ending with Glover's conviction, confession, and execution. There were other suspects as well, and Bostonians at large grew more and more alarmed. The local clergy was much involved, especially Cotton Mather. Eventually, the children's fits abated, and a kind of normalcy returned. Glover's was the first New England witchcraft case in 25 years to reach the point of capital punishment. Of course, it would not be the last.

To describe the history of witchcraft is one thing; to explain it is quite another. New England affords an unusual opportunity in both connections. Because so many hands have written about it, both then and since, and because records from the time are so copious, New England allows us to see in remarkable detail the personal, social, and historical sources of witch-hunting. On the personal level, every witchcraft case involved a clash between accusers and supposed perpetrators—one or more in each category. Always, too, there had to be victims, who might or might not act also as accusers. (Without a victim, there wouldn't be sufficient motive to pursue a case into, and through, the stage of formal prosecution.) Witch, accuser, victim: such were the essential roles in an oft-repeated, loosely scripted, real-life drama.

In many respects, the profile of the typical New England witch followed long-standing European precedent. She was *female,* first of all. On both sides of the Atlantic the ratio among the accused of women to men was roughly four to one. On both sides, too, the minority of male witches included quite a few whose status as suspect was clearly secondary—derived, that is, from connection to a previ-

ously accused woman (her husband or, less often, her son). With rare
exceptions, then, the primary witches were women. The reasons for
this certainly included the same female-inferiority principle that
held throughout the early modern English and European world,
where women were seen as inherently "weak," especially from a
moral standpoint, and thus liable to "seduction" by the Devil. Deeper
still lay the fundamentally misogynous substrate that appears quite
generally in "mother raised children": a kind of price women are
forced to pay for being chief caretakers of the very young and the
reference point for the earliest, most primitive, experiences of self
and other. Thus did witches serve, worldwide, as a variant of the
"bad mother."

In addition, she was *of middle age;* here, too, the New England pattern mirrored Europe's. A reputation for involvement with witchcraft began, most commonly, within the life decades of the 40s and
50s. To be sure, actual prosecution in court might only come years
later, after the underlying suspicions had grown and solidified. But
even at this more advanced point, when legally charged and indicted,
accused witches cannot be fitted to current notions emphasizing extreme old age.

She was *of English and Puritan* stock. New England colonists did
not, on the whole, comprise an ethnically or racially diverse population; neither did their population of accused witches. Goodwife
Glover's Irish background was exceptional; so, too, with a handful of
others (a Dutchwoman accused at Hartford, a French Huguenot on
Long Island). The same was true of religion; suspicion went not
against members of marginal groups (Quakers, Baptists, Catholics,
Jews), but rather toward people in the Protestant mainstream.

She was *married or widowed.* "Spinsters" were, in any case, a rar-
ity in early New England—and were never found in the ranks of
accused witches. Virtually all of the latter were, or had been,
"goodwives."

But, goodwife or not, her life history was likely to show a tangle
of *troubled family relationships.* Many witch suspects were chronically

at odds with their spouses and children. This could mean open disagreements, public disputes, even physical violence; not for them the Puritan ideal of a "well-ordered household."

Her family experience might also include *childbearing that fell signficantly below expectation*. Accused witches often had fewer children than the typical woman; sometimes they had none at all. Thus, in the eyes of their peers, they would seem relatively (or entirely) "barren." This may help to explain a recurrent theme in the accusations lodged against them: their supposedly "strange," envious, perhaps malign interest in the children of others. Indeed, connections between childbearing (and -rearing) on the one hand, and witchcraft on the other, are everywhere apparent in the record: children made ill, or murdered, by witchcraft; mothers bewitched while nursing or otherwise caring for infants; witches who suckled "imps" or "familiars" (in implicit parody of normal maternal function).

She was *of lowly social and economic position*. Most New England witches were the wives and daughters of farmers or craftsmen whose wealth and standing were distinctly below average. But there were also important exceptions. A few of the accused, like Boston's Ann Hibbens, belonged to the local elite. A few more were notable for having experienced extreme change in their social rank, in either an upward or a downward direction. A considerably larger number held some degree of independent control over family property—an unusual and perhaps suspicion-arousing situation for a woman.

There was a significant chance that she *professed and practiced a healing vocation*. To be sure, a considerable majority of accused witches could not have been characterized that way; like all colonial goodwives, they knew and used the rudiments of folk medicine (herbs, plasters, and a variety of age-old household nostrums), but nothing more. However, perhaps a quarter to a third of the suspect group *did* know—and do—more: making and administering special "remedies," providing expert forms of nursing, or serving in some regular way as midwives. A few were specifically described as "doctor women." ("Physicians" was a term reserved for men. There remains, of course, the more sinister category of "cunning women" whose expertise would also include healing.) The underlying linkage here is obvious enough; the ability to heal and the ability to harm seemed intimately related. A shift from one to the other might require no more than a change of motive.

She was also much more likely than New England women at large to have been *previously prosecuted on criminal charges* (separate from witchcraft). The crimes involved were, most especially, theft and various forms of verbal assault—slander, "cursing," "filthy speeches." ("Lying" and sexual misconduct also figured into this array, but at somewhat lower levels.) Theft was not, for criminals in general, a major category; so its prominence here seems significant. Assaultive speech was often experienced as a kind of theft; slanderous words, for example, might take away a good reputation. And something similar could be said of witchcraft, a perennial threat to the secure possession of property, health, and life itself.

She was, finally, *contentious in character and abrasive in personal style*. An unusually sympathetic contemporary put it this way: "Many times persons of hard favor and turbulent passions are apt to be condemned by the common people for witches, upon very slight grounds." To decode such terminology now is difficult. Quite likely, some portion of the accused were deeply troubled—even psychotic, in the language of modern psychiatry. But others come across as impressively strong and self-determined women. To most of their peers, no doubt, they seemed rather *too* strong and self-determined, *especially* for a woman. And witchcraft charges provided the means to draw a firm line of disapproval.

It was, of course, the accusers who supplied the motive power— the energy—to fuel witch-hunting. And as with witch-accusers everywhere, their own internal energy *source,* on which their actions invariably drew, was nothing more or less than strong emotion: anger, fear, excitement, distress, usually in close combination. All of this was manifest in the details of the trial testimonies given by, or about, them: "She . . . said [with] tears running down her cheeks."

"She . . . cried out with great violence." "He . . . was so affrighted [and] in such a sweat that one might have washed hands on his hair." "She said she was . . . in agony of spirit." "She trembled and shook like a leaf." Additional examples could be accumulated literally by the hundreds.

Individual accusers and victims spanned a broad range, young and old, male and female. Yet certain demographic categories were disproportionately represented among them. One major subgroup comprised middle-aged women—from the same cohort, in fact, that produced a majority of the accused. Linked by age and sex, such persons were likely to be closely acquainted through all kinds of shared experience: shared work, shared domesticity, shared participation in local trade; shared companionship, shared confidences; shared attitude, opinion, and inner preoccupation. To read the records of village-level witchcraft is to sense the power of female "gossip groups," in which enmity as well as support circulated freely back and forth.

If life-stage circumstance made certain women targets of witchcraft suspicion, life-stage anxieties prompted others to feel and to voice such suspicion. On both sides of this intramural divide, menopausal change appears to have been key. The charges leveled by accusing women expressed, most of all, their feelings of loss and deprivation—loss of health, of status, of productive (and reproductive) capacity, of personal well-being. Thus: *I have such pains in my bowels as never I felt before, and know not how to be free of them.* Or: *My child was always well, till one day he complained of cats, and lay sick; I gave him physick [medicine], and watched with him many a night, but he died a fortnight after.* Or: *I spun my wool as best I could, yet from that day forward it would never be strong.* To this category of accusers the figure of the witch stood as a kind of thief, snatching away prized elements of life and self.

A second category of accusers, at least as large as the first, included men between the ages of 20 and 40. These were, in many individual lives, years of chronic worry and stress. Every young man was obliged to negotiate a series of crucial transitional steps: leaving

the parental household and starting a family of his own, inherit-
ing property and establishing an independent stake in the local community, beginning to move toward positions of public trust and
responsibility. His concerns ran, necessarily, to competence, skills,
managerial oversight. And these were what chiefly appeared when
he, or one of his age-mates, came forward to testify against suspected
witches. *Why does my cow, as lusty a beast as ever we knew, now lie a-
wasting in the yard afflicted with vomit and griping?* Or: *By whose means
did my reaping hooks bend and break, just as harvest-time began?* Or:
*Whence came the two snakes that bit my horse, as I rode to court last Mich-
aelmas?* Here the witch was cast as a spoiler—an evil force that made
even the best-laid plans go awry.

A third group of accusers involved girls in their teen years. This
contingent did not always appear in witchcraft cases, but if present,
its impact could be decisive. Famous, most of all, for their role in the
panic outbreak at Salem, girls "in their fits" pointed (sometimes literally) toward the Devil and his witch-filled legions. Fits were, most
assuredly, their major symptom: wild, intense, altogether grotesque
outbursts of physical and emotional distress. The words of the trial
testimonies strain to convey the full measure. *Insufferable tortures
and impertinent frolics . . . Intolerable ravings . . . Preposterous courses and
mischievous designs . . . Nasty and ludicrous foolish tricks . . . Roaring and
shrieking and hallooing . . . Pinching, scratching, biting, and cutting . . .
Leaping, running, flailing about . . . Swooning and fainting away . . . Amazing postures: head twisted round, and tongue drawn out; legs and arms
stiffened, back doubled over . . . Bitter tears, sobbing and complaining . . .
Sweating and panting . . . Deadly, heartbreaking sighs . . . Noisome
smells . . . Saucy discourse . . . Threatening speeches . . . Barking like a
dog, bleating like a calf, purring like cats, clucking like hens . . . Eyes sealed
up . . . Teeth clenched . . . Mouth locked shut.* The effect on those who
stood by was huge, "representing a dark resemblance of hellish torments." In this way more than any other did "the Devil make a full
discovery of himself." And it was the witch who used her malign in-

fluence to set off fits; she would serve as instigator, and carrier, of the Devil's will.

Fits constituted a highly ritualized performance; typically, they followed a virtual script, well-known from much previous experience throughout the Anglo-American world. (Variants of the same element appeared in European witchcraft cases as well.) As such, they expressed a kind of cultural idiom, part of an evolving New England heritage. Yet, however tightly rooted in a given historical situation—this time, that place—the fits scenario also reflected universal themes in adolescent development. For one thing, the underlying dynamic, with teenage girls accusing middle-aged women, effectively relocated commonplace mother-daughter struggles. For another, fits included a large quotient of sheer personal display. In most pre-modern settings, young girls commanded less public attention than any other demographic subgroup; in witch trials that imbalance could be directly, and dramatically, reversed. Additional motivating forces came from further down in the psychological depths. Too complex for easy summary here, these fundamentally embraced the reorganization of personality that is central to adolescence everywhere (sexual maturation, identity, individuation). Of course, most young people, then as now, would manage to contain such growth challenges within socially approved limits; the witchcraft record spotlights a small but conspicuous fringe of extreme and emotionally fraught cases.

Three different source points, then, of especially potent accusation: women in midlife, young-adult men, adolescent girls. But a great many other folk, not themselves direct participants, were at least vicariously pulled in. For witch-hunting operated, always and everywhere, as a matter of collective fantasy. Indeed, the image of the witch helped shape both moral standards and cognitive understanding. Almost anyone might have sketched its leading elements. First and definitely foremost came postures of attack; witches were thought to be consumed by rage and the wish to inflict harm. (In this regard the Puritan witch stereotype contrasted markedly with its counterpart in the Catholic regions of Europe. There, the emphasis went heavily toward sexuality, with the Devil as lecher supreme, and witches as unfailingly "carnal.") Another central aspect here was blatant, and insistent, intrusiveness; witches would routinely violate conventional boundaries, so as to invade their victims' personal space. Yet another was envy, a wheedling, grasping covetousness that knew no rest. Taken together, this triad formed the very epitome of "evil" character (as the Puritans saw such things). The effect was to draw crucial markers between the bad and the good, the sinful and the sanctified—with the figure of the witch on one side, and that of virtuous, God-fearing folk on the other.

The same stereotype was, moreover, profoundly shaped by inner-life experience among many (most? all?) members of this particular population, with roots stretching far back into their formative years. Among the various human emotions, Puritans came down hardest on anger—and did so most insistently with the very young. A New England child learned virtually in the cradle that "meekness" and "forbearance" were cardinal virtues and the open expression of anger their direct, abhorred opposite. Moreover, the wilfulness that almost invariably appears during the second and third years of life (any life) was construed by Puritan parents as a sign of "original sin"; thus it must be stifled, fought back, punished at all costs. In the child's world this pressure could only be felt as a shattering breach of personal boundaries, an encroachment so strong as to leave a lasting impress on subsequent development. Not coincidentally, the same themes would continually reinvest the traditional stereotype of the witch.

Individuals might invoke the stereotype at times of acute personal need—or, better still, might invoke its nearest, most palpable incarnation, the witch in their own community. Unwanted feelings could be projected onto her: *I am not angry, or envious, or intrusive; she is.* Embarrassing failures could be laid at her door: *Last summer's poor crop wasn't my fault; she made it happen.* Unexpected and unsettling misfortune could be explained as the result of her malefic intent: *She brought the lightning that set our meetinghouse afire.* In a world where so much of experience was immediately, and intensely, personal— and where nothing was considered random, or attributed to mere chance—such ways of thinking made eminently good sense.

Indeed, whole communities, no less than individuals, derived important gains from their encounters with witchcraft. When a troublesome person had been removed, following conviction as a witch, a village or neighborhood would experience a fresh surge of unity; moreover, the process of removal might itself seem restorative: *The evil that was formerly among us is no more; we are stronger, purer, better now.* Simply to join in cosmically important struggle—God versus Satan, with their bitterly opposed followers—was a major route to self-enhancement: *We have faced down the mighty enemy, and our lives are the larger for it.*

So much for the psychological and social vectors of witch-hunting; one additional aspect has yet to be considered—nothing less, in fact, than history. Concern with witchcraft was never entirely constant; to the contrary, it rose and fell over time. Trial proceedings would represent a peak moment. And there were troughs, periods without trials, as well. Seen in retrospect, the details of this oscillating line are admittedly complex and often obscure, but the question posed is simple. What forms of community distress—anxiety, doubt, fear—proved most likely to generate concerted action against witches? Conversely, what factors served to inhibit such action?

Careful study of particular sites and regions over time does suggest a degree of patterning. Distress would be elevated, first of all, by certain obviously harmful events (epidemic disease, for example) and weather extremes (hurricanes, floods, droughts) and widespread crop failures, and also more localized happenings, like a cluster of house fires or of shipwrecks at sea. Any or all of these would be felt not only as a matter of physical loss but also as a form of "chastening" sent by the Almighty to punish sin and prompt repentance. Another, roughly parallel category involved "remarkable" events in nature, such as the sudden appearance of comets, eclipses, meteors, rainbows, and *aurora borealis*. These were not ordinarily destructive in and of themselves, but their rare and highly visible occurrence identified them as "signs" of providential intent. (Not surprisingly, the "celestial firmament" was their most likely source point.) Most often they were construed as divine warning: human, "earthly" conduct must improve, *or else*. Thus they, too, might substantially raise prevalent levels of anxiety. A third such category lay more fully within the province of human affairs; its defining element was social conflict, or "controversy," in the language of the time. Perhaps there was persistent factional struggle within a community divided around issues of religious belief, or local governance, or the division of property. Perhaps, instead, the trouble came from outside: an Indian war, or an outbreak of intercolonial violence (between the British settlers and their opposite numbers in French Canada, for instance). Since Puritans placed a high premium on "peace" and cooperative human relationships, episodes of conflict directly undermined them; the consequences were liable to include deep emotional stress, especially guilt, and a need to find some external cause.

These three elements, then, did much to shape the profile of witchcraft cases over time. Harms and signs were both predisposing to witchcraft, usually within a year or so after their occurrence. (Epidemics, in particular, seem to have preceded witch trials with some regularity.) Conflict was more ambivalent in its effects. In the moment of its actual happening, it would usually serve to suppress (or divert) concern with witchcraft; the energies it evoked were at least temporarily all-consuming. In its aftermath, however, the flow might easily turn back the other way, as guilt began to fuel an anxious search for scapegoats. To be sure, all such links, as seen from several centuries later on, are more a matter of correlation than demonstrable cause and effect. Moreover, the presence of one element by itself would not ordinarily prove efficacious. But with a convergence of two, three, or more, the likelihood of witch-hunting did indeed increase dramatically.

The Connecticut witchcraft panic of the 1660s can serve as a case in point. Between 1656 and 1660, several of the colony's leading towns plunged into religious dispute—and, for exactly that same period, experienced a complete respite from witch trials. Then, at the start of the next decade, the dispute was settled (largely because the members of one faction chose to relocate northward into Massachusetts); presumably, though, residues of guilty soul-searching remained or even increased. Moreover, springtime in 1661 brought a succession of damaging floods to the entire Connecticut River Valley, plus a virulent outbreak of influenza-like "fevers"; both were widely interpreted as punishing "frowns" of the Lord. The next year was the first of several in which a killing summertime crop blight overspread New England's farms. And in 1664 came a dramatic "blazing star" (comet) thought to foretell yet more "great and dreadful" events. These were, finally, years full of witch-hunting in Connecticut, beginning (as noted above) in Hartford and then radiating out into three or four adjacent communities. From the troubled aftermath of conflict, to providential "frowns" and "signs," to the Devil let loose in their midst: thus, for people of the time, the essential, and "awful," progression.

Listen to Cotton Mather, as he forged his own chain of connections: "I believe there never was a poor plantation more pursued . . . than our New England. . . . First, the Indian *powwaws* . . . Then *seducing spirits* . . . After this a continual *blast* upon some of our principal grains . . . Herewithal wasting *sicknesses* . . . Next many adversaries of our own language . . . Desolating *fires* also . . . And *losses* by sea . . . Besides all which . . . the devils are come down upon us with such a wrath as is justly . . . the astonishment of the world." Mather wrote this in 1693, under the direct shadow of the Salem trials, but his perspective was that of New England's entire history to date. And now we must ask—as he did—*why?* Why was this one region so much more deeply preoccupied with witchcraft than any of its neighbors? Mather's answer was sure: "If any are scandalized that New England, a place of as serious piety as any I can hear of under Heaven, should be troubled with so many witches, I think 'tis no wonder: where will the Devil show the most malice but where he is hated, and hateth, most?"

Such claims to "serious piety" should be accepted. Though never completely homogeneous in this or any other regard, New Englanders did conform their life patterns to religious principle in ways quite extraordinary even by the standard of their own time. Their church-going, their spiritual "watchfulness," their sense of transcendent "mission": such things truly set them apart, and raised the stakes of moral value—for witchcraft and much else. The Devil, in his unceasing quest to control the universe, might be anywhere around them (or among them); thus, against his "wiles" they must be ever vigilant.

Alongside their own explanation for New England's preeminence in witch-hunting, we may add another yielded by hindsight. Nowhere else in colonial America was the social web so tightly enveloping. To the south (Virginia, for example), settlement was widely dispersed, in direct antithesis to New England's typical nucleated-village plan. In the middle colonies (New York, Pennsylvania), clustered communities more generally prevailed but lacked New England's intensely intramural focus. Only in Cotton Mather's "poor plantation"—poor, yet proudly self-congratulating—was there such interactive pressure and density. "We must be knit together," John Winthrop had said long before; and so, for the most part, they were. In this context especially, witchcraft seemed plausible, if not quite a logical necessity. For witchcraft coupled one important category of events—sudden misfortune, loss, suffering—with a critical nexus of *personal* and *social*, no less than supernatural, forces.

As the 17th century's final decade began, New Englanders were feeling sorely beset by events both near at hand and far away. On the political front, a seven-year sequence of jolting changes was still in process; its effect was to challenge, and ultimately to reduce, the region's autonomy. Further upheaval seemed likely though hard to predict; hence, the outlook was, to say the least, unsettling. On the military front, the major European powers, together with their various colonial possessions, were at war. In America this meant New England versus New France (Canada), with sharp, if sporadic, bursts of fighting throughout the wilderness borderlands; targets particularly included English villages in Maine, New Hampshire, and New York, several of which suffered devastating surprise attacks.

And then came a renewal of witchcraft. Accusations surfaced—though without producing full-fledged trials—in Boston (1689 and 1691), New Haven (1689), and Northampton (1691). In 1692 a more significant outbreak gripped the coastal Connecticut towns of Stamford and Fairfield; indeed, for a time this one approached panic dimensions. It began in March, in the household of a locally prominent family, when a servant-girl named Katherine Branch suddenly "fell into fits." The details conformed to long-established precedent: wild physical contortions, trance, fainting spells, "naughty" words and looks, spectral confrontations with the Devil—all in the presence of numerous enthralled onlookers—and with the naming, finally, of supposed witch "tormentors." No fewer than six women were thus brought under suspicion. A special court was convened, and dozens of witnesses offered testimony as to their own dealings with the accused; following more lengthy precedent, they reported quarrels, threats made and received, cows that died strangely, "injuries" of every sort. The proceedings continued throughout the summer months, in an atmosphere of mounting acrimony and excitement. Local townsfolk divided into opposite camps, with some supporting, others doubting (or rejecting outright) the main charges. The doubters included several members of the court and a group of ministers whose opinion was sought and given. In the end their viewpoint prevailed; only two of the original six suspects were indicted, and the trial jury convicted but one. She, in turn, was eventually "reprieved" by a committee of magistrates.

But at almost exactly the same moment that Katherine Branch plunged into fits, something similar was gradually taking shape 100 miles off to the north, where a group of impressionable young girls had a notion to "try fortunes," hoping thereby to learn something of future husbands, by using an age-old divining trick of dropping an egg white into a glass and decoding the patterns it formed. Except that the appearance, this time, was not of husbands but of "a specter in likeness of a coffin," a sure token of death—leading, then, to shock and terror and "strange antics" and whispered accusations. All in a place with the softly beautiful, biblical name of . . . Salem.

CHAPTER VI

Mary Parsons:
A Life Under Suspicion

November 1655. Inside a farmhouse, in the village of Northampton, Massachusetts, three women fall into heated conversation.

"Mark my word, our Mary's a witch, a foresworn witch. Always was; always will be."

"Aye, Sarah, a witch indeed! Come, let us hang some bay leaves beside the doorstep to stop her from entering here anymore."

"Wait! wait! We must not think so. She's long been our friend and boon companion. The Lord says, 'Love thy neighbor.'"

"Fool! No boon of mine. I've seen too many of her tricks already. She took my child; watch that she take not yours."

"Took your child? The one we buried these two months past? How mean you, Sarah?"

"'Tis easily told. I, being kept to childbed, and having the babe in my lap, there was something gave a great blow on the door. And at that very instant, my child changed. I thought to myself and I told my girl I feared the child would die. Presently, looking towards the door, through a hole I saw Mary Parsons stand nearby with a white sheet bound to her head; then I knew my child was lost. And I sent my girl out, but suddenly the woman vanished away. And the child breathed its last the very next morn. May dear God spare me such friends hereafter."

Thus the conversation begins; thus it will continue. And there are other, similar conversations—in other farmhouses, in "yards" along the main street, in the nearby fields and byways. Mary Parsons, this; Mary Parsons, that. Mary, Mary, Mary.

By the middle of the next year, the sum of it grows very large indeed. Everyone in the village has heard the gossip, felt the tension, and—likely as not—contributed his (or her) particular piece. Their opinions are sharply divided. For many, Mary's witchcraft is a certainty—and a rising menace. (They have long suspected she was "not right.") Others find this a dubious notion at best. (They see no sure evidence of witchcraft at all. And Mary seems eccentric, yes, but nothing worse.) Some are perched precariously in the middle, wavering back and forth between the two sides.

As summer ends, Mary and her husband Joseph decide on action of their own. In August Joseph files a legal complaint against "Sarah, the wife of James Bridgman, for slandering . . . [Mary] in her name." By seizing the initiative this way, they hope to head off what otherwise might soon become a full-scale prosecution—against Mary herself for the crime of witchcraft.

The court takes evidence from two dozen witnesses, about half in support of the plaintiff, the rest for the defendant. Clearly, Sarah Bridgman has played a leading role in fostering the alleged slander. But other Northamptonites share her concerns. Their testimony covers a broad range: bizarre injuries and illnesses, "swooning fits," spectral "appearances," frightening "imps," cows that wouldn't give milk, yarn that couldn't be spun—usually following some sort of hostile encounter with Mary, from which she would "go away in anger . . . [and] showing her offense." The plaintiff's witnesses, for their part, discount such reports; in most cases, perhaps in all, "they . . . conceive nothing but what might come to pass in an ordinary way." Moreover, they stress Sarah Bridgman's extreme "jealousies and suspicion," as if to suggest that her accusations are rooted in personal spite.

The case rolls on into the early fall. Gradually the weight of local "influence" tilts toward the plaintiff; a local selectman and a county magistrate come forcefully to her aid. In due course, the court decides in Mary's favor and orders Sarah to make "public acknowledgment" of the wrong she has done. A few weeks later she complies, rising after Sabbath services in the Northampton meetinghouse to offer Mary a formal apology. And so—for the time being at least—the matter is laid to rest.

But who were Mary Parsons and Sarah Bridgman? And what chain of experiences had brought them to such a bitter point of confrontation? First, Mary.

She was born Mary Bliss, in England, around the year 1628. Her father, Thomas, belonged to a large, well-to-do, and influential family in the town of Belstone, Devonshire. There, in the first decades of the 17th century, the Blisses had joined the Puritan movement— had indeed become local leaders of the movement. For this they would eventually suffer irreparable harm to their fortune and social position. According to later reports, several of the Bliss menfolk, including Mary's father, were imprisoned after mounting a series of open challenges to the established church leadership. Additional punishment took the form of heavy fines, which greatly reduced the family patrimony. Eventually, in about 1635, a considerable number of them decided to leave home and join the exodus of their fellow Puritans to New England.

The group included Thomas, his wife Margaret, their daughter Mary, and three or four of their other children; Mary was now around seven years old. Thomas and family went first to what is today Braintree, Massachusetts, and then, by or before 1640, to Hartford, Connecticut. Hartford would remain their base for at least a decade, while Mary and her siblings grew to adulthood. Thomas died within a few years; Margaret began a long period of widowhood. Their position and property was "middling" at best, showing no hint of the Blisses' previously high rank in England. But in 1646 Mary met and married Joseph Parsons, and this marked another turning point.

Parsons lived 20 miles to the north along the Connecticut River, near Springfield, Massachusetts, where Mary joined him. He was, by all accounts, an unusually resourceful young man on the make: initially a farmer, but also drawn to "mercantile" pursuits. In 1654 Joseph and Mary moved again, still farther upriver to Northampton. There Joseph would quickly assume a role of prominence, holding numerous public offices, including those of "cornet" (leader of the local militia) and town selectman. There, too, his activities in trade and commerce would greatly expand. He opened a retail store, owned and operated at least two mills, ran an ordinary, bought and sold lands at a rapid rate, and, perhaps most important, developed a vigorous fur trade with the nearby Indians. Eventually, the range of his enterprise would extend through all the Connecticut Valley towns and eastward to the coast. In 1675 he bought a large warehouse and ship's wharf in Boston—for by now much of his trade was overseas—and obtained the privileges of a merchant in that city.

Considered as a whole, this was a success story matched by few others in 17th-century New England. And, as Joseph rose toward greater and greater heights, Mary rose right alongside him. There are hints scattered through the surviving records that the Parsonses' ascent aroused widespread comment and jealousy. Joseph was frequently in court, mostly as a plaintiff (claiming debts, enforcing contracts), but sometimes, too, as a defendant. He was prosecuted more than once for "contemptuous behavior" toward local authorities; this included episodes of "scuffling" with the constable "whereby blood was drawn between them." Mary, for her part, was resented for having a rough and "challenging" style with others. Many years later, she would be remembered as a woman "of great beauty and talents, but . . . not very amiable . . . exclusive in the choice of her associates, and . . . of haughty manners."

Their life together had its own difficulties. Testimony given in the 1656 slander trial made much of their marital quarrels. (In one such, "he had in a sort beaten [her]"; in another, he "locked her into the cellar.") However, they were notably prolific as parents. Mary's pregnancies totaled an even dozen, including two sets of twins; the last came when she was well past age 40 and already a grandmother. Her twins, all four, died young, but nine of her ten other children survived to adulthood. The latter, in turn, would populate various parts of New England with a multitude of Parsons descendants.

Whatever advantages she may have enjoyed, Mary seems to have been something of a tormented soul. In 1652, when still living in Springfield, she and the daughters of that town's minister simultaneously succumbed to "fits"; an eyewitness recalled that "just as Mr.

Moxon's children acted [Moxon being the minister], so did Mary Parsons—just all one." Together, in their "afflicted" state, they were "carried out of the meeting, it being a Sabbath day." (In fact, such fits were unusual in a fully grown person; for the most part, they happened to children. Mary was 24 or 25 at the time, the Moxon daughters a good 10 to 15 years younger.) Around the same time, Mary began to speak of harassing encounters with "spirits." Once she had been accosted "as she was washing her clothes at the brook . . . [when] they appeared . . . like poppets." On another occasion they entered her house, "and she threw the bedstaff at them and her bedclothes and the pillow, and yet they would not be gone." Such claims, from her own mouth, helped fuel additional rumor and gossip among her fellow townspeople. For example, it was said by some that she could walk on water "and not [be] wet." In this way she would come to seem less a victim than a perpetrator of magic. Even her husband supposedly remarked "that she was led by an evil spirit."

In sum, her own career was scarcely less remarkable than Joseph's. From troubled beginnings, when driven out of her English home as the child of reviled radicals (Puritans), and losing at an early age a life situation of considerable ease and high social rank, she had traveled across the wide ocean to an utterly strange "wilderness." There she passed through a seemingly modest later childhood, on a farmstead in a newly founded village—then to begin a process of recouping when, as a young bride, she shared in the mounting successes of her entrepreneurial husband, and when, too, she entered a long, fecund stretch of motherhood. But this coincided with several years of deep personal difficulty, including marital discord and the sense of being directly targeted by malign, occult forces. Finally, she arrived at the status of a woman admired for her "beauty and talents," respected for her elevated social position, envied for the same reasons, resented for her abrasive manner, and feared for her own alleged involvement with the malign and the occult.

What seemed to run through it all was the element of extreme dislocation—social, economic, psychological, and geographic dislocation. Up, down, up again; here, there, everywhere; family troubles, angry neighbors, "spirits"; a woman, a life, in zigzag motion.

Did this distinctive biographical profile, this unique package of behavior and circumstance, predestine Mary to the role of "witch"? Perhaps. However, we should not scant the complementary role of "accuser"—filled most effectively by her neighbor Sarah Bridgman. Suspicions about Mary were held, in varying degrees, throughout the Northampton community. But again and again the record shows Sarah's primacy in fueling them. Hence her story, too, deserves careful attention.

She was born Sarah Lyman, into a locally prominent family in the English town of High Ongar, county Essex, and baptized there in February 1620. Her kin included people of real distinction—for example, a lord mayor of London. Her parents, like many of their Essex neighbors, had become Puritans; hence, in 1629 her father Richard sold the family lands, in anticipation of removing to New England. The Lymans reached Massachusetts in 1631, and lived for a time in Roxbury. But five years later they again pulled up stakes, joined one of the first migrant parties to Connecticut, and resettled at Hartford.

According to later accounts, Richard Lyman had crossed the ocean "with considerable estate, keeping two servants." And his sizable land allotments at Hartford placed him in the upper tier of that town's inhabitants. However, his several moves seem to have taken a toll—first on his property, then on his morale. His Roxbury pastor described him as "an ancient Christian but weak [doubt-ridden]"; moreover, while en route to Connecticut he "underwent much affliction, for . . . his cattle were lost in driving . . . And the winter being cold, and [the settlers] ill-provided, he was sick and melancholy." Indeed, he would not survive much longer. Death took him in 1640 and his wife a few months later; thus their several children, the eldest just now reaching adulthood, were left to fend for themselves. Sarah soon married one of their Hartford neighbors, a farmer and carpenter named James Bridgman. She and James moved twice more in the ensuing years, first to Springfield (1644), then to Northampton (1654).

So far, Sarah's life track had roughly paralleled that of Mary Parsons: high-status family background, followed by a kind of plunge (just before or just after resettlement in New England), parental death, marriage at a young age, frequent removals. Indeed, their respective tracks had also *converged;* for surely they became personally acquainted, either at Hartford or at Springfield, somewhat before they both moved (in the same year) to Northampton.

But from here on, their experiences would differ dramatically. Sarah did *not* recoup and regain her birthright prominence; she and James remained in the ranks of ordinary folk, of modest means and standing. (Two of her Lyman brothers fared much better, rising to become pillars of Northampton's local elite, while a third spiraled sharply downward into "distemperature"—mental incompetence—and a "very low condition.") Nor was Sarah fortunate in her childbearing. Four of her five eldest children died young, including the infant son whose illness would figure in the 1656 slander trial.

The extant records will not disclose whatever it was that Mary and Sarah held deepest in their heads and hearts. But if witchcraft cases were typically thought to involve envy, which they were—and if Mary Parsons was later remembered as being "haughty" and a magnet for "jealousy," which she was—then the grounds for the building suspicion against her do come at least partially into focus.

And Sarah Bridgman was especially well positioned to make the most painful of personal comparisons here. *Why,* Sarah might well have asked herself, *why* had Mary prospered, both materially and maternally, so much more than she? Was it just God's will? Or was it, perhaps, Satan's?

◆ ◆ ◆

August 1674. Northampton is again abuzz with talk of witchcraft. And Mary Parsons is again at the center of it.

A young woman of the town has died rather suddenly—and, in the opinion of many, "very strangely." She was only 22 at the time of death, married a year or so before, the mother of an infant son. Her given name? Mary (yet another). Her surname? Bartlett (from Samuel Bartlett, her husband). Her maiden name (from her birth family)? Bridgman. Mary Bartlett was the daughter of Sarah and James Bridgman.

Sarah had died a few years before; James survives, though town records mention his "weakness of body." Now it is James, together with Samuel Bartlett—father and husband of the supposed victim—who press the new accusations against Mary Parsons. Within days of the younger Mary's death, they declare to the county court their shared belief that "she came to her end by some unlawful and unnatural means . . . viz. by some evil instrument." A month later the court hears "diverse testimonies" from others as well. Samuel comes forward again, "to show the ground of his suspicions." James sends a written statement "entreating that diligent inquisition be made concerning the death of . . . his daughter." Mary Parsons also comes in, albeit without a direct invitation. As the record will later note: "She having intimation that such things were bruited about, and that she should be called in question . . . she voluntarily appeared in court, desiring to clear herself of such an execrable crime."

There are still more hearings over the winter. These include numerous additional testimonies, "some of them being demonstrations of witchcraft . . . and reflecting upon Mary Parsons as being guilty that way." The accused submits renewed protestations "of her own innocency . . . and how clear she was of such a crime . . . and the righteous God knew her innocency." The court appoints a committee of "soberdized, chaste women" to conduct a body search on Mary, to see "whether any marks of witchcraft might appear." (No record of their conclusions survives.)

After all this is done, the case passes to the colony's highest legal authority, the Court of Assistants in Boston. And there, in the following spring, it enters its final stage. An imposing lineup of magistrates presides, including business associates and (presumably) friends of her husband; but her fate rests with a trial jury of ordinary citizens. The indictment is formally read: "Mary Parsons, the wife of Joseph Parsons . . . being instigated by the Devil hath . . . entered into familiarity with the Devil, and committed several acts of witchcraft on the person or persons of one or more." The evidence is reviewed yet again. And Mary, standing "at the bar, holding up her hand," again declares her innocence. After careful deliberation the jury returns its verdict: "not guilty . . . And so she [is] discharged."

Did this put an end to it? Would the long-running suspicions against Mary Parsons at last dry up? Or would they be sustained, in spite of a pair of court decisions to the contrary nearly two decades apart?

Mary had reached middle age. Joseph, considerably her senior, would die within a few more years; but she herself would live on for another 30. Throughout her widowhood, she would be more than amply provided for. Joseph's estate was one of the largest to have been probated so far anywhere in Massachusetts; it included land holdings in six different townships, together with goods, cash, and credit to a value of more than 2,000 pounds. And Mary was a chief beneficiary. Meanwhile, her grown sons and daughters were themselves moving quickly and easily into the tight circle of the provincial elite.

Might not all this wealth and social standing have served as a barrier, a shield, against further accusation? In fact, there would be no more official action linking Mary to witchcraft—no court prosecutions, certainly. She may, just possibly, have been suspected of causing the "mysterious" illness and death of a Northampton neighbor in 1678; the evidence seems murky. But *unofficial* action is, in any case, a different matter: consider the following.

In January 1702, two magistrates at Springfield hear a complaint by a certain Mr. Peletiah Glover against a slavewoman named Betty Negro, for using "bad language" to his young son. Betty has told the boy "that his grandmother . . . killed two persons over the river, and . . . killed Mrs.

Pynchon and half-killed the colonel, and his mother was half a witch."
The mother in question is Hannah Glover, née Parsons—wife of Peletiah
Glover, and daughter of Mary Parsons. If the daughter is rated "half a
witch," this can only mean that Mary herself counts even now—in local
gossip and rumor—as a full-fledged example.

She is old, and not far from her end. But clouds of mistrust surround her
still.

PART THREE

SALEM

Chapter VII approaches the notorious witch-hunt at Salem through the experience of one of its first targets, the elderly and exemplary matriarch Rebecca Nurse. Few stories in this entire array are more poignant than hers.

Chapter VIII takes a long view of the same subject, following the train of witchcraft-related events from their seemingly modest beginning, through an extraordinary peak of "panic fear," to eventual, uncertain retreat. It offers as well a survey, and summary, of the numerous different ways Americans have tried ever since to understand this dark moment in their history.

Chapter IX traces the career of Reverend Cotton Mather, a widely acknowledged leader of New England Puritanism. Long excoriated for his role at Salem, Mather emerges here as a highly complex figure—an advocate for forceful prosecution at some points, a voice of caution at others, and a rueful (though not personally apologetic) part of the community-wide postmortem that followed the end of the trials phase.

CHAPTER VII

Rebecca Nurse:
A "Witch" and Her Trials

March 13, 1692; a Sunday evening. At her home in Salem Village (Massachu-setts), a 12-year-old girl named Ann Putnam Jr. suddenly comes upon the apparition of a witch and is at once "afflicted." In the days just previous, Ann has been attacked by several other spectral witches—she is part of a little circle of young victims repeatedly driven to "fits"—but not by this one. At first she does "not know . . . her [the new apparition's] name," even while remembering "where she used to sit in our meetinghouse." Some hours later the name will come: Rebecca Nurse.

During the week that follows, Ann is further afflicted by the same appa-rition "biting, pinching, and pricking me." Meanwhile, too, her friend Abi-gail Williams (another in the victim group) is "exceedingly perplexed with the apparition of Rebecca Nurse . . . pulled, pinched, and almost choked . . . [and] hurried into violence to and fro in the room . . . sometimes making as if she would fly, stretching up her arms . . . and crying 'whish! whish! whish!' . . . and [running] to the fire . . . to throw fire brands about the house." Indeed, Abigail's encounter extends much further—to observing "this apparition at a sacrament [the Black Mass?] . . . sitting next to [a fig-ure . . . the Devil?] with a high-crowned hat," and to hearing her boast of "committing several murders."

But this is just an opener. At midafternoon on Friday, March 18, again in the Putnam household, Ann Putnam Sr. is resting in bed "after being wearied out in helping to tend my poor afflicted child," when all at once she feels "almost pressed and choked to death." Thus begins a series of excruci-ating "tortures," inflicted first by the shape of Martha Corey (another Vil-lage woman suspected of witchcraft) and then, more especially, by Rebecca

Nurse. *The worst come on Tuesday and Wednesday mornings, when (according to Ann Sr.'s later testimony) "she appeared to me only in her shift [i.e. nightgown] and brought a little red book . . . urging me vehemently to write [in it] . . . and because I would not . . . she threatened to tear my soul out of my body."*

Parts of this extraordinary scene are witnessed by a visiting clergyman, Reverend Deodat Lawson, who would write about it in a book published shortly afterward: "She [Ann Sr.] desired me to pray with her . . . but after a little time was taken with a fit . . . [and] was so stiff she could not be bended . . . but began to strive violently with her arms and legs." After some minutes, Ann Sr. gathers herself to fight back, and hurls a volley of scathing words at her spectral adversary: "Be gone! Be gone! Be gone! Are you not ashamed . . . to afflict a poor creature so? What hurt did I ever do to you in my life? You have but two years to live and then the Devil will torment your soul; for this your name is blotted out of God's book. . . . Be gone, for shame, are you not afraid of that which is coming upon you? I know, I know, what will make you afraid: the wrath of an angry God, I am sure that will make you afraid! Be gone, do not torment me. . . ." Soon Ann Sr. is again "sorely afflicted [with] her mouth drawn to one side and her body strained, for about a minute." Finally, she asks Lawson to read from a certain scriptural passage—the Book of Revelations, chapter 3—because "I am sure you [i.e. Nurse's apparition] cannot stand before that text!" At this the minister does "something scruple," since such practice seems uncomfortably close to traditional magic—in the parlance of the time, a charm—but decides to "do it . . . once for an experiment." Almost immediately, Ann Sr. is freed from her suffering.

These events—the affliction by Rebecca Nurse's apparition of at least three different persons—quickly become the subject of much agitated discussion around the Village. The fits of the victim group, some of them dating back to the previous month, have built an atmosphere of intense public concern; Rebecca is the sixth person to fall under suspicion so far. But her case is unusual in one important respect: she has numerous local supporters, friends and relatives ready to come to her defense. In due course, four of these friends—Israel and Elizabeth Porter, Daniel Andrew, and Peter

Cloyce, upstanding citizens all—are "desired to go to . . . [her] house," and speak with her personally, to break the news of the accusations made against her. The circumstances are poignant and difficult. Rebecca, age 71, has been bedridden for some time; her visitors find her "weak and low." They ask her "how it [is] . . . otherwise with her" (referring to her spiritual condition). She gamely replies that she feels "more of God's presence in this sickness than [at] some [other] times, but not so much as she desired." Indeed, her piety is fully manifest; she cites "many . . . places of scripture" that give her great comfort. Then, "of her own accord," she raises the matter of "the affliction [i.e. the witchcraft] amongst them," and expresses her sympathy for its several young victims. She regrets being too ill to visit them, for she has "pitied them with all her heart, and . . . [prayed] for them." Eventually, and as gently as possible, Rebecca's friends come to the point and tell her "that she was spoken of also [as a witch]." She feels "as it were amazed," and sits quietly trying to understand. Presently she says, "If it be so, the will of the Lord be done." But then, a moment later: "As to this thing [the witchcraft accusation], I am [as] innocent as the child unborn." She ends, in good Puritan fashion, by turning the matter back on herself and wondering aloud: "What sin hath God found out in me, unrepented of, that he should lay such an affliction on me in my old age?" An affliction it truly is—hardly less so than what the bewitched victims are concurrently suffering. And there is worse to come.

Rebecca Nurse was born in the English town of Great Yarmouth, in 1621, to a couple named William and Johannah Towne. The Townes emigrated to Massachusetts when Rebecca was still a girl, and established themselves on a small farm in Topsfield, just north of the Salem line. Across that line in years to come, William Towne would repeatedly find himself "in controversy" with various Salem Village residents, especially some from the large and locally influential Putnam clan; for the most part, the issue was poorly-drawn boundaries between one farm and another. Otherwise little is known of the family's situation in that period, except that Goodwife Towne was suspected by some of being a witch. Since witchcraft was believed to

be a heritable condition, passed through families from one generation to the next, this would be a factor in her daughter Rebecca's own
vulnerability to accusation later on.

Coming of age in the 1640s, Rebecca married a young artisan in
Salem; his name was Francis Nurse. Together they would raise eight
children. Local records afford passing glimpses of their doings: occasional lawsuits filed for and against them (debt, trespass, slander),
the taking of a foster child into their household "in charity," Francis's
occasional service as a juryman and constable. Taken together, these
bits suggest a gradual rise in status and property. Then, in 1678, came
something more substantial: Francis Nurse emerged as the pur-
chaser of a fine 300-acre "estate" from a Boston clergyman named
James Allen. The terms were unusual: Nurse was given 21 years to
discharge the principal (a hefty total of 400 pounds), while in the
meantime paying a modest annual rent. The land was in Salem Village, to which the entire family then moved from its previous home
in the Town center. In fact, this transaction would have a troubled
history, including numerous legal challenges that played out in local
courts over the next several years. Allen, who still held official title,
bore the brunt here, but inevitably the Nurses were also drawn in.
Thus, they became increasingly embroiled with various neighbors
who would later step forward among Rebecca's accusers in the witch
trials.

Still, from all signs the family prospered in its new venue. Francis
became a vigorous participant in the local economy and his wealth
as recorded on the tax rolls rose markedly. In time, he managed to
settle most of his now-grown children within the ambit of his own
property. Rebecca was a member in good standing of the church and
a figure of deep respect within the wider Village community. A contemporary would subsequently note many "testimonials of her
Christian behavior, both in the course of her life and at her death,
and her extraordinary care in educating her children, and setting
them good examples."

◆ ◆ ◆

On March 23, in the direct aftermath of Ann Putnam Sr.'s most searing affliction, two men swear out a formal complaint against Rebecca Nurse, and an order is given for her "examination" the next morning. The setting will be the Village meetinghouse, with magistrates John Hathorne and Jonathan Corwin presiding, Reverend Samuel Parris (the local minister) acting as recorder, and Rebecca's supposed victims (now numbering about ten) primed to give evidence against her.

As the proceedings begin, the meetinghouse—a simple, boxlike structure, 34 feet long by 28 feet wide by approximately 25 feet tall—is filled with onlookers from the Village and beyond. They are arrayed in rows on narrow benches, and in two balcony-style galleries overhead; the examiners and other officials sit behind a long communion table at the front. In such cramped surroundings, the mood of anxious expectation grows steadily, almost palpably, deeper. Then, as if on cue, Ann Putnam Jr. and Abigail Williams fall into fits and writhe about on the floor in apparently excruciating pain. Under questioning by Hathorne—"Have you been hurt by this woman?"— both point plaintively toward Rebecca; they mean that her specter, projected out from her person as they alone can see, is directly attacking them. Soon additional accusers rise to speak. A certain Goodman Kenny alleges that "since this Nurse came into the house," he has twice been "seized with an amazed condition." And Edward Putnam describes the previous afflictions of his sister-in-law (Ann Sr.) and niece (Ann Jr.). To every such charge Rebecca responds with heartfelt denials. Thus: "I can say before my Eternal Father I am innocent and God will clear my innocency." And: "I never afflicted no child, never in my life." But these have little effect.

Ann Putnam Sr.: Did you not bring the black man [Satan] with you? Did you not bid me tempt God and die? How oft have you ate and drunk with your own demon?

Rebecca: Oh Lord help me.

At this she spreads her hands in a gesture of despair; immediately her victims undergo fresh paroxysms of "torment."

Hathorne: Do you not see what a solemn condition these are in? When your hands are loose, their persons are afflicted.

Two more, Mary Walcott and Elizabeth Hubbard, join the chorus of *accusation. And Ann Putnam Sr. suffers another "grievous fit . . . insomuch as she could hardly move hand or foot"; presently she is "carried out." The overall result is "an hideous screech and noise" so loud that it can be heard "at a great distance" from the meetinghouse. The magistrates struggle to regain control.*

Hathorne: It is very awful to all to see these agonies, and you an old professor [of religion, i.e. a church member] thus charged with contracting with the Devil . . . and yet to see you stand with dry eyes, when there are so many wet . . .

Rebecca: You do not know my heart.

Back and forth it goes, with yet more of her accusers falling into fits. At one point Hathorne mentions "an odd discourse [gossip] in the mouths of many [Villagers]," to the effect that her recent "sickness" was actually the result of wounds received when the afflicted and others struck back at her apparition. As to "wounds," she replies, "I have none but old age." Meanwhile, the afflicted claim to see "a black man whispering in [Rebecca's] ear, and birds [her familiars]" fluttering around her.

Hathorne: Do you think these suffer voluntarily or involuntarily?

Rebecca: I cannot tell.

Hathorne: They accuse you of hurting them, and if you think it is not unwillingly but by design, you must look upon them as murderers.

Rebecca: I cannot tell what to think.

As she nervously shifts her weight from one foot to the other, the fits of her accusers are renewed in ways that mimic her own motion.

Hathorne: Is it not an unaccountable case that when you are examined these persons are afflicted?

Rebecca: I have got nobody to look to but God.

She wrings her hands helplessly, and the afflicted are beset with additional, and corresponding, "fits of torture."

Hathorne: Do you believe these afflicted persons are bewitched?

Rebecca: I do think they are.

The magistrates order Reverend Parris to read from testimony given by Ann Putnam Sr. about her prior struggles with Rebecca's apparition.

Hathorne: What do you think of this?

<u>*Rebecca:*</u> *I cannot help it; the Devil may appear in my shape.*

The proceeding is drawing to a close now, amid a bedlam of affliction and accusation. At the end of his transcript, Parris notes the difficulties he has encountered in writing, from "great noises by the afflicted and many speakers." And he adds a final "memorandum" to underscore the way the accusers have responded to Rebecca's every movement with directly mirroring torment. For example: "Nurse held her head on one side, and Elizabeth Hubbard . . . had her head set in that posture, whereupon . . . Abigail Williams cried out, 'Set up Goody Nurse's head [or else] the maid's [Hubbard's] neck will be broken,' and when some set up Nurse's head . . . Betty Hubbard's was immediately righted." Who could imagine a more vivid demonstration of the witch's injurious, and utterly coercive, power?

Indeed, for all who watch and listen there in the meetinghouse this has been a shattering experience. As Reverend Lawson would later write: "The whole assembly was struck with consternation, and they were afraid that those that sat next to them were under the influence of witchcraft." In short: no one is safe, no one can be trusted, everyone must be on guard.

It would be a mistake to make any one set of people entirely responsible for the persecution of Rebecca Nurse, but members of the Putnam clan do seem to have been disproportionately represented among her accusers. Of 18 surviving depositions given against her at her eventual trial, ten included one or more Putnams as signatories. Thus, their family's history deserves some particular attention.

Their line of descent begins with John Putnam Sr. (born 1579), an emigrant to Massachusetts from the English countryside just west of London. In 1641 this man received a handsome land grant of 100 acres in what would later become Salem Village. Over the next two decades he prospered impressively, accumulating property totaling approximately 800 acres by the time of his death in 1662. Moreover, he was in a position to assist his sons, Thomas (born 1615), Nathaniel (born 1619), and John Jr. (born 1627) in reaching the same local pinnacle of wealth and prestige. All three became major property holders, church members, and officeholders. Their lands comprised a considerable portion of Salem's northwest interior, with some overlapping into the adjacent towns of Topsfield and Rowley. (It was in this border area that various Putnams engaged in repeated legal battles with neighbors and abutters, most especially several from Rebecca Nurse's natal family, the Townes, and also somewhat later including her husband, Francis.) For the most part, they made their living as farmers. At least once they did seek to branch out in a more commercial direction, by joining in the construction of an ironworks on Putnam-owned land in Rowley. However, this venture ended in failure, with little iron ever produced or sold, numerous lawsuits among the partners and operators, and, finally, a disastrous fire (quite possibly arson).

As the second generation of Putnams gave way to the third, the family's situation began to look less favorable. By now, their abundant landholdings had been repeatedly subdivided from three main initial parcels into what would eventually become eleven, in order to meet the needs of maturing sons. Among the most conspicuous victims of this process was Thomas Putnam Jr., whose father had long rated as the single largest property holder in the entire Village. To be sure, in 1678 Thomas Jr. made an apparently fortunate marriage to Ann, the daughter of George Carr, a well-to-do shipwright, merchant, and locally prominent resident in the neighboring town of Salisbury. At this point his future must still have looked bright—resting, as it clearly did, on the prospect of substantial inheritance from the estates of his father and father-in-law. However, on both counts he would soon be badly disappointed. When George Carr died intestate in 1682, his administrators assigned the bulk of his property to his widow and two youngest sons. His other sons and his sons-in-law (including Thomas Putnam Jr.) challenged these arrangements in court, eventually winning at least partial redress. Much worse was what followed on the paternal side. Thomas Putnam Sr., upon the death of his first wife, had remarried; this woman bore him one more child, a son, to add to the eight he had previously raised. And upon *his* death in 1686, the widow and this final son became his prime beneficiaries. Once again, Thomas Jr. was caught short. And, once again, he (joined by several of his siblings) went to court—but this time without success.

This third generation of the family was, in sum, set on a markedly downward course of steadily diminishing wealth and influence. It seems striking, in retrospect, that most of Thomas Jr.'s children would leave Salem when grown, never to return (except for three daughters who remained as spinsters). In effect, his family simply disappeared and left no lasting mark on the place for later generations to remember. No mark, that is, unless one counts the devastating result of its role in the witch trials: for the two Ann Putnams, Sr. and Jr., whose charges weighed so heavily against Rebecca Nurse (and others) were Thomas Jr.'s wife and daughter.

Soon after the shocking events of Rebecca's March 24 "examination," her many friends and supporters move to create a line of defense around her. Thirty-nine of them put their names on a petition in her behalf: "We can testify that we have known her for many years, and according to our observation her life and conversation [personal conduct] was according to her profession [as a church member], and we never had any cause or grounds to suspect her of any such thing as she is now accused of." In addition, several give evidence disputing the specific charges of "injury" lodged against her.

But her accusers press on. According to testimonies given later, those in the core group continue to experience periodic bouts of affliction. Specific occasions include: March 25 (Ann Putnam Jr.); April 13 (Abigail Williams); May 2, 3, and 4 (Mary Walcott, Mercy Lewis, and Abigail Williams); May 29 (Abigail Williams); May 31 and June 1 (Ann Putnam Sr., described now as being "re-assaulted" at the exact moment her previous deposition is read aloud in court). Moreover, the accusations are broadened to include various recent deaths directly attributed to Rebecca's witchcraft. A neighbor had clashed with her because his "pigs got into her field," upon which she "fell a-railing at him"; soon afterward, he became "strangely ill" and died. An infant child (in one of the Putnam family branches) had died around the time of Rebecca's examination, after being "taken with strange and violent fits." An older man had been killed in a roadside accident; supposedly his ghost was later observed in angry dispute with Rebecca, saying "she did murder him by pushing him off the cart, and struck the breath out of his body." Finally, Ann Putnam Sr. reports seeing the ghosts of no fewer than "six children in winding sheets which called me aunt . . . and told me that they were my sister Baker's children of Boston, and that Goody Nurse [along with two other accused witches] had murdered them."

All such evidence is destined for use in a formal trial proceeding. Another part of the legal preparation is a careful examination of the defendant's body. Accordingly, she is strip-searched by a committee of local women, who proceed to identify a "supernatural mark" in her genitalia. Rebecca tries to counter this result by mentioning "difficult exigencies that hath befallen me in the time of my travails"—an allusion to physical anomalies caused by childbearing—but her claim is not heard. Meanwhile, from the other side, her kin and supporters mount new efforts to defend her by challenging the credibility of several of her leading accusers.

On June 2, the special court created for the express purpose of trying witches holds a grand jury hearing on Rebecca (and several others). The result is a set of official indictments, charging that "she . . . hath used . . . detestable arts called witchcraft and sorceries" by means of which her numerous victims have been "hurt, tortured, afflicted, consumed, pined, wasted, and tormented." The climax comes on June 29, when the court meets again and the evidence is presented to a sitting jury. Unfortunately, records of this final stage have not survived—except for the outcome. The initial verdict is not guilty. Rebecca is cleared of all charges; evidently the pleas of her supporters have proved persuasive. But almost immediately her accusers respond with a "hideous outcry"—that is, a renewal of their fits—and the trial judges themselves feel "strangely surprised."

Now comes a crucial turning point. The chief judge calls attention to a previous comment by Rebecca that some have construed as implying a link with two confessed witches; supposedly she said they were "of our company." This prompts the jurymen to ask that Rebecca clarify her meaning. But instead of explaining herself, she sits in a kind of daze, making no reply; her silence seems implicitly damning. Later she will say of the same mo-

ment: "Being somewhat hard of hearing, and full of grief, [and] none in-
forming me of how the Court took up my words . . . [I] therefore had not
opportunity to declare what I intended when I said they [the confessors]
were of our company." Elderly, deaf, distraught, confused, cornered: thus
her fatal predicament.

The jurors go out again, and decide to reverse their previous decision.
Now they find the defendant guilty, and the judges condemn her to death by
hanging. Even so some in Rebecca's family continue their struggle; apparently at their urging, the colony's governor, Sir William Phips, orders a re-
prieve. But once more the afflicted raise "dismal outcries," and Phips, too,
reverses himself; the previous sentence will stand.

There are still some loose ends to tie up. A few days after her trial,
Rebecca—presumably in chains and leg-irons by now—is brought from
prison to a meeting of her church. There the elders propose, and the congregation concurs "by a unanimous vote, . . . that our sister Nurse, being a
convicted witch . . . and condemned to die, should be excommunicated";
their purpose is to free themselves from the stain of her sin and to proclaim
her everlasting damnation in the afterworld. There will be no further efforts to save her; perhaps there is nothing left to try. Three weeks later her
life ends on the spot that later generations in Salem will call Gallows Hill.
Those same generations will preserve a "tradition" that she died in a prayer-
ful manner, asking God, from the scaffold, to forgive her accusers for the
wrong they had done her.

According to the same tradition, the members of her defiantly loyal family add a postscript of their own. On the night following her execution, under cover of darkness, some of them climb the hill and retrieve her body from
the "crevice" in which it had been rudely cast down. They bring Rebecca
back for a proper burial in a little family cemetery not far from their—and
her—home.

Her home still stands. The cemetery is still there. Gallows Hill still
rises, above the modern town center.

And now an author's postscript.

◆ ◆ ◆

July 21, 2005. We are looking for Rebecca's ghost this morning. Or at least some kind of aura. Something to connect with her. Something different from—and deeper, more direct, more personal than—all we've found on the yellowing page. Words take us only so far.

Her house seems the right place to start. We approach it from in front; its south exposure opens onto a long expanse of fields, wavy and green in midsummer, with a woodland behind, and the haze of a distant shoreline. The modern town is mostly invisible from here; thus the view may well resemble what she would have seen many a time.

We enter through the old battened door—once her door—into a little vestibule. A right turn takes us into the "keeping room": the central household space and, most assuredly, hers. The furnishings—not hers, but of the same period, and roughly equivalent to what she would have had—suggest a traditional "goodwife's" round of domestic chores: wheels for spinning, vats for brewing, buckets for churning, molds for candle making. Of course, the most important of all the activities performed here was cooking, the myriad small and delicate operations which together comprised food preparation in pre-modern times. A huge fireplace, 10 feet across, strongly evokes that part of her life, with its densely arrayed cranes, broilers, and cookpots, and two cavernous bake ovens recessed in the old bricks at the rear. There are chairs, too, and benches, and a fair-size table. Was it perhaps in this room that she received the four friends sent to report her being "cried out" by the afflicted girls?

We return to the vestibule, and climb a tight little stairway to the upper floor. This is her "chamber" (bedroom); its contents include another fireplace, a few chairs (including one purportedly made by her son Samuel), a sprawling "trundle bed" (with its retractable frame, designed for use by young children), and not much more. Was it from here that the town marshal dragged her away on the morning of her pretrial examination?

The cemetery lies in a little glen about 200 yards west of the house. Ringed with tall pines, it feels almost sublimely calm, secluded, beautiful. Her grave-marker has not survived. (We must assume she had one.) Other Nurse family headstones are scattered here and there, but none from before the time of the American Revolution. In the center of this verdant plot stands an eight-foot granite shaft. On one side is inscribed her name, the place and year of her birth and death, and some rather florid verse by the celebrated 19th-century poet John Greenleaf Whittier; on the other side, the bitter truth of her last days:

> Accused of witchcraft
> She declared,
> "I am innocent and God will
> clear my innocency."
> Once acquitted yet falsely
> condemned, she suffered
> death, July 19, 1692.
> In loving memory of her Christian character
> Even then truly attested by forty of her neighbors
> This monument is erected in 1885.

Reportedly, 600 people attended the ceremony held to mark its dedication.

Gallows Hill stands roughly four miles to the south of the Nurse homestead, on the other side of the line that once separated Salem Village (now the town of Danvers) from the Town center (now the city of Salem). It is at present a densely populated, fully urbanized space, with industrial buildings and warehouses ringing its base, residential neighborhoods along its sides, and a good-size park on its upper slope. Because the landscape is so utterly changed, we must strain to imagine what Rebecca saw as she approached it—pulled along in an executioner's cart—more than three centuries ago.

Her journey would have begun in the original town prison (long since disappeared) just off the common. From there she would have been taken down Prison Lane (today's St. Peter's Street), west along Main Street (now Essex Street), out the old Boston Road, across Town Bridge (over an inlet, now gone, below the North River), onto a path that turned sharply to cross the lower section of what was known as the Great Pasture, through little groves of pines and hemlocks, and up the fateful hill.

So far, we can follow at least the approximate route today. But then it becomes more difficult. Where, exactly, did she perish? In what part of this rather jumbled expanse would they have erected their gallows? The question has intrigued and perplexed students of Salem history for many generations. Recently something of a consensus has emerged: the site seems not to have crowned the hill at its very top (as previously thought) but to have been instead a cluster of rocky ledges partway up (between the present-day Proctor and Pope streets).

Maps in hand, we begin to scour this area. At first, we see nothing that will answer, nothing but cramped little house lots filled to overflowing with modest, wood-framed dwellings: a standard kind of urban density. But suddenly we stumble upon it. Abutting the east side of Proctor Street lies an open, entirely undeveloped, triangular section of no more than half an acre—standing out very sharply from the rest. It has thickly growing trees, luxuriant undergrowth, and, most of all, those "ledges," bold outcroppings of New England granite, set as if arranged in angled rows, with crevices (now filled) lying between. There is no sign to mark its significance, which does seem strange in a place where witchy markers abound on every side, yet feels somehow all the more satisfying for that.

In the midst of the busy cityscape, we are alone with our imaginings.

We stand on the ledges, looking out.

Looking for Rebecca.

CHAPTER VIII

The Most Famous
Witch-hunt of All, 1692–93

Salem. Witchcraft. Two words so closely identified as to seem almost twinned. Say the first, and the other comes immediately to mind.

Go to Salem today, and its witchy past is all around you. Here is a list of places to visit (for a price): the Salem Witch Museum; the Witch History Museum; the Witch Dungeon Museum; the Witch House; the Witch Mansion; the Museum of Myths and Monsters; the Spellbound Museum. Witchery is the lifeblood of local commerce. Thus (another list): the Witch's Brew Cafe; the Witch's Kettle (a restaurant); Hocus Pocus Tours; the Haunted Footsteps Ghost Tour; the Magic Parlor (offering "occult supplies, tarot readings, and more"); Crow Haven Corner ("purveyor to witches around the world"); Nu Aeon boutique ("dedicated to the Holy Arts of Magic and the Craft of the Wise"); the Witch City Cleaning Company; the Witch City Repo Services; and so on. Moreover, living, breathing, 21st-century "witches" are widely available, to see and consult—to read palms, tell fortunes, and offer intimate personal advice.

It wasn't always so. Before 1692 Salem was one among many New England towns—larger than most, more prosperous than most, and more diverse—but very much within the social and cultural mainstream. Its beginnings, in 1629, belonged to the earliest phase of colonial American history. Its fine harbor marked it as a likely hub of maritime trade; merchants would quickly assume a leadership role in its development. However, it also rested on a broad base of farmsteads, which stretched out for many miles into its hilly interior. Its initially large territorial expanse was reduced, during the middle years of the 17th century, as several of its outlying settlements broke off to become independent communities (Wenham, Manchester, Marblehead, Beverly). What remained after 1675 or so was a coastal strip, including the center and known henceforth as Salem Town, and a hinterland section variously called Salem Farms or Salem Village. It had a settled church, a town-meeting form of local governance, and an ostensibly Puritan lifestyle of the sort that prevailed all across its parent colony of Massachusetts Bay.

But beginning in the first months of 1692, and increasingly thereafter, one could not think of Salem as conforming to some larger type. On the contrary, Salem came to seem utterly special and distinctive. And it was, for certain, the witch trials that made all the difference.

Salemwitchcraft: by now virtually *one* word, whose four syllables roll together in a strangely mellifluent blend.

The Opening Phase

The trials were the outcome of a process begun long before—exactly how long would be hard to say. The personal and social tensions that found expression in legal charges went back years or decades. Witchcraft had itself been a fully acknowledged presence, with notorious suspects, irate accusers, and beleaguered victims—and even some actual trials—probably since the town's formative days. The Devil was thought to be present, too, directly tempting errant souls to "mischief" of many sorts. And everywhere "Providence" left its mark in a wide of range of baffling, apparently supernatural happenings. All this was no more true of Salem than of other parts of early New England.

Thus it did not seem initially remarkable when, sometime in midwinter, 1691 (which, according to the "old calendar" still in use, did not end until March 25), two local girls began behaving in "odd and . . . unusual" ways: "getting into holes, and creeping under chairs and stools, . . . [and] uttering foolish, ridiculous speeches, which neither they themselves nor any others could make sense of." Probably, though not provably, this pair—Betty Parris, the 9-year-old daughter of the Village minister, Reverend Samuel Parris, and Abigail Williams, her 12-year-old cousin—had participated in the egg-and-glass conjuring that produced the dark omen of a spectral coffin. Perhaps they were privy to additional "little sorceries" mentioned in some post-trials writings. And, certainly, their "antic gestures" were noticed by other young girls in their tight circle of neighborhood peers and friends. Soon, at least two of these others— Ann Putnam Jr. (age 12) and Betty Hubbard (age 17)—were behaving in similar ways. Together this group progressed rapidly toward full-blown "fits." As an eyewitness would later remember it: "Sometimes they were taken dumb, their mouths stopped, their throats choked, their limbs wracked and tormented so as might move an heart of stone to sympathize with them, with bowels of compassion for them."

Sympathy, yes; compassion, certainly; but the reaction of the adults closest to them encompassed a good deal more. There was alarm. There was anger. There was rapidly mounting suspicion. A local doctor came to assess the girls in their various "distempers": were they, after all, subject to some "natural disease"? To the contrary, the doctor concluded, no such diagnosis would hold; instead, he found them to be "under an evil hand." For Reverend Parris and other "sober-minded" folk, the meaning of this was clear—the children were bewitched. And so, too, was the appropriate response clear. Prayer, and fasting, and "earnest supplication" to God: only thus might such diabolical forces be overcome. But then one of the neighbors proposed a different strategy, based on traditional counter-magical folkways. Without Parris's knowledge, she persuaded his two Indian slaves, Tituba and John—themselves close-up observers of the unfolding scene—to bake a "witch-cake" incorporating some urine taken from "the afflicted persons," to feed to the family dog. This procedure did nothing to lessen the symptoms of bewitchment, but apparently helped to identify its source. For within a short time, Betty and Abigail "cried out of the Indian woman" as the cause of their "grievous afflictions."

Thus, in early March, was Tituba pushed to center stage. It is tempting to think that without her—or, to be more accurate, without the suspicions and pressures directed against her—the rest might never have happened. Tituba's personal history is now mostly obscure; what seems clearest is her slave status, her Indian descent (with a probable connection to the Arawaks of northeastern South America), and her childhood within the "creole" society of the West Indies (specifically, Barbados). There she had imbibed a lively mix of cultural traditions, African as well as Indian, together with some from the English slave-owning class. This background no doubt made her seem quite exotic when, with her minister-master, she arrived in Salem in the late 1680s.

Pushed hard (perhaps beaten) by Parris to confess to witchery, she at first resisted but then yielded at least partway. She admitted to baking the witch-cake, which good Puritans like the Parrises could only regard as a "devilish" act, and also to having been familiar with witchcraft "in her own country" (the Caribbean). Meanwhile, the afflicted girls were naming two additional Village women, Sarah Good and Sarah Osborne, as additional witch-attackers. Crucially, they attributed more and more of their torment to "specters"— apparitions not visible to others, but imbued with supernatural powers and inseparably identified with the accused.

The Investigation Phase

This was enough to move the process of "examination" from private to public auspices, from the Parris household to the Village meetinghouse. With formal complaints duly filed, and local magistrates henceforth in charge, the three accused were closely interrogated before a large and clamorous "multitude" of the local citizenry. Sarah Good went first.

The magistrates' opening questions set a definite pattern. "What evil spirit have you familiarity with?" they asked—immediately followed by, "Why do you hurt these children?" In short, guilt was assumed; the aim was simply to obtain confirmation. When Good responded with firm denials, the magistrates "desired [the afflicted] . . . to look upon her, and see if this was the person that had hurt them." They did as directed, and showed their assent by becoming again "tormented." This, too, would become an important pattern: eye contact with the accused causing fits in the supposed victims.

Sarah Osborne came next, and the same sequence was repeated for the first of many times. Then it was Tituba's turn. Initially hesitant, she was threatened and coaxed, step by step, into an astonishing set of confessions. Her long tale of malefic activity included her own reluctant participation, but shifted most of the blame elsewhere. She spoke of blasphemous conversations with the Devil and "persuasions" to sign her name in his "book," of strange spectral creatures (a yellow bird, a red cat, a "great black dog," a "thing all over hairy . . . that goeth like a man"), of riding through the sky on a pole to a witch meeting in Boston, and of being forced by some witch confederates to attack her master's child and niece. Before she was done, she had amply confirmed the guilt of the previously accused pair (Good and Osborne) and had also implicated a half-dozen others whom she did not name.

From this dramatic account emerged two immediate and important results. First, Tituba saved her own life, apparently because her accusers and judges hoped to continue using her as a witness against future suspects (the start of yet another enduring pattern). Second, the sense of a broad witchcraft "plot"—not just the *maleficia* of a few scattered miscreants—began to take hold within the community at large. That very same evening, local folk variously heard "strange noises," saw "a strange and unusual beast," encountered apparitions of the accused, and so forth. From now on, Salem Village would feel itself to be in a state of siege.

As part of her confession Tituba had mentioned seeing nine separate signatures inscribed "in red blood" in the Devil's book—in effect, a kind of enrollment list. Whose were they? The magistrates made every possible effort to find out, questioning Sarah Good, Sarah Osborne, and Tituba herself through five consecutive days. The anguished performances of the bewitched continued apace, and the tumult carried over into Sabbath services (held, of course, in the same meetinghouse) whenever Parris and other clergy tried to carry on in the usual way. Their preaching and prayer was repeatedly interrupted by renewals of "howling fits," and a rising mood of terror undercut their strained efforts of reassurance. The victim group grew, as other local girls (and two married women) fell "under affliction." New names were added to the list of the accused. The previous three had come from the outer margins of local society: a down-on-her-luck vagrant and occasional beggar (Good), a quarrelsome misfit (Osborne), an enslaved Indian (Tituba). But the next few were more favorably positioned: Elizabeth Proctor, wife of the local innkeeper; Martha Corey, church-member wife of a prosperous (though conflict-prone) farmer and landowner; and the elderly, widely-admired matriarch Rebecca Nurse.

The accusation of "gospel witches" (church members) was only the first in a series of crucial changes. Encounters with spectral shapes spread from the households of the original victims to the Village at large—and to all sorts of people, young and old, male and female. Two new elements emerged in the "complaints" of the afflicted: the hovering presence of a "black man," obviously a Devil figure; and the holding of large witch meetings at which participants consumed "red bread and red drink," in evident parody of Christian worship and the Christian sacrament. (This was, of course, a Protestant counterpart to the notorious "Black Mass" as described in the witch trials and witchcraft-related literature of European Catholics.)

The ministers, for their part, stressed the cosmically significant stakes of "this infernal assault" on the Village, and Satan's "malicious designs" therein. Salem, they said, had become "the rendezvous of Devils"; in response, right-thinking men and women must "ARM, ARM, ARM." Such overheated rhetoric would both build on and enhance a sense of *conspiracy* that was wide, deep, and still unfolding.

By this point the process of "discovery" had developed a pattern as well. Afflicted victims, mostly teenage girls, were the immediate source of accusation. (As such, they stepped far out of the modest role prescribed for persons of their age and sex, overshadowing even the magistrates who were officially in control. Within their families they engendered a similar reversal, as regular household routines became reorganized around their ongoing "torments.") But they responded to cues that reached them from many different directions, especially through the gossip and rumor that swirled ever more thickly within their community. Their specific charges had to be accepted by a variety of adult men who served, in a sense, as gatekeepers: first, the heads of their own households; second, the local authorities responsible for the preliminary hearings; and third, the judges and juries in full court proceedings.

At about the same time, the web of suspicion began to push out across the borders of Salem Village toward neighboring communities; "witches" were accused in Salem Town, in Ipswich, in Malden, and in Topsfield. Farther away, in Boston, topmost colony officials felt increasing pressure to intervene. Thus, in mid-April a second venue for examination was opened, this time in the Town center. Here the audience would become much larger—indeed, "a very great assembly," according to one account. And here the prosecutorial role fell not to local magistrates but to members of the colony's ruling Council, newly arrived from the capital and led by Lieutenant Governor Thomas Danforth.

Yet another turning point came in mid-April, with the accusation and examination of an apparently wayward teenager from Topsfield named Abigail Hobbs. Ever since Tituba's extraordinary revelations two months earlier, the examiners had been trying to secure a second major confession; they had succeeded only with a four-year-old child (Dorcas Good) and clearly needed more. Hobbs gave them exactly what they were looking for: a detailed account of meeting with the Devil, of making an explicit covenant with him (in exchange for his promise to give her "fine things"), and of agreeing to allow him the use of her "shape" when afflicting his victims. She also admitted to (invisible) collaboration with others among the accused, thus enlarging the conspiracy theme.

Strikingly, none of the key victims experienced "torments" while Hobbs was in the midst of her confessing. Indeed, when she finished, they expressed "compassion [for her] over and over again." Hobbs was then remanded to prison for subsequent trial; found guilty, she was nevertheless reprieved. She had, perhaps unwittingly, discovered an escape route for those who might later fall "under accusation": confess, and you may gain some traction with your accusers; confess, and save your skin. A few weeks later this linkage was, in effect, officially ratified when the magistrates advised another suspect that "if I would not confess I would be put down into the dungeon and . . . hanged, but if I would confess I should have my life." As events played out over the coming months, many confessors to witchcraft were indicted, tried, convicted, and jailed; but none of them were executed.

A recurrent theme in the Hobbs confession, the ministers' sermons, and the formal investigations was the Devil's intense determination to gain additional recruits to his nefarious cause; the witch plot would surely grow as weak-minded persons came, one after another, under his sway. And here lay an opening for local gossip to weave a spreading dragnet of accusation. For example, Bridget Bishop, of Salem Town, had been tried for witchcraft some 12 years before. Though officially acquitted on that previous occasion, the suspicions about her had lingered; now they resurfaced in the explosive atmosphere emanating from the Village nearby. In mid-April she was summoned for examination—whereupon several of the previously afflicted girls immediately "fell into fits." Her examiners then invoked long-standing rumor that "you bewitched your first husband to death." This she met with "angry" denials—which, how-ever, availed nothing against the effect of her "evil" reputation.

The list of the accused caught in the same web also included:

Rachel Clinton, of Ipswich. She, like Bishop, had been prosecuted for witchcraft years before; several of her neighbors had accused her of afflicting them, especially a young woman repeatedly "pricked with pins."

Sarah Wilds, of Topsfield. A deceased sister of her husband's first wife had complained that Wilds "assaulted [her] by witchcraft . . . and afflicted her many times grievously."

Dorcas Hoar, of Beverly. Her minister would later comment that "when discourses arose about witchcrafts at the village [of Salem], then I heard discourses revived of Goody Hoar's fortune telling." This latter practice seemed dangerously close to witchcraft; more-over, Hoar's "shape" had appeared at untimely moments here and there in the local community.

Giles Corey, husband of Martha. (As was true elsewhere, most of the men prosecuted in the Salem trials were the spouses of women already charged.) Corey was known for his persistent "miscarriage" (bad conduct), some of which verged on the supernatural.

Wilmot Redd, of Marblehead. She was believed to have bewitched one Mistress Syms following a lengthy quarrel over a missing parcel of linens.

Roger Toothaker, of Billerica. He was a "physician" and adept in the use of counter-magic, supposedly for combating *maleficia;* yet according to local rumor, he had turned those skills around so as to become himself a witchcraft practitioner. (His wife and daughter would also be accused.)

Susanna Martin, of Amesbury. Her alleged bewitchments went back more than three decades, including attacks on a number of her neighbors with invisible but deadly "nails and pins."

Margaret Scott, of Rowley. Her fellow townspeople remembered the long-ago sufferings of a man named Robert Shilleto, and how he "complained of [her] . . . for hurting of him, and often said that she was a witch . . . until he died."

Mary Bradbury, of Salisbury. She had allegedly targeted a ship at sea eleven years previously. Sailors blamed her for raising storms, causing "a leak in the hold," and spoiling their food supplies; moreover, they "would often say they heard she was a witch."

Sarah Cole, of Lynn. According to local gossip, she had occasionally bewitched cows in the town herd.

"Discourses" here, "discourses" there: before it was over, many, if not most, Essex County communities had disgorged their own particular witch suspects into the rapidly spiraling mix. The sequencing of these charges within the 1692 witch-hunt was variable; some came earlier, some later. A few were not much pursued, but most led to full-scale trials. Several produced verdicts of guilty, and death on the gallows (Wilds, Corey, Redd, Scott).

On the evening of April 20 came the most astonishing, and frightening, development so far: Ann Putnam Jr. was suddenly confronted with "the apparition of a minister." She was "tormented," just as she had been by others before. This time, however, it was much worse: "He tore me all to pieces." After initially refusing to reveal his identity, her assailant opened up. "He told me that his name was George Burroughs . . . that he had three wives . . . [and] that he had bewitched the first two of them to death . . . that he had killed Mistress Lawson . . . and also killed Mr. Lawson's child . . . [and] had bewitched a great many soldiers to death . . . [and] had made Abigail Hobbs a witch, and several witches more . . . and also . . . that he was above a witch, for he was a conjuror."

Nothing could have seemed more shocking than to have a minister unmasked as a witch—in fact, "above a witch . . . a conjuror," or (as was said elsewhere) a wizard. Abigail Hobbs would quickly confirm this revelation; from then on, the awful details poured out. In addition to his numerous killings, Burroughs was accused of organizing large meetings of his witch confederates, of going about in company with the Devil (in typical guise as "a black man"), of recruiting many additional witches, and of becoming himself a primary afflicter of the accusing girls.

Who was George Burroughs? He had been born in Virginia, in 1653, the son of a prosperous English merchant, but through most of his childhood had lived with his mother in the town of Roxbury, Massachusetts. He had attended Harvard College, graduating in the class of 1670. He had then begun a career in the ministry, though without being formally ordained. He had spent most of his adult years in the province of Maine (which was then annexed to Massachusetts), serving several local congregations there. Additionally, and crucially, he had served for three years (1680–83) as pastor of Salem Village, in the course of which he and some of his parishioners became bitterly antagonized; his tenure at Salem ended with lawsuits and his decision to return to Maine. He had indeed been married three times, and widowed twice, and was described as being "very sharp" toward each of his wives. His failure to gain ordination, his occasional absence from communion, his apparent disinterest in baptizing his children all made good grist for local gossip mills. Further suspicions were raised by his unusual, even "preternatural" physical strength. (He was reported, for example, to have shouldered large casks "of molasses or cider" without difficulty, and to have lifted a "very heavy gun . . . of six-foot barrel [by] putting the forefinger of his right hand into [its] muzzle, and so held it out at arm's end only with that finger.") Seen in retrospect, he was something of a marked man.

The charges against him came to the fore at an extraordinary examination of other witch suspects before a large crowd gathered in the Village meetinghouse on April 22. Deliverance Hobbs, mother of Abigail, was herself accused—and was then persuaded to offer her own elaborate confession. She recounted, in particular, "a meeting [of witches] yesterday" where Burroughs "was the preacher, and pressed them to bewitch all in the Village . . . assuring them they should prevail." Eight more suspects were examined at, or just after, the April 22 hearing; never before had such a large number been brought in at once. By month's end the total of the newly accused had reached 15; in May and early June another 39 were added to the list. Given a total population (for Town and Village together) of just over 1,000, these figures were extraordinary. They reflected, as well, a steady climb in the social position of those accused. Among the new targets were Philip English, an extremely wealthy Salem merchant with trading contacts all around the Atlantic basin, and his wife, Mary; Mistress Elizabeth Cary, of Charlestown, wife of a prosperous shipowner and mariner; Captain John Alden, son and namesake of the famous Pilgrim settler and himself a leading merchant; and others whom the record did not specifically identify, but including "some [with] great estates in Boston" and even certain "gentlemen of the Council, Justices of the Peace, ministers, and several of their wives."

As accusations mounted, so too did the pace of spectral sightings, especially within the core group of young accusers. At home, along the roadways, in the local tavern: "apparitions" might accost them at any time. Moreover, the format of these encounters was changing, at least in part. Previously, witch-specters were bent simply on attack: now, however, they would often pause to boast of their various crimes (especially killings). Indeed, some of the specters were actually victims of those crimes—returned now to inform the living of what they had suffered. Thus, George Burroughs's two deceased wives appeared before Ann Putnam Jr. and others, "in winding sheets and [with] napkins about their heads," and described the manner of their deaths in gruesome detail. ("He stabbed her under the arm, and put a piece of sealing wax on the wound," and so on.) Soon such ghostly visitations would become a regular part of the larger crisis.

The effect was to elevate still further the role of the afflicted, since their access would henceforth extend to both sides of the spectral combat—to witches and victims alike. They ranked now as witch-*finders* supreme, while the importance of formal examination shrank in direct proportion. Increasingly, the very purpose of the meetinghouse hearings was to provide a stage for the "actings" of bewitchment. And these grew ever more loud, more abandoned, more insistent, more terrifying. Special investigatory techniques were added to the standard repertoire, including, for example, a "touch test." Magistrates would order a suspect to touch the afflicted as a means of relieving their torments—usually with instantaneous and gratifying results.

As always, the impact of such vividly personal dramas rippled out into the community at large, where ordinary citizens pursuing their everyday business might come to see themselves as additional victims of Satanic assault. Thus, one Salemite was mysteriously "struck . . . a very hard blow . . . on my breast" while traveling on horseback with his wife; later, by the roadside, he observed a woman in the process (so he later said) of turning herself into a cow. Another man, upon entering an unlighted room in his home, "did see very strange things appear in the chimney . . . which seemed . . . to be something like jelly . . . and quavered with a strange motion." Yet another found his mare in a strangely injured state, as if "she was ridden with a hot bridle." And another believed "my sow was bewitched . . . [for] on a sudden she leapt up about three or four feet high . . . and gave one squeak, and fell down dead"; moreover, when he touched the corpse, his hand became "so numb and full of pain . . . that I could not do any work . . . [for] several days after." And still another, after being (supposedly) stared down by one of the witch suspects, was "taken in a strange condition, so that I could not dine, nor eat anything . . . for my water [urine] was suddenly stopped, and I had no benefit of nature, but was like a man on a rack."

These misadventures went on and on, regenerating and deepening the climate of fear. There were also anxieties of a different sort. In late May rumors flew about that several local residents of French background were plotting to "go for Canada and join with the French . . . [to] come down . . . upon the backside of the country to destroy all the English." Mortal peril on every side, assault from

both the visible and the invisible worlds: such was the prospect confronting them. There was but one plausible line of response. *Be
vigilant. Trust no one. Fight the Devil, and his dastardly minions, with
all your strength.* The Salem witch-hunt has often been described,
through the succeeding centuries, as an instance of "mass hysteria";
and, for the events of that fateful spring, the term does seem to fit.

The Trials Phase

Meanwhile, the process was moving toward a new stage—from accusation and investigation to actual trial proceedings. But before
these could begin, certain institutional arrangements must be put in
place. The Massachusetts Bay Colony was just now emerging from
several years of political turmoil, during which its charter—its very
right to exist—had been revoked, and its system of governance temporarily suspended. In 1691 a new charter was secured, followed soon
after by the appointment of new leadership. The governor would be
a one-time gunsmith and ship captain named Sir William Phips.
(Born and raised in the province of Maine, Phips had recently been
knighted for various services to the Crown.) The designated members of the Governor's Council were all familiar figures in the local
elite, including several magistrates at the center of the witch-hunt.

Phips arrived in Boston from England in the tense days of mid-
May, with the jails already full of the accused and further charges
emerging nearly every day. It was up to him, with the assistance of
his councillors, to craft legal machinery for resolving the crisis. Their
choice was a "Commission of Oyer and Terminer" (a term borrowed
from French legal parlance, meaning "to hear and determine"). Nine
judges were appointed to sit on this special court; at its head was the
new lieutenant governor, a famously stern and uncompromising
lawmaker named William Stoughton. (One of the others was Boston
merchant Samuel Sewall, whose diary would provide a lasting—and
very personal—commentary on key courtroom events.) While these

preparations went forward, witnesses and confessors were asked to confirm their previous testimonies. Further accusations were added to the original list, and several of the core accusers underwent a fresh round of affliction.

With the empaneling of a jury at month's end, all was in readiness for the first full-fledged trial. The setting was an upstairs courtroom in the Salem Town House. The proceedings opened at midmorning on June 2, in an atmosphere of the keenest possible anticipation. The lead-off defendant, chosen because the evidence against her seemed especially broad and damning, was Bridget Bishop of Salem Town. Unfortunately, the official records of this and succeeding trials have not survived, but important details are known through subsequent writings. Typically, the proceedings began with an appearance by several of the afflicted, whose "torments" might now be reenacted for the benefit of both judges and jurors. Next came the confessors, primed to reconfirm their crucially important accounts of spectral collaboration with the accused. The final part of the prosecution's agenda involved the calling of witnesses attesting to various *maleficia* in years past. All in all, it made for a tight and potentially unanswerable case.

The trial of Goody Bishop included each of these elements. The afflicted accusers thrashed about in anguish, all the while complaining that "the shape of the prisoner did oftentimes grievously pinch them, choke them, bite them." The confessor Deliverance Hobbs described Bishop's participation in "a general meeting of the witches, in a field at Salem Village," an event that had featured "a diabolical sacrament in bread and wine." No fewer than ten neighbors and acquaintances recalled past misfortunes—illnesses in people and cows, accidents, disappearances—following quarrels with the defendant, some dating back nearly two decades. There were some additional flourishes, too: the supposed discovery in her cellar of "poppets," and a report by a court-appointed committee about "preternatural excrescences" (witch marks) appearing on her body. Cotton Mather would comment later that her guilt was "evident and notorious to all beholders." In very short order, the jury brought in its verdict—guilty as charged—and the magistrates pronounced sentence. A week later, she was hanged.

Bishop's trial was followed by the first real pause in the pace of the witch-hunt. Over the next several weeks, spectral sightings, afflictions, and accusations became much less frequent (though they did not cease entirely). Perhaps the elimination of an important suspect brought a sense of relief, a generalized lowering of tension; or perhaps some participants were sobered by the high stakes of what they were about. Indeed, it was now that an initial round of doubts and questions began to rise, however tentatively, toward the surface of public consciousness.

In mid-June the governor and his Council asked members of the clergy for their opinions about the proceedings to date. (This in itself implied the beginnings of doubt.) The result was a long, carefully worded, and manifestly ambivalent document entitled "The Return of Several Ministers." On the one hand, the ministers praised the court's "exemplary piety and . . . agony of soul . . . [in seeking] the direction of Heaven." On the other, they raised some troubling questions about the "principles" behind the actual conduct of the trials. They seemed especially concerned that persons "of an unblemished reputation" were becoming ensnared by the witch-hunt; in such cases, they affirmed, "a very critical and exquisite caution" must be exercised. But their most pointed and difficult question—one that would loom increasingly large in the weeks to come—was about the reliability of spectral evidence. Chief Justice Stoughton (like many others) believed that God would not allow the Devil to represent innocent people as specters; hence, wherever and whenever such representation occurred, guilt was certain. But the ministers demurred, declaring it "an undoubted and a notorious thing that a demon may, by God's permission, appear in the shape of an innocent, yea, and a virtuous, man." To take such a position was to challenge a vital weapon in the hands of the prosecution.

And there was more. At around the same time another minister (not involved in the "return") gathered signatures on a pair of petitions to the colony's legislative assembly. These, too, noted the way "persons of good fame and unspotted reputation" had come under suspicion. And these, too, construed "bare specter testimony" as liable to mean "that the innocent will be condemned." A third line of opposition emerged in the struggle of the Nurse family to defend its own Rebecca; there the main strategy was to attack the credibility of the foremost accusers.

But the thrust of these convergent efforts was decisively—if temporarily—turned back. The Court of Oyer and Terminer simply ignored the questions put forward in the ministers' "return." The two petitions meant for the assembly were officially condemned as being "scandalous and seditious"; their chief author was rebuked and put on notice against further attempts of the same sort. And the trial of Rebecca Nurse proceeded as before. The time for wholesale reconsideration and regret would come, but not yet.

On June 28 the court met for its second full session; there would be five separate trials this time. The defendants, in order of their appearance, were: Sarah Good (one of the three initial suspects at Salem Village), Susanna Martin (Amesbury), Rebecca Nurse (Salem Village), Elizabeth Howe (Topsfield), and Sarah Wilds (also Topsfield). All were convicted, on the usual mix of evidence—"torments" in the core accusers, charges by one or more confessors, testimony about past *maleficia*. All were condemned to die. Moreover, hearings were conducted and indictments handed down for four additional suspects, and new examinations begun with several more. A few days later a Dutchman temporarily living in Boston wrote to a friend in New York, describing at length the panicked atmosphere that now prevailed "throughout the countryside." He particularly lamented "the gullibility of the magistrates" in allowing "trivial circumstances to be taken as substantially true and convincing testimony against the accused." The root of it all, he felt, was nothing more or less than "superstition and mistakes."

But his was a lone voice, impossible to hear amidst the rising gale

of accusation. On July 12, two weeks after their trial, the court issued
death warrants for the five women most recently convicted; a
week later they were hanged. This was the first of several multiple
executions—and it produced a tumultuous scene. There was the
usual procession to Gallows Hill, where crowds of onlookers jostled
for position. Clergy were present as well, hoping to extract last-
minute confessions. When Reverend Nicholas Noyes, minister of
the church in Salem Town, pressed that idea on Sarah Good, it
brought a scathing—and unforgettable—retort. "I am no more a
witch than you are a wizard," she shot back, "and if you take away
my life God will give you blood to drink." *God will give you blood
to drink:* soon there would be enough to gag on.

After another brief pause, the trials moved into their truly cli-
mactic phase. The entire crisis has been associated ever since with
Salem, its undoubted source point. But it also encompassed many of
the neighboring Essex County communities, and now it made its
most far-reaching impact, on the town of Andover. There, throughout the summer months, a constable's wife named Elizabeth Ballard
lay ill from mysterious causes. In due course, the possibility of witchcraft was raised, and two of the young accusers from Salem (probably Mercy Lewis and Elizabeth Hubbard) were invited in "to tell
what it was that did afflict her." (The source of this information is a
letter from a Boston merchant, written some months after the fact.
The same man would also comment that "poor Andover does now
rue the day that ever the said afflicted went among them.")

After a half-day's journey by carriage through the intervening
countryside, the witch-finders reached Andover and began their
work on July 14. They directed suspicion toward three women in
a single family: an elderly widow named Ann Foster, her married
daughter, and her teenage granddaughter. Under harsh questioning,
the widow confessed, the others followed suit shortly thereafter.
Then, together, the three of them spun out a vast web of incriminat-
ing testimony. Once again the primary focus was spectral activity

with other witches. Their accounts overflowed with lurid details: of large witch conclaves ("near a hundred in company"); of encounters with Satan, appearing sometimes "in the shape of a horse" or as "a black man . . . [with] a high-crowned hat," and always exhorting them "to make more witches if we can"; of making and using "poppets"; of traveling about "above the trees . . . upon a pole"; of hearing a kind of roll call of "77 witches' names"; of watching their confederates suckle "imps"; of child-murders, and magical swords, and the infamous "red book," and extravagant talk of "throwing down the kingdom of Christ, and setting up the Devil on his throne." It went on and on, prompted at every turn by eager questions from behind the magistrates' bench.

Meanwhile, in Salem, the Court of Oyer and Terminer was preparing to hold its third session; begun on August 2, and lasting four days, this one would yield five more convictions. The most important—not to say sensational—of the new trials was that of Reverend Burroughs, by now considered "the head and ringleader of all the supposed witches in the land." Burroughs went into the dock on August 5 before "a vast concourse of people"; the latter included clergy from several neighboring towns and, quite likely, Governor Phips himself. According to subsequent accounts, "about thirty testimonies were brought in against him." There were the usual "actings" of the afflicted girls, with special emphasis on injury from "biting." (Their bodies appeared to show imprinted wounds exactly corresponding to Burroughs's teeth, "which could be distinguished from those of other men.") There were spectral sightings of the "ghosts" of his deceased victims, some of whom "looked red, as if the blood would fly out of their faces with indignation at him." There were new accounts of his "preternatural strength"; though of small stature—one witness called him "puny"—he had performed such "extraordinary lifting" and other feats "as could not be done without a diabolical assistance." Finally, there were lengthy reports of his central role at the numerous witch gatherings: of his preaching the

Devil's message and administering a kind of inverted "sacrament."
(He was even said to own a "diabolical trumpet" useful in summoning his "horrible crew" of followers to action.)

Once again warrants of execution followed conclusion of the trials within a scant few days. Thus, on August 19, this latest group of convicts made their own final journey up Gallows Hill. But the scene that unfolded then was quite different from the one of a month before. From the same platform where Sarah Good had cursed her persecutors so bitterly, Burroughs made a dignified speech "for the clearing of his innocency" that won "the admiration of all present"; his concluding prayer "drew tears from many." Others among the condemned explicitly "forgave their accusers" and cast no blame on the judges and jurymen; they wished only that theirs "might be the last innocent blood shed on that account." All this proved "very affecting and melting to the hearts of . . . spectators." As Burroughs finished speaking and was about to be "turned off" (hanged), some in the crowd seemed of a mind to "hinder the execution." But at that critical moment, Reverend Cotton Mather, watching from astride his horse, spoke out "to possess the people of his guilt, and saying that the Devil had often been transformed into an angel of light." This did "somewhat appease" their doubts, and the proceedings reverted to plan. Burroughs's corpse was then dragged off "by the halter," and stuffed into "a hole . . . between the rocks . . . [with] one of his hands and his chin . . . left uncovered." Even in death, a witch deserved the utmost ignominy.

With this latest batch of executions behind them, the magistrates could turn their full attention toward Andover, where afflictions, accusations, and confessions were fast piling up. Fits of the familiar sort had begun in several local girls; these led on to official complaints. Examinations followed, with many, if not most, of the accused apparently ready to confess their guilt. Presumably, it was clear by now that straightforward denials availed little against the rush to prosecute, whereas cooperation might at least gain the advantage of delay. Indeed, some of those examined, having once confessed, would subsequently join the ranks of the afflicted to accuse still other suspects. Moreover, community pressure wore down any lingering impulse to resist; confessors would later recount how they had been "urged and affrighted" into saying "anything that was desired." The Andover cases, unlike the rest, set close kin against one another—a child accusing a parent, a brother condemning a sister, a husband suspecting a wife. It was as if all protective human structures—village, neighborhood, and family itself—had caved in under the weight of raw panic.

By late August, some 40 Andover residents had been examined and charged, while dozens more lay "under suspicion." Then came a turning point—for Andover, for the trial process, for this entire history. Its exact nature is obscure (since the surviving records grow vague just here). But apparently, the magistrates ordered some version of a touch test, with several of the leading suspects put in blindfold and obliged to lay hands on one or another of the accusers—thus to relieve their "torments." Did the procedure somehow miss its mark? Did the accusers respond in ways not anticipated—become confused, try to change course, fall into dispute? Did they then retreat into renewed affliction? We can only imagine, for the records are silent. (Did the record-*keepers* feel chagrined, or embarrassed, by what they had witnessed? And were they, as a result, wont to omit crucial details?) What we know for certain is that the Andover magistrates declined thereafter to order additional arrests. For this, one of them was himself accused as a witch and obliged to flee the town.

The Reconsideration Phase

By now, "objections" were being raised, and "objectors" heard, at the highest levels of provincial governance: among members of the Council, for example, and within the clergy as well. The key issue, as before, was spectral evidence, about which much of the leadership

inclined toward doubt, or outright denial. And if the previously in-
criminating specters were now considered fraudulent, how should
the "afflicted" accusers be viewed? Did they bear some personal responsibility for initiating, and spreading, a deadly series of false
charges? The predominant view supported them; both their "complaints" and their "torments" seemed genuine enough. However, in
some quarters suspicion was growing that "they do but counterfeit."
Several of the accused had suggested as much long before; at least
one had charged them with telling "lies," another with using "wiles
and subtlety," yet another with resort to "juggling tricks, falling
down, crying out, and staring in people's faces." In fact, it seems
probable that skepticism about the trials—most of it covert, ambivalent, checked by fear and doubt—had been present virtually from
the start. To express such attitudes directly was, of course, to risk
being accused oneself. Still, as summer passed into fall, the skeptics were becoming both more numerous and more emboldened.
Governor Phips, upon returning from a trip to the Maine frontier,
found Boston and the surrounding towns in "a strange ferment of
dissatisfaction." And the region was soon to witness an open print
war between critics and supporters of the trials.

First, though, there would be one more round of prosecutions,
with Lieutenant Governor Stoughton and his fellow judges determined to press ahead regardless. Indeed, this fourth and (as it turned
out) final session of the Court of Oyer and Terminer claimed more
victims than any of its predecessors. Within a span of eleven frenetic
days, the court tried 15 suspects, and convicted them all; then it
brought another group out for indictment and subsequent trial. For
the first time, the convicts included several confessors; all but one
of these, however, were eventually reprieved. (The exception was a
man who recanted his confession.) Among the more notable defendants was old Giles Corey, who "stood mute" before the bar and refused to enter a plea. The court then ordered him to undergo an
ancient procedure known as *peine fort et dure* (strong and hard pain)
designed to force a response. He was laid flat while large stones were

piled on his chest; this would continue until he spoke as required or died. According to legend, his only words before succumbing were a whispered but defiant "more weight."

In very short order, death warrants were issued for most of the others, and September 22 brought the largest of the mass executions. The process was delayed when a cart carrying the condemned became temporarily stuck in the roadway; some thought "the Devil hindered it." Then, as one after another was finally "turned off," there were solemn prayers and affecting farewells; according to an eyewitness, "Tears [flowed] from the eyes of almost all present." But not entirely all. Reverend Noyes, of the Town church, is said to have remarked with evident scorn, "What a sad thing it is to see eight firebrands of hell hanging there!"

By the end of the summer, fourteen women and six men had been executed, and accusations were still coming in. (Among the new names mentioned was that of Lady Phips, wife of the governor.) Examinations continued, with many of the accused languishing in prison for weeks, even months, more. Several escaped in nighttime jailbreaks with the active assistance of family and friends. Meanwhile, Boston and the adjacent towns were abuzz with witchcraft debate, "in the coffee-houses and elsewhere." The talk was fed by a spate of fresh writings, some in published form, others in manuscript but intended for general circulation. Two of these were by Boston ministers, Increase Mather (father of Cotton) and Samuel Willard. Both men sought to straddle the jagged fence between opposing viewpoints on the trials. They questioned the use of spectral evidence, believing as they did that the Devil could assume the shape of innocent persons; by the same token, they disapproved touch tests as amounting to "the Devil's testimony." Yet they drew back from criticizing the current court in any direct way. It seemed possible, even probable, that Satan had used the trials as a means of "deluding and imposing on the imaginations of men"; this meant that "the witnesses, judges, and juries were all to be excused from blame."

Another careful observer (and author), the Boston merchant

Thomas Brattle, drew a more sharply negative picture. He, too, discounted spectral evidence and such "superstitious methods" as touch tests. But he added strong criticism of the court's reliance on the testimony of confessors, whom he viewed as "deluded . . . and under the influence of an evil spirit," and thus "unfit to be evidences against themselves or anyone else." He noted a troubling compromise of "distributive justice," in that several persons of high social rank had escaped persecution even though "much complained of by the afflicted"; this, he said, had occasioned "much discourse and many hot words" among more ordinary folk. He concluded by listing various "men of understanding, judgment, and piety . . . that do utterly condemn the said proceedings," including a former governor, a former lieutenant governor, and several justices, as well as "reverend elders almost throughout the country."

Against such critics stood the redoubtable Cotton Mather, whose impassioned defense *The Wonders of the Invisible World* was published in mid-October. But Mather was swimming against a steadily rising tide. The momentum for prosecution did not collapse all at once; rather, it disintegrated piece by piece, day by day, person by person. Petitioners urged that those still in jail be released; confessors recanted their previous testimony; and at least one of the afflicted accusers came forward to say that "now she believeth it is all a delusion of the Devil." The Court of Oyer and Terminer was scheduled to resume prosecutions at the start of November. However, the Council had begun, in the meantime, to debate its future, and the assembly declared a public day of fasting, with a "convocation of ministers" appointed to reflect on the entire crisis. On October 29, Governor Phips responded to a questioner by stating flatly that the court "must fall."

In fact, the Court of Oyer and Terminer had been from the start a special creation, designed to meet the exigencies of the witchcraft "outbreak" in particular. There was always an expectation that its duties would someday be taken over by one or another part of the regular judicial system. And that is what happened in December, when the Superior Court of Judicature (freshly constituted following a renewal and revision of the colony's charter) went into full operation.

The Concluding Phase

Even now the witch-hunt mentality had not fully abated; prosecutions would continue under new auspices. In fact, when the superior court was officially convened in early January, with Lieutenant Governor Stoughton again in charge and other members of the previous court sitting alongside him, it confronted a backlog of more than 50 cases from the previous summer and fall. To be sure, the rules had changed; from now on, spectral evidence would be effectively disallowed. There was also a sense, among some of the judges themselves, that "their former proceedings were too violent, and not grounded upon a right foundation." Thus many in the latest group of defendants were quickly dismissed without even an indictment, while others were tried and acquitted. Only three were found guilty. Each of these had previously confessed, so spectral evidence was not at issue. Stoughton was perhaps the last holdout for an inflexibly hard line: almost immediately he signed death warrants for the newly convicted trio, plus five others (from earlier trials) whose sentence had not yet been carried out. A date of execution was set—February first—and preparations begun. And workmen began hacking fresh graves out of the frozen ground.

   In the meantime, however, the king's attorney for Massachusetts had given the governor an advisory opinion that the case against those under sentence seemed little different from what had been alleged with others now freed. Phips thought it over for the next two weeks, and then, with just a day to spare, revoked the execution orders and issued a set of reprieves. Predictably, Stoughton responded with fury. "We were in a way to have the country cleared of these," he exclaimed; but now, thanks to the governor's ruling, "the kingdom of Satan is advanced." He stormed from the court and refused for a while thereafter to take any part in its regular work.

And still it dragged on. The jails in Salem and Boston housed perhaps two dozen additional suspects, most of them under indictment and awaiting trial. Five of these would be acquitted in early February. (In one case, the verdict contravened some 30 witnesses, ready even now to attest to "malicious and felonious" acts of witchcraft.) Over the weeks and months that followed, several more would be released, quietly and without official formalities. A final burst of court proceedings came in mid-May, some resulting in simple dismissals, some in trials, but none in convictions. Among this group of defendants was Tituba, Reverend Parris's Indian slave, who had remained in jail since the time of her extraordinary and explosive confession more than a year earlier. Upon being released, she was (according to later reports) put up for sale and purchased by a new owner, since Parris declined responsibility for the costs of her imprisonment. The inability to reimburse such costs, assessed for meals and other necessaries provided by the prison-keeper, kept a few more unlucky souls confined until midsummer. The last such case was concluded only at the end of August, when Mary Watkins, a onetime accuser and subsequent confessor, went off to Virginia as an indentured servant.

Reverend John Hale of Beverly had been both an observer and a participant in the trials; his little book *A Modest Enquiry Into the Nature of Witchcraft* (published several years later) provided a kind of postmortem on the entire crisis. His view of its ending commands attention even now. Alongside the learned debate about questions such as spectral evidence and the extent of Satan's power, Hale noted a widespread public perception of "going too far in this affair." It had become harder and harder to believe that "so many in so small a compass of land should so abominably leap into the Devil's lap at once." Moreover, "the quality of several of the accused was such as did bespeak better things, and things that accompany salvation." In sum: on grounds of both quantity and quality, "those that were concerned . . . grew amazed"—and finally disbelieving. The witch-hunt had overreached, and, in effect, destroyed itself.

The Aftermath

Trials finished, jails emptied, time at last to reckon the costs. Twenty dead, over a hundred imprisoned, dozens more cast under suspicion; neighbors set bitterly against one another, families sundered, property and reputations lost or destroyed. It was, by any measure, a heavy, shattering toll. Recovery would proceed in small increments over long periods of time.

Bits and pieces of the aftermath lie scattered through local and provincial records, beginning with the homecoming of dozens among the accused. Many of them had been in prison for months; some had fled to escape prosecution; a few had gone into hiding. Their reintegration cannot have been easy; imagine, for example, the situation of a woman whose husband or other relatives had joined the list of her accusers. (Imagine, too, the situation of such a husband.) In some cases, especially those involving the joint prosecution of a married couple, household property had been confiscated by the authorities (or simply pilfered by neighbors); now there would be lawsuits to gain restitution. When the wealthy Salem importer Philip English and his wife returned to their home in the spring of 1693, having been forced previously "to fly for our lives," they found "a considerable body of household goods . . . taken away," including family portraits, wines, clothing, five pigs, and "a certain cow with a bob tail." Moreover, the warehouses from which English had carried on his extensive trade were stripped almost bare. The list of his losses went on for pages, and amounted in value to more than £1,000; his efforts to obtain redress, through the courts, would continue for decades. At the opposite end of the social scale, an impoverished widow from Lynn named Mary deRich—also accused and long imprisoned—had "lost her bed and pot"; she, too, would seek legal remedy. Elizabeth Proctor, meanwhile, had been tried and convicted along with her husband, John; he was executed, but she was spared because she was pregnant. Her eventual release ignited a bitter struggle with her stepchildren over the terms of John's will; years later she petitioned the General Court for relief, saying that "they [the stepchildren] will not suffer me to have one penny of his estate." The courts were also a logical site for handling many smaller *residua* of the trials, such as payments to constables, sheriffs, and jail-keepers, and even to tavern-keepers who had supplied judges and jurors with needed "refreshment" as they went about their grim task.

Doubtless the trials remained for years a lively, if painful, topic of both public and private conversation; references to such moments appear from time to time in Samuel Sewall's diary. In June 1693, for example, Sewall went to see his old friend John Alden, who had recently come home to Boston following prosecution, escape from prison, and several months of life on the lam in New York. "I was sorry," Sewall told Alden and his wife, "for their sorrow and temptations, by reason of his imprisonment, and I was glad of his restoration." Some time later Sewall reported visiting with another Bostonian named Jacob Melyen, who "spoke to me very smartly about the Salem witchcraft." In particular, Melyen ridiculed the accusations touching Reverend George Burroughs's supposedly supernatural strength, saying that "if a man should take Beacon Hill on his back, carry it away, and then . . . set it in its place again, I should not make anything of it." In November 1697, Sewall wrote that "Mr. Hale and I lodged together. He discussed with me about writing a history of witchcraft." (The reference was to Reverend John Hale, minister in the town of Beverly.)

Indeed, reevaluation of the witch trials proceeded not only in conversation, but also—and perhaps more significantly—in print. Cotton Mather's *The Wonders of the Invisible World* was answered by merchant Robert Calef's highly skeptical and sardonic *More Wonders of the Invisible World*. Thomas Maule, a Quaker shopkeeper in Salem, authored another, equally critical work, entitled *Truth Held Forth and Maintained* (1695). And at roughly the same time Reverend Hale was preparing his *A Modest Enquiry*. In it, he reconsidered his early support for the trials, admitting to "errors" and "the sad consequences of mistakes" and "grief of heart . . . to have been encouraging of the sufferings of the innocent."

Some of this discussion crossed the ocean. Mather's *Wonders* was advertised in London within weeks of its Boston publication; the diarist John Evelyn read it right away and remarked on the "considerable" interest it aroused among other English readers. Calef and Hale were published there as well. Phips, meanwhile, was sending lengthy accounts of the trials—part description, part self-justification—to leading officials in the king's government. In midsummer 1693, just as the last of the suspects were being released from prison, he decided to let his prior reprieves stand indefinitely. "Next to divine providence," he declared in a letter to his superiors in London, "it is the stop to these proceedings which has averted the ruin of this province."

A *stop:* yes and no. To be sure, the actual witch-hunt was over. But in Salem Village the fallout from the trials—divisions, recriminations, a feeling of *ruin*—would continue well into the future. Even as the trials were unfolding, some local residents had begun to withdraw from participation in the church. Prominent among them were the families of the accused: the Nurses, for example. Their objection, as they later described it, was straightforward enough. They deplored the "tumults and noises made by . . . persons under diabolical power and delusions" and feared that they, too, might be accused "as the Devil's instruments." Most of all, they felt helpless to protect their loved ones from a lethal attack that had the approval, not to say the encouragement, of the minister himself. In their view, several of Reverend Parris's sermons, during the crucial springtime weeks in 1692, had expounded "principles and practices" that greatly accelerated the rush to prosecution.

But this was just a beginning; after the trials had concluded, the anti-Parris "dissenters" formed a solid, unappeasable bloc. They consistently "absented from communion" with the Village church. They refused to pay any share of the minister's salary, contested his residence in the parsonage, and worked with increasing openness for his dismissal. The struggle went on for three years, with countless internal meetings, bitterly fought campaigns for control of local governance, and strenuous efforts of mediation by outsiders, including a grand "council" of Massachusetts ministers brought to Salem in April 1695—all to no avail. At every juncture, the core issue remained the witch trials, the injustice done to the accused, and Parris's alleged role as their "great prosecutor." In response, the embattled minister flailed this way and that. Occasionally he proffered olive branches: for example, a post-trials sermon on the theme of "kisses . . . among friends that have been long absent" and a subsequent writing entitled "Meditations for Peace." He expressed sympathy for the families of all who had suffered, and even made a (heavily qualified) apology: "I do most heartily . . . beseech pardon of all my mistakes and trespasses . . . wherein you see or conceive I have erred or offended." But he also threatened legal action to throttle his adversaries and repeatedly denounced the "factious and seditious" lies made out against him.

The dissenters would not relent and finally succeeded in bringing him down. In 1696, under pressure from other clergy, Parris resigned his pastorate (though even then he stayed on in the parsonage until awarded a hefty sum in back pay). The Villagers were spent, bruised, and exhausted—but at last they could move on. Their church hired a new pastor in 1698 and immediately took steps to reconcile with the leading dissenter families. The excommunication of at least one accused church member (Martha Corey) was now posthumously reversed, mistakes acknowledged, sorrow expressed. "We were at that dark day," the congregation declared in a formal statement of apology, "under the power of those errors which then prevailed in the land"; as a result, their actions had not been "according to the mind of God."

A spirit of apology grew apace, both within the town borders and beyond. A group of a dozen men who had served as jurors during the witch trials offered a public statement of their own to "signify to all in general (and to the surviving sufferers in especial) our deep sense of, and sorrow for, our errors, in acting . . . to the condemning of any person." Looking back, they considered themselves to have been "sadly deluded and mistaken"; they wished to "heartily ask forgiveness of you all whom we have justly offended." At around the same time the members of the General Court ordered a "day of prayer, with fasting, throughout this province" in order to seek God's absolution for "the many sins prevailing in the midst of us." At the heart of their official proclamation was an oblique but unmistakable reference to the witch trials as "the late tragedy raised among us by Satan and his instruments." Then, on the day appointed—January 14, 1697, almost exactly five years after the "rise and beginning" of the whole affair—came another striking act of apology. In the course of the services in his Boston church, Samuel Sewall passed a note to the minister (Reverend Willard) to be read aloud to the full congregation. In it, Sewall acknowledged the "guilt contracted" from his participation in the Court of Oyer and Terminer, and his readiness to shoulder "the blame and shame of it." On the same midwinter date in years to come, Sewall would hold a private fast at his home, without exception, to the end of his life.

To be sure, other central figures—Chief Judge Stoughton, for example—did not apologize and resumed the course of their previous lives without apparent difficulty. And even the apologies that did come excluded full personal responsibility. The proximate cause of the "tragedy"—always a tragedy, never a killing spree—was "delusion," not vengeance or ill will or simple inattention. And the root cause was the malign force of "Satan and his instruments."

The aftermath would drag on for decades. In 1703 came the first in a torrent of petitions on behalf of the accused "that something may be publicly done to take off the infamy from their names." In 1709, as part of seeking membership in the Salem church, Ann Putnam confessed her own responsibility for the shedding of "innocent blood"; she made special apologies to the family of Rebecca Nurse, in whose trial she had been so active, desiring now "to lie in the dust, and be humbled for it." In 1710 the General Court arranged to pay reparations to many of the families involved. In 1711 the court passed a bill of attainder, directly nullifying most of the convictions from two decades before. As late as 1738, and again in 1740, the authorities were considering measures to help "the families as were in a manner ruined in the mistaken mismanagement of the terrible affair called witchcraft" that was now nearly a half century behind them.

The element of "ruin" may have touched even some among the accusers and prosecutors. Several of the famously afflicted girls were reported to have gone on to lives of "dissolution and profligacy." One (Mercy Lewis) is known to have borne a bastard child. Another (probably Abigail Williams) was said by Reverend Hale to have been "followed with diabolical manifestations to her death"; he meant that she was not thereafter of sound mind. Ann Putnam Jr. never married, was in chronically frail health, and died at age 37. Then, finally, there was Reverend Noyes, a stern and unwavering advocate for the trials, and the man at whom Sarah Good—just prior to execution—had flung her bitter curse *God will give you blood to drink*. Noyes remained for many years a figure of importance, still on duty as minister of Salem Town, until one day in December 1718, when a sudden and massive brain hemorrhage struck him down. According to local lore, he did indeed die with his mouth full of blood— which caused at least a few of his parishioners to wonder whether Good had not been something of a witch after all.

What happened at Salem?

That question has reverberated across the generations, from theirs
to our own. What happened? And why did it happen? *How could
they . . . ?* The answers proposed by literally dozens of writers—
historians, novelists, playwrights, poets, scientists, physicians, and
witchcraft enthusiasts of every stripe—span an enormous range.
Taken together, they amount to a template of changing values,
changing ideas, changing times.

Salemwitchcraft as divine retribution

John Hale, the Beverly minister, can perhaps be considered the first
in this long procession. Though himself directly involved and in-
vested in the trials, he had, during the five years that elapsed prior to
writing his *A Modest Enquiry*, achieved a certain distance from them.
No longer able to take the multiple accusations at face value, but unwilling to discredit the leaders (judges, clergy, government officials)
who had done exactly that, Hale reframed the underlying question
as "what the Lord speaks to us in his letting loose Satan upon us in
this unusual way." Why, in short, had God allowed the Devil to or-
chestrate such an "awful tragedy," full of lethal "errors and mistakes"? Hale's answer would become sufficient, indeed standard, for
many of those in his own particular cohort (and the one or two that
immediately followed). It was, simply: punishment for sin, especially
"an inordinate love of the world" and "contempt of God's worship
and . . . ordinances." Put differently: "The Lord sends evil angels to
awaken and punish our negligence." In making such connections,
Hale adapted the well-worn Puritan trope of "declension." The ill-
gotten witch trials, like other "chastening strokes" on 17th-century
New England, were the Lord's retribution for moral decline among
His chosen people.

Salemwitchcraft as deception

For almost a century, "declension" and "chastening" remained the favored way of understanding the witch-hunt. But then, in the third quarter of the 18th century, as the European Enlightenment made itself felt across the ocean in America, this religious paradigm began to crumble. A two-volume history of Massachusetts, written in the 1760s by Thomas Hutchinson (soon to become the colony's governor) served to mark the change. For Hutchinson, unlike Hale, belief in witchcraft was fundamentally "superstitious." And for him the Salem "tragedy"—he, too, favored that word—admitted of only two possible explanations: physical illness ("bodily distempers") or outright deception. The first idea struck Hutchinson as "kind and charitable," but also as a way of "winking the truth out of sight"; he much preferred the second. "A little attention," he wrote, "must force the conviction that the whole was a scene of fraud and imposture, begun by young girls, who at first perhaps thought of nothing more than being pitied and indulged, and continued by adult persons who were afraid of being accused themselves."

Salemwitchcraft and class conflict

Another significant contributor to this gradually building discussion (several decades later) was George Bancroft, author of an immensely popular, multivolume *History of the United States*. Bancroft had imbibed, and forcefully contributed to, the buoyant, "go-ahead" spirit of Jacksonian democracy. His *History* (composed in the 1840s and '50s) was celebratory in both theme and tone, and the place of Salemwitchcraft within it took shape accordingly. On one side stood "the authority"—the colony leaders, especially the clergy—a "party of superstition," blinded by "self-love," "zeal," "vanity," and "self-righteousness," and bent on dominance through the workings of an "illegal commission" (the Court of Oyer and Terminer). On the other side, "the common mind of Massachusetts was more wise."

Common *mind,* common *people,* common *sense:* to be "common" was, for a man of Bancroft's ideals, a strongly favorable point. Fortunately, proponents of the common had prevailed against "the delusion of witchcraft" and its upper-class sponsors. Indeed, Bancroft declared, "the responsibility of the tragedy, far from attaching to the people of the colony, rests with a very few, hardly five or six . . . [who had] for a season unlimited influence."

Salemwitchcraft and village factionalism

In 1867, Charles W. Upham, a Salem resident who served as both the town's minister and its mayor and who was an avid local historian besides, published the first full-scale work devoted entirely to the history of the witch trials. Upham followed Bancroft in setting a scene where "credulity, superstition, and fanaticism" loomed large (at least among the leadership); in the same connection, he stressed "an ignorance of the many natural laws that have been revealed by modern science." He also followed Hutchinson in charging the afflicted children with "imposture," with "deliberate cunning" and "cool malice," as they pursued their work of destruction; "there can be no doubt," he concluded, "that they were great actors."

But Upham added some new elements of his own. For one thing, he shone a highly pejorative spotlight on Tituba and her fellow slave (and husband) John Indian; in fact, he wrote, "these two persons may have originated the Salem witchcraft." Coming as they did from the Caribbean islands, they "in all probability contributed, from the wild and strange superstitions prevalent among their native tribes," opinions and emotions to which Betty Parris, Ann Putnam Jr., and others in the initial group of accusers were fatally drawn. Here Upham was directly projecting the predominant racial attitudes of his time: Indians, like blacks, were seen as biological and cultural inferiors, liable under suitable conditions to infect "civilized" white folk with their primitivism. Finally, and most important, Upham presented the fruits of some extremely diligent local research on the workings within 17th-century Salem of deep-seated "factionalism." He had uncovered evidence of bitter "quarrels and controversies," of long-lasting "feuds"; these, he argued, shaped specific patterns of accusation. The girls at the center were "under the guidance of older heads . . . all the way through"; thus, their targets reflected enmities long established in the town. Perhaps this emphasis on social division, in a work written just after the close of a colossal Civil War, was more than a matter of simple intuition. Little Salem Village had once endured its own civil war.

Salemwitchcraft as mental illness

Occasionally, Upham gestured in yet another direction, by offering "the supposition that they [the afflicted children] were more or less deranged." From conscious and calculating imposture, they had gradually been led into a kind of "sickly mania." To be sure, they were "sinners" first and foremost, yet "sin . . . in all cases, is itself insanity." (This last came straight from Upham the clergyman and Christian moralist.)

The same theme—derangement, or, in a phrasing more congenial to our own day, mental illness—would be taken up by George M. Beard, author of *The Psychology of the Salem Witchcraft Excitement of 1692*, published in 1882. Beard was a physician; his book was designed to reflect then-current trends in clinical practice. The keyword in its title was "excitement"; the afflicted girls, he believed, had been so overstimulated by Puritan tales of "the invisible world," of devils and hellfire, that they became "partly insane and partly entranced." (The latter term referenced a growing public interest in hypnosis.) Beard also introduced the concept of hysteria, which was just then beginning to acquire serious professional currency and would later become central to witchcraft interpretation.

The larger motive behind *The Psychology of the Salem Witchcraft Excitement* was to buttress the use of the insanity defense for murder suspects; this, in turn, had been prompted by the recent trial and conviction (and execution) of Charles Guiteau, the assassin of President James A. Garfield. Beard's sympathy for the Salem accusers was somewhat tempered by his belief that in their case (unlike Guiteau's) "the genuine symptoms of real disease were supplemented by malignity and crime"; like other commentators before and after, he read an element of "intentional deception" into the mix.

Salemwitchcraft and cultural "provincialism"

As a new century opened, Americans were caught up in what became known as the Progressive Movement, with its burgeoning spirit of change and reform. The rise of "modern science," to which Upham had so confidently referred decades before, was continuing apace; under its bright light, traditional perspectives of every sort were being fundamentally reconsidered. The newest part of modern science was the systematic study of societies, including their histories. And when the "progressives" turned, in particular, to American history, they quickly identified Puritanism as a special sort of bogeyman. Never previously had the repute of the New England colonists sunk so low, linked as they now were with ignorance, intolerance, and across-the-board cultural backwardness. Moreover, the Salem witch-hunt seemed, by this reckoning, the very epitome of its time and place.

Among the many writers who advanced such views, two can be seen as representative: the historians James Truslow Adams and Vernon L. Parrington. Adams, for his part, saw "the witchcraft frenzy" as a matter of "superstitious fanaticism" brought on chiefly by the "ravings and goadings" of the clergy. It reflected throughout "the extraordinarily large sphere accorded to the devil in Puritan theology, and that theology's virtual repudiation of science." The result, in addition to "shedding the blood of innocent victims," was "lasting political and intellectual damage" to the community as a whole. Parrington hit virtually the same note. New England culture, he wrote in his masterwork *Main Currents of American Thought*, was "in-

fected . . . [by] a common provincialism." In this regard, "the ministers were no better than their congregations; they were blind leaders
of the blind, and they lent their sanction to the intolerance of mass
judgment." The result was a building wave of "stark reaction"; and
"the Salem outbreak was the logical outcome of the long policy of
repression, that had . . . destroyed independent thought, in its attempt to imprison the natural man in a strait-jacket of Puritan righteousness." There was, in this bleak portrayal, no single gleam of
redemption.

Salemwitchcraft as period piece

But redemption would come in due course, as the Puritans gained a
new set of revisionist interpreters. Among professional historians
the leader (at least in chronological sequence) was Samuel Eliot Morison, whose pathbreaking work, *The Puritan Pronaos: Studies in the
Intellectual Life of New England, in the Seventeenth Century,* appeared
in 1936. Morison strove, above all else, to take the Puritans on their
own terms, without superimposing modern (and "progressive")
standards of value. Seen in that light, their achievements, intellectual and otherwise, were distinctly impressive. And also in that light,
witchcraft beliefs—even witch trials—did not appear incongruous;
to the contrary, they were "typical of the seventeenth-century situation." The Salem trials, moreover, were the product of an especially
"troubled period" in New England history, when "the people were
uneasy with rebellions, changes of government, and Indian attacks."
The "afflicted children" had acted an insincere part, while their elders "kept a cowardly silence." Such moments of "mass madness"
had occurred also in other times and places. Indeed, Salem recalled,
for Morison, "a recent miscarriage of justice . . . in the same commonwealth [Massachusetts]," the Sacco-Vanzetti trials of the 1920s;
this parallel "compels us to be charitable" to the perpetrators. All
things considered, the 1692 "outbreak" was no more than "a small
incident in the history of a great superstition." And, when it was

done, New England was "left . . . much as it had been before." In short: unfortunate, yes; regrettable, yes; but not very significant overall.

Morison's colleague on the faculty at Harvard, Perry Miller, took a more complex and nuanced position. Miller would eventually become the most important of all contributors to Puritan studies; in ways unimagined by his predecessors, he plumbed the depths of a collective "New England mind." The witch trials, however, left him in a somewhat divided frame. At certain points he seemed impatient with the popular interest they inevitably aroused—a product, he thought, of rank sensationalism. In that connection he could say, with a faint air of contempt: "The intellectual history of New England can be written as if no such thing ever happened. It had no effect on the ecclesiastical or political situation, it does not figure in the institutional or ideological development." Like Morison, Miller hoped to wish the matter away by denying its importance. The elaborately developed Puritan theology, on which he lavished his own extraordinary powers of analysis, counted for so much more.

Yet in other parts of his oeuvre, a different, and less dismissive, assessment appeared. He sensed in some of his clergymen subjects—Hale, for one; Cotton Mather, for another—a virtual crisis of faith in response to the witch trials. Hale, of course, had come to acknowledge "error," and Mather had approached the same point without quite getting there. Both had been led, in Hale's words, to "a more strict scanning of the principles . . . [they] had imbibed." Once such a process began, Miller wondered, where would it stop? He concluded as follows: "The onus of error lay heavy upon the land; the realization of it slowly but irresistibly ate into the New England conscience." The passing years brought "an unassuageable grief that the covenanted community should have committed an irreparable evil. Out of sorrow and chagrin, out of dread, was born a new love for the land which had been desecrated, but somehow also consecrated, by the blood of innocents." For Miller, the witch-hunt had finally been transmuted into a strange kind of romantic myth.

Salemwitchcraft and the vulnerability of children

A slender article, little noticed at the time of its publication in 1943, deserves at least brief mention here, if only because it anticipated later developments. Entitled "Pediatric Aspects of the Salem Witchcraft Tragedy," it appeared in a scientific journal; its author, Ernest Caulfield, was a medical doctor. Caulfield's chief aim was to counter the still-prevalent emphasis on "fraud" in explaining the witch-hunt; his approach reflected his professional specialty in pediatrics. A foremost point about the accusers, he believed, was simply their position as children subject to the extreme pressures created by a "gruesome theology" of sin and death. Key Puritan doctrines such as predestination "involved a complex mental process that no child could experience, much less enjoy." As a result, young New Englanders were obliged to live in a state of "constant, gnawing fear." Some, for whom the demands were too great, plunged into "the worst sort of mental distress." And the bizarre antics seen at Salem were "only the outward manifestation of their feeble attempts to escape from their insecure, cruel, depressive . . . village world."

Salemwitchcraft as hysteria

The cumulative effect of witchcraft-related writing through the first half of the 20th century was almost to remove the topic from public view. The progressive historians had buried it, along with everything else in Puritanism, as being unworthy of serious consideration. The opinions of revisionists like Morison and Miller were at best ambivalent; moreover, embedded as they were in a scholarly literature, they could not command wide attention. Hence it fell to a nonscholar, Marion L. Starkey, to bring Salem back out where general readers might again take its measure. Her book, *The Devil in Massachusetts: A Modern Enquiry Into the Salem Witch Trials*, was published in 1949, and quickly gained a large audience.

Starkey was a writer of considerable imaginative gifts, and she tried especially to develop the dramatic possibilities inherent in the story. Her focus throughout was the "circle" of afflicted girls. In this, she reinstated the emphasis of the 18th- and 19th-century writers on Salem, and her question was also theirs: How to explain the "fits" and similar "actings" that had proved so crucial to the entire affair? Her answer, however, was diametrically opposed. Where many others had seen "fraud and imposture," Starkey (like Caulfield a few years before) diagnosed involuntary, not to say unconscious, motives at work; her circle was composed of true hysterics. The modern in her "modern enquiry" was a quick shot of Freudianism, flavored with a dollop of developmental psychology. The special "adolescent" status of the afflicted accusers seemed to Starkey a key element. They were at the mercy of biological and hormonal change, familial stress, and community neglect (this last because teenage girls were so little acknowledged in pre-modern culture); at one point she referred to them as "a pack of bobbysoxers on the loose." They sought excitement, notoriety, adventure—and their fits did, in addition, convey a certain protest—but all without any form of planful intent.

Salemwitchcraft as political repression

Starkey's work was also shaped, at least implicitly, by the political environment of the post–World War Two era—the aftermath of violent struggle against Nazism, and the beginnings of the Cold War. Soon this environment would inspire another treatment that was both similar and different. Its form would be that of the theater, its creator the playwright Arthur Miller. The play itself, an immediate sensation when first performed in 1952, was entitled *The Crucible*. Miller's version of the witch trials was a superbly crafted parody of the Red Scare—the government investigations of Communism—in the late 1940s and early '50s. Indeed it joined, to an astonishing degree, the history of those two widely separated periods.

Miller had begun his preparations for the play with a careful reading of Upham (all 1,000 pages); he had also spent a week at the old courthouse in Salem itself, wading through the trial records. He altered certain of the original facts in order to suit the needs of the stage—elevating John Proctor, for example, to a central role, and adding a love interest. But the play as a whole remained remarkably faithful to the spirit and emotions of actual events; even the speech patterns rang true. (There is no better way to "hear" the people of 17th-century New England than to attend a performance of *The Crucible*.)

The play took no position on the motives of the afflicted girls; they might, or might not, have been *bona fide* hysterics. But it strongly suggested that much of the community, judges, clergy, and ordinary citizens alike, had succumbed to a particularly malignant form of *group* hysteria—and then, in the name of conformity, had carried out a ruthless program of social and political repression. Rampant suspicion, spiraling panic, a thirst for vengeance: thus the ingredients of witch-hunting, in the 1690s and again in the 1950s. As Miller would put it many years afterward, his aim was to spotlight "the primeval structure of human sacrifice to the forces of fanaticism and paranoia that goes on repeating itself forever as though imbedded in the brain of social man." The important word here is "forever"; the stakes were now raised to a level approaching universality.

Taken as a whole, *The Crucible* has done more to shape popular perceptions of Salem witchcraft than any other single writing; for many in the present day, it is the only real source. It has, at the same time, greatly enhanced the metaphorical power of the *term* witch-hunting. And it continues to remind us that, behind the term, there does indeed lurk something spanning many otherwise disparate historical and cultural circumstances.

Salem witchcraft and shifting cultural boundaries

In 1966, Kai T. Erikson published an important work of historical sociology, *Wayward Puritans: A Study in the Sociology of Deviance,* in which the witch trials played a conspicuous part. Erikson's main theme was social and cultural "boundary-setting." He decided to take 17th-century Massachusetts as a "laboratory" for investigating the way communities, during periods of crisis, seek to redefine themselves and redraw their cultural boundaries; Salem would serve as a test case. His conclusion, after careful examination of the pertinent records, was that Massachusetts in 1692 had indeed reached a crucial turning point. Its imperial charter was in doubt, its cultural fulcrum was shifting from the spiritual to the secular, outbursts of "angry dissension" were on the rise, and so forth. Ministers, for their part, had developed a distinctive sermon type appropriate to such difficult times, the so-called jeremiad, with lament over moral shortcoming as its dominant motif; this, in turn, served only to heighten the general mood of anxiety.

The cumulative result was a loss of the special "sense of mission" that had inspired the colony's founding. The "yardstick" against which "the original settlers . . . measured their achievements" was gone, and, in the convulsive process of witch-hunting, their descendants wrestled with a host of unsettling consequences. Ironically, the subsequent collapse (and discrediting) of the trials enabled the community to reorient itself and mark out new boundaries—and thus to birth a new identity, built around the prototype of "the practical, self-reliant Yankee." Whatever the value of this conclusion for sociological theory, it did jibe with some leading facts of early New England history: the undeniable, seemingly intractable, stresses— political, social, and psychological—the region had faced during the years and decades preceding the trials.

Salemwitchcraft as actual practice

Chadwick Hansen was the next important entrant in this increasingly crowded field; his book *Witchcraft at Salem* (1969) was designed to offer "a fresh and objective review of the entire matter." Hansen began by adopting the position of Starkey, that the afflicted were nothing more (or less) than hysterics. "Their behavior," he stated flatly, "was not fraudulent, but pathological. . . . They were mentally ill." Moreover, he extended this diagnosis to include many confessors as well; thus the whole amounted to "an outbreak of epidemic hysteria."

But the truly new piece in Hansen's "review" was his idea that "witchcraft actually did exist and was widely practiced in seventeenth-century New England." From his own reading of the courtroom records he had concluded that several of the accused were "in all probability" guilty as charged. On this point he referred especially to evidence for the use of "image magic"; as an example, he cited the testimony given at the trial of Bridget Bishop about "poppets" found in her basement. From here he took a further step, arguing that witchcraft "worked" as intended by its practitioners, but "through psychogenic rather than occult means." It was extreme fear in the victims that brought on their "symptoms," energized their fits, and produced other disabling conditions up to and including death. Here Hansen invoked an important group of studies by medical anthropologists, on certain present-day West Indian communities, where severe, occasionally fatal, illness appears to have no identifiable cause apart from a dread of attack by magical means (voodoo).

Hansen's work seems, in retrospect, a transitional moment in the overall sequence of these histories. To some extent, it followed established patterns. Like most of its predecessors, it took the witch trials essentially as a set piece, without much connection to any wider historical forces; it also retained the old concern with the possibility of fraud (on which, however, it gave an emphatically negative verdict). But its careful research base, and, in particular, its interdisciplinary thrust—reaching out toward clinical psychology and anthropology—pointed in a new direction.

In fact, the study of Salem witchcraft was about to undergo a dramatic transformation in both quantitative and qualitative terms. The sheer volume of work on the subject would soon leap upward, as professional historians reclaimed it for their own. At the same time, the center of interest shifted to matters of context: how to situate witch-hunting in relation to other elements of time and place. This does not mean that previous questions were abandoned altogether: *What happened at Salem?* would always, perhaps inevitably, remain a lively point of concern. But there arose a second set of questions, parallel yet different, as to what witchcraft history might reveal about pre-modern life in a variety of related dimensions. In a sense, this history was no longer simply an end in itself; it was also a means to other ends. There was, too, a further implication here— that changing scholarly trends and fashions, as much as events in the world at large, would henceforth shape the approach taken by leading contributors.

Salemwitchcraft and the coming of capitalism

The most powerful such trend, during the 1970s, was the so-called new social history, a broad-gauge revisionary movement centered on the systematic (even scientific) analysis of the day-to-day lives of ordinary people. This provided the frame for the next major contribution to Salem studies, a brilliantly innovative work by a pair of young scholars, Paul Boyer and Stephen Nissenbaum, published in 1974 as *Salem Possessed: The Social Origins of Witchcraft*. Both title and subtitle announced a difference. The Salem community, not the witch-hunt as such, would be the chief focus. And questions of social organization, not blow-by-blow details of the trial proceedings, would set the main lines of investigation. In fact, *Salem Possessed* relegated the trials almost to a prefatory role—summarized in its opening chapter and mentioned thereafter only tangentially.

The authors began by following up on a lead from Upham's work of more than a century before. Through careful analysis of land deeds and other local records, Upham had succeeded in creating a detailed map of Salem at the time of the trials, with every household carefully plotted in. He had then noted an interesting geographical pattern, which Boyer and Nissenbaum were able to confirm and to interpret. Salem was divided between its original nucleus, abutting the shoreline and known as "the Town," and another section, a few miles back to the west and north, called simply "the Village." The Town was strongly oriented to the sea and trade, while the Village was made up predominantly of small-scale farmsteads. This difference had widened steadily through several decades. By the end of the century, the Town represented (for its time) a "capitalist" way of life, with a cadre of busy merchants at the top of its steeply graded social and economic pyramid.

The witchcraft accusations began, it is clear, among residents of the Village. Moreover, Upham's map showed that virtually all the key accusers lived in the most *interior* part of the Village, while the accused came largely from households in the section bordering the Town. Boyer and Nissenbaum used this discovery as a stepping-off point for developing detailed "profiles" of two sharply antagonized factions in Village life. (The theme of "factionalism" had also appeared in Upham, but *Salem Possessed* would take it much further.) The group based in the interior consisted of old-style farmers of below-average means and highly traditional values. In direct contrast, its opponents displayed an "entrepreneurial" bent; they included tradesmen, innkeepers, and farmers who were at least partially oriented to the market (as befitted their location close to the Town). Boyer and Nissenbaum summed up the difference as follows: "From the evidence . . . the [interior] faction emerges as by far the more vulnerable of the two: less wealthy, . . . owning less land, quite literally hedged in by more flourishing . . . neighbors, and less able to benefit from developments centered in Salem Town."

The struggle between them went back nearly 20 years before 1692. Its most visible aspect was a succession of controversies involving the Village ministers: first, Reverend James Bayley (hired in 1672, fired in 1679); followed by Reverend George Burroughs (1680–83); and then Reverend Deodat Lawson (1684–87). The level of feeling, in each case, was remarkably high; as one Villager described the situation in 1679, "Brother is against brother, and neighbors [are] against neighbors, all quarreling and smiting one another." A final, crucial phase began with the arrival in 1688 of Reverend Samuel Parris, around whom the old "contentions" immediately flared anew. The traditionalists were, by and large, Parris's loyal supporters, their more entrepreneurial counterparts his persistent detractors. The points of conflict were political rather than ecclesiastical, especially the desire—again, among the traditionalists—to separate the life of the Village as much as possible from the capitalist ethos of the Town.

Seen in full context, then, the trials constituted a kind of backlash phenomenon, an effort by the traditionalists to forestall and to punish the "evil" forces of change pushing outward toward the far corners of the Village from the Town. In Boyer and Nissenbaum's own words, the witch-hunt reflected (and was greatly energized by) one of the "central issues of New England society in the late seventeenth century: the resistance of back-country farmers to the pressures of commercial capitalism, and the social style that accompanied it." To be sure, such folk were themselves of divided mind—both attracted to, and repelled by, the "pressures" at hand. In this, they "were part of a vast company, on both sides of the Atlantic, trying to expunge the lure of a new order from their own souls by doing battle with it in the real world." Presumably, the goal was misguided, the effort futile, and the results (at least for Salem) devastating. But Boyer and Nissenbaum were not inclined to condemn; instead, they described feelings of "real sympathy" for the beleaguered Villagers. Here they made a connection to their personal experience of "living through the 1960s, the decade of Watts and Vietnam," and thus coming to realize "that the sometimes violent roles men play in 'history' are not necessarily a measure of their personal decency or lack of it." Not for the first time, or the last, did a retelling of the Salem story find echoes in the teller's own present.

In sum, *Salem Possessed* offered much more than a new answer to the familiar question of what caused the witch trials. As the authors put it in a startling bit of metaphor, "We have . . . exploited the focal events of 1692 somewhat as a stranger might make use of a lightning flash in the night: better to observe the contours of the landscape which it chances to illuminate." The landscape thus observed was broad, deep, and hugely significant: nothing less than the approach of the modern era.

In the 30-odd years since the time of its publication, *Salem Possessed* has faced a number of scholarly challenges, most recently on empirical grounds. Its portrayal of the two warring Village factions may be overdrawn; reinvestigation and reanalysis of some parts are still ongoing. Nonetheless, it remains the single most influential paradigm we have for understanding the Salem witch trials—not to mention its portentous "lightning flash" revelations.

Salemwitchcraft as "acid" trip

Now the publishing floodgates opened wide; since 1974 books and articles on Salem witchcraft have poured forth at such a rate that only a portion of them can be noticed here. One conspicuous example— sufficiently conspicuous that it would find its way onto the front page of some newspapers—first appeared in the journal *Science*, in 1976, under the title "Ergotism: The Satan Loosed in Salem." The author was a young biologist named Linnda R. Caporael. The argument was drawn from clinical pharmacology. And the inspiration (or so one might speculate) was a rising public fascination with hallucinogenic drugs.

It was Caporael's basic contention that "the physical symptoms of the afflicted and many of the other accusers are those induced by convulsive ergot poisoning." Ergot, she explained, is a fungus containing "powerful pharmacologic agents." (In fact, it bears a close relation to lysergic acid diethylamide, also known as LSD or in street parlance, simply, acid.) Its usual hosts are cereal grains, most especially rye, from which it may eventually be carried into baked breads. It grows under many conditions of soil and climate, but dampness and warmth suit it best. The matchup with Salem and the witch trials, Caporael argued, was exceedingly close. The spring and summer of 1691 had been mild and rainy. Lots of rye had been grown in the Village fields. Harvesting would have occurred in the late fall, with baking and eating of ergotized bread following soon thereafter; the witch-hunt started up just a short while after that. Moreover, details of the fits in the core accusers—"convulsions" and all the rest—closely tracked the clinical picture for ergotism. Presto! A longtime mystery solved by medical science.

It seemed almost too good to be true. And, in fact, it was. Barely six months later, another issue of *Science* contained another article presenting a point-by-point refutation. According to the authors of this second piece, a pair of psychologists named Nicholas P. Spanos and Jack Gottlieb, the "general features . . . of ergotism" and "the events that occurred at Salem" did not make for such a good fit, after all. Prominent among the "features" they listed were vomiting, diarrhea, a "livid" skin color, "contractures of the extremities," and a ravenous appetite—none of which appeared, to any significant degree, in contemporaneous accounts from the trials. Moreover, the timing was off, since many of the accusers became "afflicted" only in the late spring. Finally, the spread of accusations beyond Salem to numerous other communities would seem to have required "a concurrent spread of ergotized rye"; and for this, there was no plausible evidence at all.

Surprisingly, a new round of claims for ergotism began several years later (1982), with the publication of yet another article by another author. Mary K. Mattosian resuscitated Caporael's argument, with some modest reshuffling (for example, cold weather, rather than warm, was now deemed essential) and with the Spanos-Gottlieb "objection" ruled "not as valid as originally perceived." Mattosian would subsequently extend the same theory to a vast range of historical events, in a book fetchingly entitled *Poisons of the Past* (1997). But by then the culture had changed; LSD was passé, and witchcraft study had moved on.

Salemwitchcraft and other witchcraft

Indeed, the 1980s brought a different direction entirely. Perhaps because the Boyer-Nissenbaum model proved so powerful an explanation of the Salem affair, historians shifted their attention toward earlier New England trials. The new goal was to unravel a general "system" of witchcraft belief (and of behavior based on such belief). The work proliferated along several different tracks: ideas of witchcraft in relation to other cultural phenomena, such as magic, fortune-telling, and astrology; anxiety about witchcraft as a reflection of "inner-life preoccupation" (in short, its underpinnings in psychology); charges of witchcraft as a measure of "social strain." The Salem witch-hunt had a place in this interpretive enterprise, and lent it useful material, but made no claim of special preference. As one historian put it, "Salem was unique in its quantitative dimension—witch-hunting gone wild—and for that reason alone has exercised a disproportionate hold on the public imagination." There was nothing unique, however, about its qualitative patterning. In matters such as the style and substance of accusation, the types of people involved, and the occasions leading up to an actual court proceeding, Salem was broadly consistent with witch trials at other times and places in early New England. Salem *alongside* others, Salem *together with* others: thus the framing of the new approach.

Salemwitchcraft and patriarchal privilege

Of course, these inquiries might still throw valuable light on the events of 1692. And one of them, especially, merits further description here: Carol Karlsen's *The Devil in the Shape of a Woman* (1986). Karlsen began by asking to what extent, and in what ways, economic difference might have contributed to fueling witchcraft charges against particular women. Her conclusion, after much painstaking local research, was that women of all economic levels were at least potential targets; then, as she refined her evidence, she discovered something more. The *most* likely targets were those whose direct control of property went well beyond the usual expectation—for women. The culture at large was frankly patriarchal; for example, it everywhere affirmed a principle of male inheritance. Married women could not ordinarily hold property in their own right; a widow was granted simply the "use" of her late husband's estate with no right of transfer to others. Yet exceptions were inevitable, especially in families lacking male heirs; there, the women involved might gain a measure of real economic independence. And that seemed unnatural—or, at any rate, unacceptable—sufficiently so to ground suspicions of witchcraft.

A considerable portion of the women accused at Salem did fit, quite closely, the profile of "independent women" traced by Karlsen (Bridget Bishop, Martha Corey, Rachel Clinton, and Alice Parker, among others, together with many from earlier cases). Her point, at bottom, was about gender more than economics—and it was compelling. Since no other aspect of this entire subject-area has seemed so obvious, but at the same time so resistant to explanation, as the fundamental equation of witch and woman, Karlsen's work was quickly, and widely, acknowledged.

Salemwitchcraft as anniversary pageant

The 1990s produced a renewed surge of Salem witchcraft histories: no fewer than five major books, plus a host of anthologies and shorter writings. In part, this was an anniversary phenomenon. Nineteen ninety-two marked three hundred years since the start of the trials; and modern-era denizens of "the witch city" made the most of it. There were learned conferences (and some not so learned), elaborate museum exhibitions, carefully staged tours of the leading physical sites, vivid "re-enactments," and a great deal of heavily hyped marketing: in short, a veritable outpouring of pageantry. How does one commemorate—even celebrate—a "tragedy"? Salem showed the way.

On the whole, the new book-length studies offered narrative re-tellings of the trial sequence, rather than sweeping reinterpretations. There were, however, differences of emphasis and some challenges to prior work. Larry Gragg's *The Salem Witch Crisis* (1992) stressed the importance of "particular decisions made by the individuals in-volved" (as opposed to broad structural conditions). Bernard Rosen-thal, in *Salem Story: Reading the Witch Trials of 1692* (1993), used his textual expertise as a literature scholar to cast doubt on portrayals of the "afflicted" as hysterics; with many of them, Rosenthal argued (echoing others, as far back as Hutchinson), outright fakery came closer to the mark. Peter Charles Hoffer, in *The Devil's Disciples: Makers of the Salem Witch Trials* (1996), focused very closely on "the girls' circle," and, even more sharply than Rosenthal, questioned their honesty. They were not very different, in Hoffer's view, from "a gang of juvenile delinquents"; in most cases, they "knew that they were lying." Frances Hill's *A Delusion of Satan: The Full Story of the Salem Witch Trials* (1995) proposed a line of interpretation midway between "deliberate fraud" and "clinical hysteria." Eschewing any sort of one-size-fits-all approach, Hill summed up the motives for accusation as "a mixture of hysteria, vengeful fury, evil mischief, and longing."

Salemwitchcraft as epidemic illness

One book in the 1990s crop did bring forward a truly novel idea. Lau-rie Winn Carlson's *A Fever in Salem: A New Interpretation of the New England Witch Trials* (1999) argued that epidemic encephalitis (or "sleeping sickness") was the fundamental cause of the 1692 "out-break." Carlson seized on a little-noticed aspect of the trial evidence: the fact that animals had supposedly experienced "afflictions . . . eerily like those of the 'bewitched' people." Indeed, the records said as much; cattle, in particular, were described as falling into convul-sions, "roaring" and "dancing" as if possessed, and occasionally dy-ing in strangely "tortured" ways. From this Carlson inferred that "a biological pathogen was afflicting both people and livestock." Then, following the method used by Caporael and Mattosian to advance their ergotism hypothesis, Carlson canvassed a host of medical and epidemiological authorities in order to match the "symptoms" of witchcraft victims with the clinical picture for encephalitis. Her specific point of reference was a worldwide pandemic during the years 1918–20, in which she claimed to have found a host of close similarities. Moreover, she extended her interpretive line to include flocks of migratory birds carrying microbes across oceans and continents; hemispheric wind patterns and storm tracks; mosquitoes, ticks, and other ground-level transmitters; and relationships among the various human sufferers themselves. Ultimately, however, this apparatus became so large and cumbersome, and so remote from specific bits of historical evidence, that it seemed to topple of its own weight. It covered both too much and too little; as a result, the proposed link—witchcraft to encephalitis—slowly came apart, one little piece after another. Put differently, the Devil was not in these particular details, after all.

Salem witchcraft and fear of Indians

As three decades thick with witchcraft studies came to an end, one might well have expected a pause in this long progression. Indeed, what more could possibly be said about the "causes" of the Salem trials?

Surprisingly, there *was* more to say. In 2002, the distinguished colonial historian Mary Beth Norton published the fruits of a decade-long research project in a book entitled *In the Devil's Snare: The Salem Witchcraft Crisis of 1692*. Norton had achieved an across-the-board mastery of the materials beyond anything seen before; her work offered the most rounded and comprehensive treatment of its subject yet. Simply as a narrative—sorting out the basic sequence, establishing the links between key persons and events—it was unsurpassed. Moreover, it effectively revised certain of the chief interpretive issues: the central role of confessing witches, for example, and the complex collaboration between afflicted accusers on the one hand and the magistrates in charge of the courtroom proceedings on the other. But these important gains in understanding were themselves overshadowed by a major research discovery involving a host of dynamic connections between the witch-hunt and the northeastern New England frontier.

On setting out, Norton had "no idea" about the importance of this latter dimension. But the evidence kept leading her away from Salem and Essex County, and toward the coastal communities of New Hampshire and Maine. There, starting in 1675, English settlers and their Wabanaki neighbors had engaged in repeated warfare. The initial round, part of the larger King Philip's War, lasted until 1677. Its successor, begun in 1689 and linked to what participants called King William's War, was focused more closely on the frontier regions; the fighting would last into, and beyond, the period of the witch trials. Along the northern coast these were also described as, simply, the First and Second Indian Wars. They attained throughout an extraordinary level of ferocity, with attacks and counterattacks piled rapidly one upon another. Whole communities were burned to the ground; hundreds of men, women, and children were killed (on both sides, sometimes after gruesome torture); captives were taken and held for months or years. Armies came up from Massachusetts to defend the beleaguered English villagers; there was French support (via Canada) for the equally desperate Indians. Battle reports—including full-blown atrocity stories—traveled back with some regularity to points above and below. The result, especially in the affected region but also in nearby Essex County, was a steadily mounting wave of "panic fear."

All this had long been known to historians; what hadn't been known was its many-stranded linkage to Salem and the 1692 trials. One strand, as Norton discovered through meticulous genealogical sleuthing, was simply and directly personal; in short, many individuals who played key roles in the trials had previously resided on the Maine frontier, or had familial or business connections to it. This was the case with some among the afflicted accusers. Mercy Lewis, for example, had spent most of her childhood in the community of Falmouth, Maine, and had lost family members to the fighting there; Mercy Short had actually been for several months a Wabanaki captive. Key confessors had similar backstories. Abigail Hobbs, like Lewis, had lived for several years in Falmouth; indeed, her confession began with an account of meeting the Devil in the woods outside that town in the late 1680s. And several of the accused were merchants accustomed to trading along the frontier: Philip English, John Alden, John Floyd, and Nathaniel Cary, among others. English was of French background and a French speaker; accordingly, some of his Salem neighbors suspected him of dealings with Frenchmen friendly to the Wabanakis. Alden had occasionally served as a negotiator with both French and native leaders; and when Ann Putnam Jr. confronted his specter in the course of an agonizing fit, she shouted out the remarkable charge that "he sells powder and shot to the Indians and French, and lies with Indian squaws, and has Indian papooses." George Burroughs, the supposed "head and ringleader" of all the New England witches, had served as minister first in Falmouth and then in Wells (also in Maine). Governor Phips himself had been born and raised in Maine.

Beyond these personal connections, the very language and imagery of witch-trial accusation evoked Indians. When, time after time, accusers and confessors described the Devil's skin color as "black," they were referencing not Africans, of whom they had as yet only limited experience, but Native Americans. (One accuser spoke of "a short black man . . . not of a Negro, but of a tawny, or an Indian, color." And Cotton Mather noted that when confessing witches described Satan as "the black man . . . they generally say he resembles an Indian.") Another common tendency was to describe the agony of affliction through images of being "torn to pieces" and "knocked in the head"—thereby recalling lurid tales of Indian captivity, in which prisoners underwent physical dismemberment, scalping, or killing by blows from native hatchets. Even the timing of the witch-hunt corresponded to events in the frontier war. Its beginning, in late winter, followed closely on a major assault by French and Indian forces against the Maine town of York, and its springtime surge coincided with a similar attack on nearby Wells. Moreover, contemporaries recognized the underlying connection here; many would have approved Cotton Mather's assertion that "the prodigious war made by the spirits of the invisible world upon the people of New England in the year 1692 . . . might have some of its original among the Indians, whose chief sagamores [leaders] are well known to have been horrid sorcerers and hellish conjurors and such as conversed with demons."

This was the tableau Norton laid out in abundant, and altogether persuasive, detail. Her final, summative point drew the two concurrent "crises" even more closely together. New Englanders faced "an alliance of their enemies in the visible and invisible worlds"—with witches and Indians, Satan and "sagamores," virtually morphed into one. Indeed, "had the Second Indian War on the northeastern frontier somehow been avoided, the Essex County witchcraft crisis of 1692 would not have occurred."

New Englanders blamed themselves for committing the sins that had prompted the Lord to allow such a devastating, double-barreled assault. But Norton, for her part, was more inclined to blame their leaders. *"It must always be remembered,"* she wrote, using italics for emphasis, *"that the judges of the Court of Oyer and Terminer were the very men who led the colony both politically and militarily."* Responsible, as they mostly were, for failure to stem attacks by "visible" enemies, these men welcomed the opportunity to "shift responsibility . . . to the demons of the invisible world." And then, as a direct result, "they presided over the deaths of many innocent people."

What happened at Salem? A reprise

Divine retribution. Fraud. Class conflict. Village factionalism. Mental illness. Cultural provincialism. Vulnerable children. Hysteria. Political repression. Shifting social boundaries. Actual witchcraft. Approaching capitalism. Ergot poisoning. Patriarchal privilege. Encephalitis. Fear of Indians.

One inevitable, irrepressible question, with many different answers. Yet the answers are not of equal weight; indeed, some can be discarded completely. Forget class conflict. Forget ergotism. Forget encephalitis. The match with the evidence is too weak to support any of them.

Several others seem obvious and unexceptionable—and thus not very helpful. Yes, a few of the "afflicted" may have been acting, or lying, or cleverly dissembling—even while their fellow accusers were in the grip of true, and harrowing, psychopathology. And yes, Puritan belief and practice was hard on young children. (For that matter, it was also pretty demanding for adults.) It seems likely, too, that certain individual suspects did actually attempt the practice of witchcraft; but we have no plausible way to distinguish them from others who were falsely accused.

When the list has been suitably trimmed, a number of entries yet remain. They need not compete with one another; to the contrary, they can be joined so as to create a powerfully inclusive whole. Witch-hunts, like most large social and historical phenomena, invariably show a pattern of multiple causation; in scientific language, they are overdetermined. And the case of Salem, because it is so well documented, allows us to identify a broad array of causes—and also to observe the manner of their joining.

Start around the year 1675. By then Salem (both Town and Village) already shows signs of incipient factionalism. There are small farmers, geared to old-style "subsistence" production. There are other farmers, somewhat more prosperous and forward-looking, who are beginning to produce for the market. There are tradesmen and artisans, who operate on a community-wide basis. Finally, there are merchants, whose economic horizons extend all around the Atlantic basin. Each of these groups represents a different way of being in the world. They continue, of course, to share a great deal; they live at close quarters; they interact frequently; they directly cooperate from time to time. But they also feel—and actually are—distinct from one another. Viewed from our perspective, they stretch across a spectrum: from peasantlike to entrepreneurial, from "traditional" to "protomodern." Soon Salem will see them directly counterposed in a series of bitter, internecine conflicts that will stretch through almost two decades. The underlying issue here is social and economic change. New modes of production and trade—amounting, roughly, to early capitalism—are increasingly important and *visible*. These, in turn, create new interests, new values, new expectations, new lifestyles. But the old ways die hard. And in places like Salem Village, they find a corps of especially determined defenders.

As part of the same scenario, and in common with many neighboring communities, Salem feels the deep moral reproach encapsulated by the term "declension." Leaders and plain folk alike lament their losing touch with the spiritual wellsprings that had once fed their "errand" and shaped their core identity. Meanwhile, too, a political crisis looms, as administrative changes enacted by royal authority overseas steadily erode the self-governing traditions passed down from their forebears. Indeed, when New England's official charters are temporarily revoked (1684–91), title to the very lands they live on is potentially at risk. Their Puritan religious establishment is also under challenge, as Anglican churches, with direct ties to the mother country, rise alongside their cherished congregational meetinghouses. Yet another kind of crisis comes with an outbreak of smallpox in 1689, perhaps the most severe of the many 17th-century epidemics to strike their region. And in 1690, their long-standing project to evict the French from control of Canada ends in abject failure, when a Quebec-bound fleet carrying thousands of their soldiers and sailors founders off the coast of Acadia (Nova Scotia). Take it all around, and New Englanders of the 1680s and early '90s— including those living in Salem—may easily come to feel a *general* movement of "Divine Providence" against them.

Finally, there is the pressure of Indian enemies. This, too, is felt throughout New England, but with special force in those places lying closest to nodes of actual warfare. Essex County is positioned exactly so; its northern sector abuts the coastal communities of New Hampshire and Maine, where the specter of conflict with native peoples is omnipresent. The First and Second Indian Wars destroy both lives and property on a massive scale; and even in the intervals between wars, episodic violence continues. Essex County residents are directly involved, some militarily, others as traders, land speculators, and would-be settlers. Still others are pulled in through the suffering of kin and friends who live in the affected areas. The current also runs in the opposite direction, as refugees seeking to escape the devastation flee southward into Massachusetts. All this is accompanied by the widespread dissemination of horrific war stories, rumors, and threats. The cumulative result is nothing less than an overwhelming and highly toxic climate of fear.

In sum: an entire region teeters on the edge. And if this configuration points toward one place more than others, it would have to be . . . Salem. There, the two factors of greatest causal significance— rising capitalism and Indian terror—fully converge. The ensuing ripples circle well out into the surrounding countryside, but their center and source point is clear. Thus does Salem become, in Arthur Miller's perfectly chosen image, the "crucible" for early America's most far-reaching, deadly, and lastingly famous witch-hunt of all.

CHAPTER IX

The Reverend Cotton Mather:
A Minister and His Demons

The reputation of witch-hunter hangs like a noose around the ghost of Cotton Mather. More than anyone else from his time and place, Mather has been held responsible for the "zeal," the "fanaticism," the "bigotry" and "prejudice" that drove the Salem trials to their lethal end. His reported intervention at the execution of "wizard" George Burroughs—perched on a horse, exhorting a large crowd of onlookers to suppress any last-minute feelings of doubt or sympathy—has long been seen as emblematic.

In fact, this picture is overdrawn. The "discovery" of witches and witchcraft was important to Mather, especially during the first dozen or so of his adult years. But it did not define his life and work; rather, it formed one strand in a remarkably variegated career. Viewed overall, Mather's involvement in witch-hunting was as prudent, as nuanced, as ambivalent even, as that of any of his contemporaries. He seems, then, less an extreme case of witch-hunting than an exemplary one.

He is born in February 1663, the first child of Reverend Increase and Maria (Cotton) Mather. Almost at once he shows signs of precocity, especially in his spiritual development. He begins to pray as soon as he can speak; at age two and a half, having fallen dangerously ill, he declares to Increase, "Father, Ton [his nickname] would go see God." He learns very early to read and write, and is composing prayers for his playmates by the time he turns seven. He becomes a favored pupil of the famed Boston schoolmaster Ezekiel Cheever, from whom he learns Latin, Greek, and Hebrew (among other things); eventually, he will master no fewer than seven different languages (including Iroquois). He is admitted to Harvard at age 12, performs with distinction there, and becomes at 15 the College's youngest graduate of the entire 17th century.

He feels, from the start, destined for a life in the clergy—certainly his parents expect as much—and his immediate postgraduate years are shaped accordingly: further study, guest preaching here and there (he delivers his first sermon at age 16), an increasingly close relation to his father's ministry at Boston's Second Church. In due course, that church invites him to serve as a regular assistant; then, in 1683, as its pastor. Increase Mather's official title is "teacher"; in effect, the two of them become co-ministers—when Cotton is barely 20.

This progression, though extraordinarily swift, is not without difficulties. At 14, he falls into a state of spiritual "melancholy," and around the same time (or a little before) develops a severe stammer. As a result, his prospects as a clergyman are temporarily dimmed; it takes much determined effort to resolve the problem. An anxious temperament will remain with him, to some extent, for the rest of his life. But he does also achieve an inward "assurance" of "saving faith" (conversion) at age 18, and at 22 he has the supremely uplifting experience of a direct visitation by angels. Shortly thereafter (1686) he marries Abigail Phillips, the 15-year-old daughter of a prosperous merchant and public official in nearby Charlestown. A child is born to them the following year but dies within a few months. It is the first of many sorrows Cotton Mather will endure as a parent; by the time of his own death he will have outlived all but 2 of his 15 children.

Mather's personal history and the history of Boston were intertwined in many ways—not least through his lineage. His grandfathers, John Cotton and Richard Mather, had been leaders in the settlement process—as ministers at Boston's First Church and nearby Dorchester, respectively. His father, meanwhile, was a notably rising star among the younger clergy.

Boston was founded in 1630 at the start of a so-called great migration of dissident Puritans from Old England and would remain at the edge of religious reform for several decades thereafter. Its earliest ·

years were marked by a mood of special hope and excitement—
one might almost say a spiritual "high," embracing the entire
community—as churches were "gathered," conversions announced,
and farmsteads raised on the newly claimed land. Indeed, the New
England settlers, including their Boston contingent, have some claim
even now to a place at the head of what would later become a long
line of American "utopian experiments."

By the time of Cotton Mather's birth, however, that initial élan
had begun to wane. The Puritan Revolution in the mother country
was over—reversed and repudiated by the Restoration of the Stuart
monarchy in 1660. The aging and eventual disappearance of the
founders' cohort proved particularly unsettling. A hotly contested
decision in 1669 to lower the standard for admission to church membership (known, then and since, as the Halfway Covenant) appeared
to signal a general "declension" of religious purpose. There followed,
in rapid succession, a devastating race war (King Philip's War, 1675–
76), the revocation by the king of the Massachusetts charter (1684),
and the installation of a new "Dominion" government (1686) in order to exert a stronger, fuller measure of imperial control. The latter
was overturned three years later, when news reached Boston of the
Glorious Revolution in the motherland (1689). A bloodless coup ex-
pelled the royal governor and set in motion a chain of events that
would lead to yet another, less restrictive, political charter for the
Bay Colony (1691).

*His own experience of the 1680s brings Cotton Mather to a position of great
prestige and influence. He plays, for example, a leading role in the political
crisis of those years. He and his father help form a party of covert opposition
to the Dominion authorities. And when Increase goes off to London to plead
the colony's interest at the king's court, Cotton moves to the very center of
Boston's resistance. He is involved in secret meetings to prepare for the ouster
of the administration. When the crucial moment arrives, it is he who drafts
key public documents announcing, and justifying, a change of governance.
(One of these, officially titled A* Declaration of Merchants and Minis-

ters, *anticipates both the spirit and substance of the Declaration of Independence nearly a century later.)*

All these changes—coinciding, as they do, with recurrent smallpox outbreaks, devastating house fires, and other such unanticipated "catastrophes"—seem, from Mather's viewpoint, to portend a far greater transformation. He can sense the approach of "End Time," that long-awaited moment when human history will give way to an entirely new dispensation, including divine judgment, Christ's second coming, and the start of an everlasting millennium. He tries to calculate its most likely date, and arrives at the figure of 1697.

In this context, and in response also to a rising spirit of secularism, religious leaders are stirred ever more strongly by "providential" concerns. In 1684 Increase Mather publishes an important work entitled An Essay for the Recording of Illustrious Providences, with the aim of demonstrating the power of the supernatural world; among its numerous chapters are several devoted to witchcraft. And Cotton is poised to make his own contribution to the same cause.

Opportunity soon comes to him. In the fall of 1688, four children of a Boston stonemason named John Goodwin begin quite suddenly to experience "fits." The two oldest, a girl named Martha (age 13) and a boy named John Jr. (11) are most fully affected, their younger siblings intermittently so. Hour after hour, day after day, they are drawn into bizarre "antics"; swooping about, with their bodies fixed in strange, contorted positions; shrieking uncontrollably; eyes bulging; mouth snapping open and shut; aping the behavior of animals (cats, dogs, and cows). A physician is called to examine them, but finds no evidence of "natural maladies." Frightened neighbors urge the use of "tricks"—counter-magic—to end their affliction. But John Goodwin prefers a more orthodox approach; thus he solicits the help of local ministers, including Cotton Mather, who, predictably, stress the power of prayer.

Mather then goes further, proposing that Martha be removed to his own home for a period of intensive pastoral care; her father readily agrees. In the weeks that follow, Mather watches over her, prays with her, endures her recurrent "naughtiness" and "impertinencies," comforts her, questions her, and through it all strives to discover the source of her difficulties.

Meanwhile, in the community at large attention focuses on a local Irish-woman named Glover, long suspected of practicing witchcraft. (The Good-wins have recently quarreled with Glover and her daughter over some missing property.) A trial follows, and Glover makes a full confession; a witch she most certainly is. For this she goes to the gallows. But still the children continue "in their fits." Martha then offers Mather the name of an-other local woman as her new witch-tormentor. But the minister does not publicly reveal it; in such matters, he feels, extreme caution is necessary.

As time passes, the Goodwin children will gradually recover their nor-mal lives (and selves). And Cotton Mather will turn from hands-on work with witchcraft victims to writing and publishing about them instead. His book Memorable Providences, Relating to Witchcrafts and Posses-sions *appears just months later. (He is a prodigiously fluent and prolific writer. The list of his published work will eventually swell to 383 different titles.)* Memorable Providences *includes a long account of the Goodwin case and a careful description of Mather's own part in it. Significantly, young Martha's second accusation is mentioned only briefly and without specific detail. Mather's goal is not, after all, to encourage or instigate proj-ects of witch-hunting. Instead, he aims to refute, from "my own ocular ob-servation," those who would "deny . . . the being of Angels either good or evil." "Go tell Mankind that there are Devils and Witches," he writes in an oddly triumphant tone. "Go tell the world what prayers can do beyond all devils and witches."*

The years immediately following the Goodwin case found Mather involved on many fronts simultaneously. Not yet out of his 20s, he was responsible both for his own growing household and for that of his absent father; he was leader of the largest church congregation in Massachusetts; and he was public champion, spokesman, and strate-gist for the colony's revamped administration. (He would quickly emerge as a close confidante of the incoming governor, Sir William Phips.) His days were filled with pastoral visits, composing and de-livering sermons, writing and publishing tracts and books on sub-jects both spiritual and secular—all mixed with his regular round of private meditations and everyday familial cares. Sometimes it seemed almost too much for him, and a petulant edge began to emerge in his dealings with the world around him. He might complain in his diary about "the calumnies of the people against poor me" or "the spirit of lying that prevails so generally around us."

But his most urgent preoccupation was still the approach of the new millennium. Growing signs of "blessedness" on the one hand and of imminent disaster on the other pointed equally in the same direction. During the unusually harsh winter of 1691–92 he felt certain that the Last Judgment was "at the door." Indeed: "I do, without any hesitation, venture to say 'the great day of the Lord is near . . . and it hastens greatly.'" At such a time a new outbreak of witchcraft, on a scale unprecedented for New England, would not seem altogether surprising. That, too, might well be a forerunner of apocalyptic change.

Cotton Mather's participation in the Salem witch-hunt will be mostly indirect, inherently complex, painfully conflicted—and undeniably important. He does not attend any of the actual trials; instead he follows their course as closely as he can from his base in Boston. To be sure, he is notoriously present on that crucial occasion when five convicts, including Reverend Burroughs, are executed in August; otherwise he does not visit Salem during the entire year of 1692.

Certainly, he has good correspondents—such as Stephen Sewall, clerk of the Court of Oyer and Terminer—to supply him with regular reports from, and about, the scene of the action. And he is not reluctant to offer his opinions in return. In April he delivers (and then publishes) a powerful sermon entitled A Midnight Cry, *stressing the convergence of recent and current "calamities," including attack by devils. A short while later, he proposes a personal intervention in the Salem affair. He would have several of the "afflicted girls" brought to his own home for close-up pastoral supervision, just as he had done with Martha Goodwin. Does he imagine that he might thereby close off the rapidly deepening vortex of public accusation? After all, he has succeeded before. No matter—for this time his offer is not accepted.*

In May he composes a long letter of advice to one of the trial judges. His chief aim is to discourage undue reliance on spectral evidence, since "it is very certain that the devils have sometimes represented the shapes of persons not only innocent but also very virtuous." Should such testimony be allowed, "a door may be . . . opened for the devils . . . to proceed with the most hideous desolations upon the repute and repose" of perfectly upstanding citizens. He believes that only "a credible confession" can provide a clear and solid basis for establishing guilt. At the same time he condones harsh prosecutorial tactics: for example, the use of "cross and swift questions" and forced body searches for "witch-marks." Moreover, he will not impeach the trials as a whole. "The business thus managed," he writes, "may not be called imaginary. The effects are dreadfully real. Our dear neighbors are most really tormented."

The same divided attitude will inform other Mather writings in the months to come. When, in mid-June, leading Boston clergymen are asked for counsel on trial procedure, Mather becomes the author of their written response. This is the (previously noted) "Return of Several Ministers," which emphatically disapproves "things received only upon the Devil's authority"—in short, spectral evidence—and urges "exceeding tenderness towards those that may be complained of." Retreating somewhat from Mather's previous endorsement of harassing interrogations, the "Return" also argues against allowing "such noise, company, and openness as may too hastily expose" the accused. Furthermore, touch tests and similar "experiments" must be firmly excluded as "liable to be abused by the Devil's legerdemains."

These cautions take Mather and his colleagues almost to the end of their chosen agenda. If they stop there, the "Return" might serve to check the momentum of prosecution—and be hailed later on as an admirably liberal statement. But they don't stop there. Instead they declare, in conclusion: "We cannot but humbly recommend unto the government the speedy and vigorous prosecution of such as have rendered themselves obnoxious, according to the direction given in the laws of God and the wholesome statutes of the English nation for the detection of witchcraft." Here is a ministerial license for the court to continue as before.

Mather will reiterate both his concerns about procedure and his general approval of the witch-hunt in additional comments made through the remainder of the summer. At one point he suggests a moderating tactic: the use of banishment—instead of trial, conviction, and capital punishment—for persons who may have been "innocently" represented by specters. (He even volunteers to accept such a fate for himself, should he too be implicated that way.) At the same time, he repeatedly and strenuously summons the faithful to uncompromising struggle against the Devil's "infernal" designs.

In August his father publishes yet another cautionary work, Cases of Conscience, Concerning Evil Spirits Personating Men, *with the strongest critique yet of spectral evidence. Fourteen ministers sign a preface of endorsement—but Cotton Mather is not among them. His own focus has shifted by now. He is racing to complete his witchcraft apologia; its full title is* The Wonders of the Invisible World: Observations, as Well Historical as Theological, Upon the Nature, the Number, and the Operations of Devils. *This work, suggested by "the direction of His Excellency, the Governor," and stitched together at intervals between the beginning of June and the end of September, will become one of Mather's best-known writings and the chief basis in subsequent years for assessing his involvement with witch-hunting.*

The immediate context is a surge of public opposition to the trials; Wonders *is Mather's response. In it he assembles a broad range of affirmative materials, including two of his own recent sermons, accounts of witchcraft cases from overseas, some scattered reportage on "enchantments and apparitions," and finally—at its heart—detailed summaries of the trial proceedings against five "of the principal witches that have been condemned" at Salem. Doubts about spectral evidence do not appear; the central theme is other, presumably more credible, means of "discovering" and convicting the guilty. Indeed, Mather never wavers from a goal he announces at the start: "to countermine the whole plot of the Devil against New England, in every branch of it." Taken in its entirety, the book is nothing less than a full-throated vindication of the work of the Salem judges—whose leader, William Stoughton, is moved to contribute for the front matter a*

fulsome letter of "thankfulness to you for so great pains, and . . . [for your]
singular approbation."

   Even as Mather is completing this text, showing it to colleagues, and
packing it off to the printer, he finds himself suddenly face-to-face with an-
other living specimen of witchcraft. Mercy Short, a girl of 17, recently ar-
rived in Boston from the Maine frontier where she had been for a time a
captive of Indians, begins in the summer of 1692 to show the unmistakable
signs of "affliction." The link to concurrent events in Salem is direct; Sarah
Good, one of the convicted witches there, is being temporarily held at the jail
in Boston, where Mercy encounters her in the course of an errand. The two
of them exchange "ill words," following which Mercy is "taken with just
such . . . fits as those that held the bewitched people in the county of Essex."
Thus begin months of torment—and notoriety—for this latest young vic-
tim. Her fits run the usual gamut, from "swooning" (fainting episodes), to
"fasting" (inability to eat), to many sorts of physical hurt (pinches, pricks,
sensations of "burning" and "roasting," forced ingestion of poisonous
liquids), all at the hands of a vividly personified Devil and a host of his
spectral "confederates."

   Mather is nearby, and eager to take charge. For him this is another
chance to demonstrate the correct way of responding to such "assaults."
(To that end he will record the entire performance in a carefully-kept jour-
nal, for the benefit of posterity.) The gist of his treatment approach, as in
the Goodwin case, is sustained prayer and fasting. Indeed, this becomes a
community-wide project, involving several different ministers and numer-
ous "pious people in the north part of Boston." Mather's personal atten-
tions to Mercy remain foremost, however; she is in and out of his house
and church on a regular basis. He endures, as a result, not only the recur-
rent "spectacle" of her sufferings but also her occasional "insolent and
abusive . . . frolics"; at some points, she seems "as extravagant as a wild-
cat." Then, after four months, her assailants suddenly vanish, affording
her a "complete deliverance." And Mather feels a rush of triumph. As he
will later write in his diary, "I had the satisfaction of seeing her . . . so
brought home unto the Lord that she was admitted unto our church." His
accomplishment extends also to "many other . . . young people [who are]

awakened by the picture of Hell exhibited in her sufferings, to flee from the wrath to come."

Through it all Mather maintains his principle of discretion about the identity of the witches supposedly involved. Several of the attacking specters take "the shape of [actual persons] . . . who are doubtless innocent as to the crime of witchcraft"—while others represent "as dangerous and damnable witches as ever there were in the world." The problem lies in deciding who is who (or which is witch!); just there the Devil's "legerdemains" prove impossible to sort out. "For my part, I did all I could that not so much as the name of any one good person in the world might suffer the least ill report on this occasion": herewith a centerpiece of Mather's "example" to other witch-hunters in Boston, at Salem, everywhere.

If his work with Mercy Short seems a triumph, a similar experience just a few months later will prove the exact opposite. It begins when another young woman "in the north part of Boston," named Margaret Rule, falls into "odd fits" that quickly blossom into "an affliction . . . marvelously resembling" that of Short. There are pinchings, prickings, force-fed poisons, and "exorbitant convulsions," inflicted once again by the Devil and a group of "cruel specters." Mather's response, as he will describe it in yet another journal, is just as before: prayer and fasting, and an absolute determination "to prevent the excessive credit of spectral accusations." (He will claim later to have explicitly "charged the afflicted that they should cry out of nobody for afflicting 'em.")

The difference this time is a growing public skepticism about all these "sufferers"—and about Mather's personal efforts of exorcism. The lead is taken by Robert Calef, a local cloth merchant who has visited Margaret Rule while she lay "under affliction" in Mather's care—and who then writes a highly critical account of what he observed. According to Calef the victim was repeatedly drawn into giving a set of coached responses and indulged in "merry" behaviors, while the minister "rubbed her stomach, her breast not covered with the bed clothes." (This intimation of sexual impropriety is especially wounding.) Mather is appalled—and outraged—that "a sort of Sadducee in this town . . . hath written a volume of invented and notorious lies" about him. But Calef is not, evidently, alone in his opinions.

When Mather vents his deep resentment in the privacy of his diary, he speaks of "this unworthy, ungodly, ungrateful people" and the "hard representations some ill men [note plural usage] have given my conduct." He and Calef exchange hotly-phrased letters, and Mather begins a lawsuit for libel (which he will subsequently drop). Calef's book is published in London some years later; its title, More Wonders of the Invisible World, *mockingly riffs Mather's own work.*

All of which leaves Mather feeling bitter and bruised, and more than a little self-pitying. In writing about the Rule case he defends "all my unwearied cares and pains to rescue the miserable from the lions and bears of Hell," and compares the "danger attending me" to a trek of "ten thousand steps over a rocky mountain filled with rattlesnakes."

He lived on for more than three decades. (He died in 1728.) His ministry continued, as did his writing and involvement in public affairs. But he never again returned to a front-line position in the battle against witchcraft. He would attempt no more exorcism of "the miserable" victims; give no further advice on such matters to magistrates and other officials; offer little, if any, preaching about them from his pulpit. His leading modern biographers agree that the apex of his life—his greatest influence and widest acclaim—came just *before* his direct participation in witch-hunting. Calef's viewpoint— "that there are witches . . . but what this witchcraft is, or wherein it does consist, is the whole question"—would, with the passage of time, become the dominant one. And Mather's rather different view would, for generations, cast a shadow on his public standing.

But what, finally, *was* Mather's view? And how should we summarize his career as a witch-hunter? All in all, it made something of a zigzag; depending on the circumstances, he could be a force for restraint—or for unsparing attack. His aim to "prevent the excessive credit of spectral evidence" lest "any one good person . . . suffer the least ill report on this occasion" was real, was principled, was consistently maintained, was put into action. Yet he unwaveringly believed that actual witches—and undeniable witchcraft—posed the deepest

possible threat to "the people of God," especially those in New England. His language, which always tended toward hyperbole, reached
new heights in discussing these dangers. Thus: the Salem witches
aimed at nothing less than "rooting out the Christian religion in this
country, and setting up instead of it perhaps a more gross diabolism
than ever the world saw before." And: "I believe there never was a
poor plantation more pursued by the wrath of the Devil than our
poor New England." And: "This people . . . [must] make a right use
of the stupendous and prodigious things that are happening among
us . . . [and] the amazing dispensations now upon us." *Ever saw, never
was; stupendous, prodigious, amazing:* he could scarcely find a sufficient standard of comparison. Given such extremities, the response
must be total, with "all due steps taken for the utter extinction of
witchcraft."

There was, finally, an additional source for his vigilance—
something more personal, more practical, yet no less urgent. To
credit the activity of witches, and of the Devil alongside them, was
to acknowledge the immanence and power of the entire "invisible
world." Conversely, to discount such things was to call that world
into question. God and Satan, angels and demons, divine miracles
and diabolic witchcraft belonged to opposite halves of the same
package; remove one, and the other would disintegrate. Ironically,
then, faith in God *depended* (at least in part) on belief in witchcraft.
"Go tell Mankind that there are devils and witches," Mather had
urged after finishing his work with Martha Goodwin. For him, and
for many others too, this blunt affirmation was a barrier and bul-
wark against a different kind of specter—the awesome, awful, deeply
undermining possibility of religious doubt.

*Will he, in later years, reflect on—perhaps even reconsider—his role in the
Salem witch-hunt?*

*In December 1696, with a new round of "calamities" engulfing New En-
gland (Indian warfare, epidemic illness, the loss of ships at sea, an unusually poor autumn harvest), the governing authorities of Massachusetts*

approach the local ministry for help in preparing a public fast. The ministers then invite Cotton Mather to compose a draft for an official proclamation detailing "the sins whereby divine anger has been provoked against this
country." He responds with the usual sort of list, including worldliness, evil
business practices, the prevalence of social contention and "controversy,"
and so on. But he does add something else: "The late inexplicable storms
from the Invisible World [meaning the whole Salem affair] . . . whereby . . .
we were led unto errors and great hardships were brought upon innocent
persons and (we fear) guilt incurred, which we all have cause to bewail with
much confusion of face before the Lord."

The fast is held a few weeks later. People flock to their churches all over
the land. A spirit of profound sorrow and contrition is everywhere apparent. In Boston's First Church, Samuel Sewall's famous apology is read aloud
to the full congregation.

At roughly the same hour, in Boston's Second Church, Cotton Mather
turns his fast-day proclamation into a sermon, with further reference to
"errors," and "guilt," and "confusion . . . before the Lord." But, unlike Sewall,
he offers no personal retraction. At home that evening he seems uncertain
and anxious; he writes plaintively in his diary of "the Divine displeasure"
manifest in the illnesses of several in his family, and links this to "my not appearing with vigor enough to stop the proceedings of the judges, when the in-
extricable storm from the invisible world assaulted the country."

In 1709 he addresses the colony's House of Deputies to urge approval of a
new petition "to restore the reputations . . . of the sufferers [in the trials]"
and make reparation to their survivors. After all, he notes, the same body
had previously announced a "General Day of Humiliation . . . to bewail the
errors of our dark time."

As late as 1711, he is still holding private vigils about Salem, to ponder
"the meaning of the descent from the invisible world."

In sum: reconsideration, yes. Regret, yes. Acknowledgment of "error,"
even of "guilt," yes. But apology? no—almost, but not quite. And for that,
history will not easily forgive him.

PART FOUR

MODERN AMERICA

After the 17th century, the history of American witch-hunting becomes harder to follow. At that point trials and other officially recorded proceedings against witches came virtually to a stop. However, the central beliefs continued in at least attenuated form. And so, too, did the emotional basis continue—the projection of fear, hatred, contempt. This, in turn, was sufficient to fuel *in*formal, *un*official actions against witchcraft, lasting through the 18th century and beyond.

Meanwhile, there began a series of events with characteristics strikingly similar to witch-hunts; hence the term itself has survived, as a way to describe these (figuratively) even now. Chapter X offers a close-up account of one such episode, an angry struggle to suppress the Order of Freemasons in the early 19th century. Though ostensibly a political and social movement, anti-Masonry's moral tone and countersubversive theme strongly evoked the Salem "hysteria" of the early 1690s and the long, bitter "craze" years in Europe.

Chapter XI traces the same theme—what some have called, from a different perspective, a "paranoid" strain in American public life—across a broad historical canvas from the Revolutionary era to the present. Six public "scares" are singled out for special consideration. In the last of these, Satan himself (if not quite witchcraft in the old sense) makes a startling reappearance.

Chapter XII, another close-up, treats matters so recent as to be within the memory of both author and a good many readers. Here, indeed, is as clear a viewpoint on witch-hunting as any of us personally will ever come to.

CHAPTER X

Anti-Masonry:
A Politics of Panic

June 1826; the town of Batavia, in the northwest corner of New York State. William Morgan, a local stone-worker, and David C. Miller, a newspaper editor, announce plans to publish an exposé of the "secret rites" of the fraternal Order of Freemasons. (Morgan is an order member, now apparently on the outs.) Nearby Masonic lodges respond with alarm; some, indeed, are said to be "in a kind of frenzy." Their leaders move to head off the Morgan-Miller project by any means possible: pleading, social pressure, threats of force.

In September they resort to vigilantism. On the 10th, a gang of Masons tries, unsuccessfully, to torch Miller's printing office. On the 11th, a similar group comes to Morgan's home at dawn and seizes him in what amounts to a citizens' arrest. They take him 40 miles east to the town of Canandaigua and commit him to jail there, on thinly based charges of debt. The following night, yet another group of Masons arrives to reclaim—in effect, to abduct—the prisoner. Under cover of darkness they convey him in a closed carriage back to the west, via Rochester, to his last known destination—Fort Niagara, on the Canadian border near the southern tip of Lake Ontario. Beyond this, he simply vanishes.

At year's end Morgan's pamphlet, Illustrations of Free Masonry, *is printed and offered for sale. Its "revelations" are relatively tame—most concern initiation procedure—and fail to arouse widespread interest. Morgan's disappearance, however, is another matter; by now this has become a sensation in its own right. Citizens' committees form throughout the region to protest the "outrage" of abduction—and of an apparent cover-up. Local authorities, many of them longtime Masons, are suspected of shielding the perpetrators and suppressing evidence.*

Beginning in October and stretching through the next five years, court-rooms in several different New York counties will host a variety of Morgan-related proceedings, including some 20 grand-jury inquiries. These spawn motions to the state supreme court, vigorous debates in the Assembly, and the appointment of three separate special counsels with broad powers of investigation. A prolonged spate of publishing activity—books, newspaper articles, official reports—serves to inflame opinion throughout the state and beyond. (A visitor to Albany in the spring of 1827 comments that he "hears nothing talked of in the stages and barrooms but Morgan"; the affair is "alarming the whole country.")

The eventual results will include indictment of at least 26 Masons, on grounds of false imprisonment, perjury, and kidnapping. But only six of the accused are actually brought to trial, with just four convicted. And these four receive light sentences: from three months' to one year's imprisonment. This, in turn, fuels further public indignation and a deepening belief in the corruption of the courts. Masons have reportedly sent some potential wit-nesses into hiding and bribed others not to testify. Prosecutors, sheriffs, and judges are said to have betrayed their official responsibilities; thus, accord-ing to one of the special counsels, "Difficulties which never occurred in any other prosecution have been met at every step." Although no definite trace of Morgan has come to light, his murder—most likely by drowning in the Ni-agara River—is widely assumed.

The roots of organized Freemasonry lie deep in Europe's medieval past. Clearly, there was some long-range tie to traditional guilds of stonemasons and cathedral builders. With the passage of centuries, as their work diminished, these evolved from an "operative" to a "speculative" (and social) mode. By the start of the 18th century, especially in Britain but also across many parts of the European continent, an elaborate web of "lodges" had formed around essen-tially fraternal aims. An early account of Masonry described it as "a peculiar system of morality, veiled in allegory and illustrated by symbols."

In about 1730, the movement jumped the ocean with the founding in Philadelphia of the first lodge on American soil and entered a period of remarkable growth. On the eve of the American Revolution, roughly 100 lodges lay dotted across the 13 colonies; their members included George Washington, Benjamin Franklin, and others among the founding generation. By 1800, the total of Masons nationwide had reached at least 16,000. To be sure, the order was not universally appreciated. Critics focused especially on its code of secrecy, its seemingly "aristocratic" spirit, and its somewhat ambiguous relation to religion. In the 1790s, amid rising alarm over the radical tendencies of the French Revolution, Masons were occasionally accused of nurturing a "Jacobin" conspiracy.

But in the opening years of the 19th century, Masonry expanded faster than ever and achieved a new public prominence. Its recruitment drew heavily on local leadership groups: young professionals, businessmen, aspiring politicians, and others touched by the "go-ahead" spirit of the age. Its avowed goal was mental and moral "improvement"; in that respect it conformed to Enlightenment values. But its appeal was based, most of all, on "comradely feeling." Moreover, it served to provide a place of retreat from "the cares of the world"—plus, one can be sure, the practical advantages of ready-made networking. Its membership standards, and its not inconsiderable dues, fostered a sense of social elevation, while its commitment to secrecy proved an effective means of bonding. Its allegiance to Christianity was broadly ecumenical; Masons came, to a disproportionate extent, from the more "liberal" churches—Unitarians, Universalists, Episcopalians—but all denominations were at least somewhat represented. (Indeed, even Jews and Muslims could be accepted; only atheists were officially barred.) Its elaborate ritual enactments, the focus of Morgan's exposé, added a special touch of aesthetic and emotional reward.

By the mid-1820s, Masonry had reached a pinnacle within the rapidly growing galaxy of American "associations." Lodges were found in more than 1,000 cities and towns, while the sum total of members had climbed well past 100,000. In 1825 one particularly enthusiastic

spokesman asked the rhetorical question, "What is Masonry now?"—
and then gave his own answer: "It is POWERFUL. It comprises men
of rank, wealth, office, and talent . . . in almost every place where
power is of importance . . . so as to have the force of concert throughout the civilized world."

*"Power," "force," and "concert": these are, from the first, animating issues
in the Morgan affair. The power to seize, and destroy, a self-proclaimed op-
ponent. The force to turn back a criminal investigation. The concert of control over jurymen, judges, and the legal system in general. The means, even,
to shape the flow of public information. (Newspapers owned and edited by
men who are Masons seem suspiciously reluctant to report key events in the
unfolding sequence.) Masonic power looms everywhere—or so large numbers of ordinary folk are ready to believe.*

*How should they react? Presumably, with "power" and "concert" of
their own. The period of the various judicial hearings and trials (1826–31) is
also a time of mobilizing against Masons. Print constitutes one kind of
power—as a torrent of fledgling anti-Masonic newspapers and tracts will
soon attest. Public denunciation is a second; thus comes a burst of meetings,
speech making, and other demonstrative actions. (Some of these feature dramatic "secessions" by previously loyal Masons.) Indeed, organized anti-
Masonry begins as a moral crusade with strongly evangelical undertones;
from early on advocates refer to it as "the Blessed Spirit." Clergy are often in
the lead, and churches serve as centers of protest. And much of the rhetoric
heard on such occasions has the flavor of revival "enthusiasm."*

*In the long run, however, politics will prove the best and most effica-
cious line of response. Starting in New York, but spreading quickly to New
England, governance is convulsed by anti-Masonic agitation. The goal is to
purge public life of any and all influence by Masons. Masonic charters of incorporation must be voided, Masonic oaths outlawed, Masonic officeholders defeated at the polls. "We refuse to vote for a Mason because we believe
their adherence to Masonic oaths disqualifies them from civic trusts": thus
the credo, a virtual counteroath, of the Antis.*

◆ ◆ ◆

Political anti-Masonry makes a unique chapter in American history. Though relatively short-lived (scarcely more than a decade from first breath to last gasp), it was at its height a force to be reckoned with. Its timing—birth and early growth in the midst of a transitional period between the first party system (Federalists versus anti-Federalists) and the second (Democrats versus Whigs)—opened special forms of opportunity.

It was, at the outset, very much a grassroots movement, sprung from a host of local initiatives. These would soon coalesce, through the workings of Revolution-style "committees of correspondence," to yield county- and state-wide gatherings, and, eventually, the first national party convention ever. Indeed, political conventions as we know them today—in contrast to the older "caucus" tradition—were largely a brainchild of the anti-Masons.

The movement's greatest impact was felt at the state level. In Vermont, anti-Masons became the dominant party, electing the governor four times running (1831–35) and controlling both legislative chambers. In Massachusetts, Rhode Island, Pennsylvania, and New York, they were a powerful minority, in the legislatures as well as many local communities. This enabled them to exert direct influence on the day-to-day political process; for example, in several states they engineered official "investigations" of Masonry, with witnesses summoned under power of subpoena and subjected to decidedly hostile questioning. They also managed to gain passage of laws outlawing extrajudicial oaths, denying (some) Masonic lodges a civil charter and tax-exempt status, and imposing regular patterns of public oversight. Even in more remote areas such as Ohio and the Michigan Territory they made their mark. In general, they were most successful wherever mainstream party organization was weak, in the Northeast rather than the South and West, and in rural or small-town communities more than in major urban centers.

They attracted, too, some notable political personalities. Former president John Quincy Adams joined the anti-Masons and ran unsuccessfully as their gubernatorial candidate in the Massachusetts

election of 1833. Their New York leaders included William Henry
Seward, future secretary of state in the Lincoln administration, and
Thurlow Weed, who, like Seward, would be among the founders of
the modern Republican Party. In Pennsylvania they were headed by
Thaddeus Stevens, later to become a mainstay of the radical Republicans in the post–Civil War Senate. Indeed, a corps of rising young
politicians passed through anti-Masonry enroute to prominence
among the Whigs in the 1840s and the Republicans in the 1850s
and '60s.

On the national level, 25 congressmen would at one time or another call themselves anti-Masons. But the party's single independent
foray into presidential politics, in 1832, was a shattering disappointment. Its nominee, William Wirt, a leading Maryland lawyer and
one-time attorney general of the United States, proved to be an utterly inept—in fact, unwilling—campaigner. The only state carried
by the anti-Masonic ticket was Vermont (and that by only a bare
plurality).

The movement was hampered, from start to finish, by deep divisions within its own ranks. On one side stood a firm band of purists,
refusing any compromise of principle; on the other, a more loosely
affiliated group of pragmatists sought to form strategic coalitions for
the sake of electoral success. The so-called National Republican
Party, precursor to the Whigs, seemed an especially likely partner,
but "union" slates of candidates invariably provoked conflict among
anti-Masons themselves.

For all that, they achieved striking success with their primary
goal: to reduce Masonic presence and power. Lodges shrank, or disappeared entirely, all across the country, as individual members "se-
ceded" by the thousands; by 1840, Freemasonry seemed but a shadow
of its former self. And this, not surprisingly, was a chief cause for the
concurrent decline of the anti-Masons.

*Always and everywhere, for anti-Masons, Morgan's abduction is the start-
ing point; words sufficient to describe it can hardly be found. As one leading*

spokesman writes: "I challenge the Spanish Inquisition to exceed it. I boldly invite a search into the archives of that engine of ferocious despotism . . . to produce a case that goes beyond it. . . . The iron clamps that were probably prepared for the feet and hands of Morgan aptly compare with the chains in which the victim of the Inquisition was habited . . . whilst the pictures of devouring dogs and serpents that were hung round his neck completely pre-figure the horrid gang of murdering conspirators who plunged their hands in the blood of Morgan." Yet, when seen in the widest perspective, "the Morgan affair . . . [is] but a comparatively small thing"—whereas the pattern it reveals, a spreading conspiracy against fundamental American virtues and values, is of "terrific character."

Masons are, according to their opponents, determined foes of "republican equality." Indeed, their entire tendency goes the opposite way—toward "haughty aristocracy." The titles they bestow on themselves—"Master," "High Priest," "Most Excellent General," even "Grand King"—are obvious examples of that; so, too, is their elaborate internal hierarchy of "ranks" and "degrees." In everyday political practice, Masons are sworn to promote "a brother's advancement" in preference to the common good. As a result, they have gained power at a level "ten times" what their numbers alone would suggest; by one estimate, they control three-fourths of all public offices. The same pattern of cliquish loyalty also undermines the legal system; time after time, in courtrooms across the land, "Masonic influence has turned the scale in favor of the brethren of their craft."

All this stands in stark opposition to the principles upon which the nation was founded. Invariably, then, anti-Masons see themselves as guardians of a sacred tradition; it is their duty, in this hour of peril, to rescue "for posterity . . . the republic we inherited from our forefathers." Consider, too, that Morgan's abduction has followed by mere weeks the nearly simultaneous (and providentially timed?) deaths of two of the last surviving "forefathers"—John Adams and Thomas Jefferson—on July 4, 1826, the 50th anniversary of the Declaration of Independence. By putting Freemasonry to rout, the nation may reaffirm their legacy, and attain "a Second Independence."

Masonry subverts not only the polity but also revealed religion. "In its whole length and breadth," declares an anti-Masonic convention, the order "is as anti-Christian as it is anti-Republican." To be sure, Masonry frequently masquerades as "the handmaiden of religion," but, in reality, it operates as a virtual counter-faith. At bottom, it amounts to "pure Deism," even "blank Atheism." Indeed, "you might as well expect religion in a brothel as in a Masonic lodge." Churches no less than governments must be fully purged of its influence; otherwise it will "corrupt and destroy all our . . . religious institutions, and spread infidelity . . . throughout the earth."

Home life, too, is gravely threatened. Masonic lodges are, of course, an exclusively male preserve; as such, they withdraw men from the "tender influence" and "moral sense" of women and "the duties of the family circle." The typical Masonic wife is left unprotected "in solitude . . . in the shadow of night, [and] ignorant of the employment in which her husband is engaged." And what might such "employment" be? To anti-Masons, the lodges are "cages of uncleanness" and thus a probable setting for "unseemly orgies . . . and Bacchanalian revels." Their meetings are said to include freely flowing drink, lavish gambling, lewd song, and nudity. Lodge members are explicitly pledged not "to violate the chastity of a Master Mason's wife, mother, sister, or daughter," which anti-Masons construe as a license to prey on women who lack Masonic connections.

State, church, family: three separate, yet interconnected, fronts in a high-stakes "war." The enemy's methods—his strategy, his tactics—are especially devious and difficult. Oath taking, for example, is a weapon of great power. Other loyalties fall away: Masonry first, Masonry last, Masonry forever. But secrecy is worst of all. Whatever transpires behind the closed doors of the lodge must not be revealed—on pain of death—even to one's "dearest relations." (Thus, according to widespread belief, the fate that has befallen poor William Morgan.) Masonry flourishes in the dark, at "midnight assemblies." It slithers like "a wily serpent which [has] crept insidiously into the Eden of this happy Republic." Such serpent imagery is pervasive and telling. At least occasionally, anti-Masons will directly connect the dots—to witchcraft and Satan, in days of yore.

◆ ◆ ◆

Did such rhetorical heat reflect a genuine threat? Or was it a kind of social paranoia?

In certain respects, Freemasonry was—as both sides contended—"powerful." The reason anti-Masons could never penetrate the mainstream political parties was that most party leaders were Masons. (This was true from Washington right through to Andrew Jackson and Henry Clay.) Local politics, too, were frequently dominated by men who belonged to the order. But it would be hard to prove that Masons acted, in their political roles, *as Masons,* or sought to advance particular Masonic interests. And there is no good evidence whatsoever that they aimed to transform established patterns of governance, religious practice, or family life.

However, the feeling expressed by the anti-Masons seems genuine enough. And feeling did lead, at least occasionally, to action. Quite apart from the political movement (including the laws passed and the investigations carried out), anti-Masons would sometimes resort to informal, even extralegal action. The surviving evidence is anecdotal and has never been carefully assembled. But Masonic buildings were vandalized, Masonic gravestones were defaced, and individual Masons were threatened with harm. In some communities (according to a contemporaneous account), "Neighbor was set against neighbor, friends separated, families made enemies, and . . . peace and harmony . . . almost wholly destroyed." The sum of this fell far short of witch-hunting in the older, more lethal sense; but its emotional basis was recognizably similar. Fear, anger, envy, "outrage": these were the central, propulsive elements, bridging the Salem trials of the late 17th century and the anti-Masonic fervor of the early 19th. Another link across time was the fantasy of secret conspiracy, including sexual libertinism and a complete inversion of traditional social arrangements. Paranoia does not, after all, seem too strong a word here.

Political anti-Masonry was finished by 1840 or so. And "the Blessed

Spirit" that had inspired it appeared also to evaporate (or perhaps was diverted into the several reform movements of midcentury, especially antislavery). Yet the story does not quite end there. Freemasonry made a strong comeback after the Civil War, albeit in a quieter, less conspicuous mode. And anti-Masonry came back, though it, too, was much toned down. Indeed, a certain tension has continued to swirl around the order virtually to the present day; some leading religious groups—the Roman Catholic and Mormon churches, for example—maintain an attitude of open antagonism.

Moreover, after nearly 200 years, the mystery of William Morgan's disappearance remains unresolved.

CHAPTER XI

Saga of Scares, 1700–2000

The effects of the Salem affair were deep and lastingly traumatic. The terror of 1692 would echo in the attacks on the Freemasons and on numerous other groups for many years to come.

In the immediate aftermath of Salem, New Englanders of every rank and station came to think that appalling "errors" had been made and together bemoaned "the guilt of innocent blood." They blamed the Devil for having "deluded" them. They blamed the difficult times. They even, in some cases, blamed themselves. And, whatever their preferred way of explaining the "tragedy," they were determined that nothing like it should happen again. Few were inclined to doubt the existence of witchcraft; the difficulty lay in identifying specific practitioners. Always, there were likely suspects nearby. But how could one separate those who were bona fide witches from others whom Satan had wrongfully "represented" as such? A leading New England minister wrote in 1728, "Although I firmly believe [in] . . . the agency of Satan and his instruments in afflicting the children of men, yet I fear the world has been wretchedly imposed upon by relations of such matters. . . . Many things have been dubbed witchcraft, and called the works of the devil, which were nothing more than the contrivance of . . . men." The problem of "proof" had troubled expert theorists of witchcraft long before 1692; now it came to seem virtually insuperable.

The 18th century brought a gradual decline in the strength and salience of witchcraft belief. People of more than average wealth and education made up an advance guard of skeptics. For them, this was a period of "enlightenment" led by the steady growth of modern scientific ideas. The latter included: an orderly universe (with the deity reduced to the role of benevolent, but distant, "watchmaker"); the natural, and ultimately discoverable, causation of particular events; and what one historian has called "a new faith in the potentialities of human initiative." The cumulative result was gradually to erode traditional worldviews, among which witchcraft had loomed so large.

Still, with plain folk of the same era, the old attitudes hung on for several generations longer; their traces are evident now chiefly through folklore and what scholars call "oral tradition."

Littleton, Massachusetts; 1720. Three young sisters in the Blanchard family fell "under affliction"; their "torments" included "wounds and pinches and prickings," interspersed with "trances and visions." Many "conjectures" were offered as to the source of their difficulties, but "the greater number [of townspeople] thought . . . they were under an evil hand, or possessed by Satan"—whereupon the sisters jointly accused "a certain woman . . . of afflicting them." Presently the suspect "fell ill and died within a few weeks," and the Blanchard children returned to a normal condition. Some saw this sequencing itself as proof of guilt. Yet discussion continued, and several "of the good neighbors . . . suspected . . . falsehood." The children insisted they had offered "nothing but the truth throughout." Eventually, however, "their consciences contradicted them"; the eldest, when grown to womanhood, confessed to having concocted the whole affair, led by "folly and pride" into a course of "deceit." The parallels here to the earliest phase of the Salem witch-hunt were obvious—and may well have contributed to the neighbors' doubts. The outcome, however, proved very different.

Fayette, Maine; the summer of 1800. A Massachusetts minister visited this town as part of a missionary tour and wrote about it in his diary: "Lodged with Dr. Hall. Here was witchcraft in plenty. A man had been troubled six months, and it was thought he must die. He is emaciated and often horribly distressed. . . . A Baptist teacher, soon to be ordained, has lost his milk for some time. The end of a cheese would come and go, and boil off from the fire, and finally come to nothing. Etc. Etc."

Cape Cod, Massachusetts; 1793. Another New England minister offered the following, more general observation: "There are but few towns, if any, but at one time or other have not had one or more [inhabitants] in suspicion of witchcraft, as if the place were not complete without some well-versed in that occupation."

Long Island, New York; 1802. A farmer composed a careful account of "strange occurrences . . . in the course of my life," many of which he attributed to a local "gang of witches." He admitted to doubts about the whole idea of witchcraft, which seemed "contrary to my senses and my reason." Nonetheless, "what has happened to me and fallen in the way of my observation" forced the conclusion that "spirits" are indeed able "to act or operate on the minds or bodies of creatures."

Bristol, Connecticut; about 1810. According to a local historian, "witchcraft caused much excitement . . . and greatly frightened some of the good people." A girl named Norton claimed to have been enchanted by one of her aunts, who "put a bridle on her and [drove] her through the air to Albany, where great witch-meetings were held." A sympathetic neighbor took her into his house in an effort to "exorcise her," and was immediately beset by "awful sights and sounds"; a friend who tried to assist was "frightened into convulsions." Others "were tormented by unseen hands, pinching them, sticking red hot pins into their flesh, and bringing strange maladies upon them."

New Hampton, New Hampshire; the early 19th century. A certain "Granny Hicks" was suspected of using witchcraft to cause illness in a child of some neighbors with whom she had been recently at odds. Five young men of the town decided to retaliate by demolishing her house "with axes"; they then set its remains on fire. Hicks stood by and begged them "for mercy"—but to no avail. When the deed was done, she "pointed . . . to each one in turn, and . . . prophesied the manner in which death would come as judgment upon him." Years later, her "prophecy of that fateful night . . . was wholly, and literally, fulfilled."

Stories like these are studded through dozens of local histories, especially from New England. To be sure, they *are* stories, not trial records or government statutes or detailed parish transcripts; hence they lack the "official" status of witch-hunting evidence from an earlier time. Still, they are valuable for the light they throw on popular mentality; taken as a whole, they provide the clearest available view of witchcraft history in its post-trials phase. They show, for one thing, that women of middle and old age remained the most likely suspects. They show, too, that episodes of conflict—threats, neighborhood spats and squabbles, petty jealousies, the refusal of cooperation or charity—were, as before, the usual triggers for suspicion.

In other ways, however, they suggest change. Many stories shift the focus from harm caused *by* the witch to injury done *to* her. Put differently: they express a growing emphasis on counter-magic— on measures taken to ward off, or even to reverse, the effects of witchcraft.

New Salem, New Hampshire; the early 19th century. On a summer day, a farmer went out to his barn and noticed one of his cows "looking strangely," and immediately suspected its "bewitchment" by a local woman. Adopting a time-honored strategy, he took the unfortunate creature and cut off its ears and tail; shortly thereafter the woman in question was found dead in a house fire.

Exeter, Rhode Island; the early 19th century. A woodcutter set out to cart a load of lumber to market. While he was en route, a cat scampered across the road, badly startling his team of horses. He immediately inferred "mischief" by one of his neighbors who might, through witchcraft, have assumed the shape of the offending cat. So he shot and killed the cat with a silver bullet (a well-known countermagical tactic). At virtually the same moment, on the other side of town, the supposed witch took a bad fall and broke her hip.

The conceptual basis of witchcraft was changing, too. Alongside her 17th-century predecessor, the stereotypical witch of the 18th and 19th centuries seems a much diminished figure. From the enactment of invisible, life-altering, sometimes death-dealing *maleficium,* to occasional bits of local "mischief": this was the basic trend. (To be sure, killing was still theoretically within the witch's power; but very few of the later stories include this element, or anything close to it.) Crucially, the essential, enabling tie to Satan was broken—and, along with it, the idea of a cosmically scaled "conspiracy" against Almighty God and his forces of righteousness. Witchcraft had become a freelance activity performed by individual miscreants.

Even the stereotype of witches was different now. The post-trials period birthed the figure of the "hag-witch," who remains with us in popular culture today. She appears in a thousand different variations—but with a core of central features found nearly everywhere. The hag-witch is *old,* and on that account *decrepit.* She walks with a stagger, leaning on a gnarled cane. She is physically *repulsive.* Her back is bent, her complexion a pallid gray; her face is grotesquely wrinkled, her eyes beady, her nose crooked, her mouth toothless—and so on. She is also *eccentric.* She seems disorganized, confused, a trifle "dotty." Finally, she is *an isolate.* She lives alone, in a remote location, without regular, supportive human contact. In sum, she is pathetic rather than powerful—a victim more than a victimizer. She may still, under some circumstances, elicit fear; but contempt, disgust, even ridicule, are the more likely reactions to her.

How and why witches and witchcraft became weakened this way is a complex question touching many broad currents of historical change. One of these was surely the altered position of women in society at large, including a process of disempowerment through which the robust "goodwife" of the colonial era evolved into the spotless, but relatively constricted, "True Woman" of the 19th century. Now, even though the ancient and ubiquitous witch/woman equation remained intact, it lacked the punch it had packed in an earlier time.

Another closely-related element was the rise of a new cultural ethos, in which competition and conflict became approved routes to social betterment; this, in turn, was paralleled at the level of individual experience by a growing acceptance of personal assertiveness (even openly expressed aggression). In short, qualities which had once served as deeply negative referents—and which were directly linked to witchcraft—no longer felt so threatening.

A third important line of change was the loosening of community ties and a corresponding reduction in the social density of everyday life. As pre-modern villages grew into fully developed towns and cities, it made less and less sense to attribute misfortune to personal factors such as motives of attack in one's neighbor next door.

Finally, the old "providential" view of history—the readiness to see all events as tightly linked in a grand design controlled by the Almighty—was, with the passage of time, steadily scaled back. Insofar as witchcraft had been part of that design, it became displaced, disorganized, unmoored.

Vestiges of old-style witchcraft belief could be found well into the 20th century—and perhaps, here and there, even in the 21st. They have survived in the play of children, in folklore, and (rarely now) in the lives and attitudes of people little touched by modernizing forces. To be sure, a new style of witchcraft has emerged in just the past few decades. But this is an altogether different thing—call it witchcraft with a smiling face. Its shape and substance must be outlined here, if only to separate it from the main lines of the present inquiry.

"Wicca" is its currently popular name, though some adherents prefer to be called "witches" plain and simple. It appears in many versions, all of which can be broadly grouped under the rubric of "neo-Paganism." Because it is highly decentralized, and also because it has until recently followed a code of secrecy, its dimensions—its total of supporters and sympathizers—are hard to come by; some estimates push toward a million worldwide. Its rapid expansion, since a modest beginning in the 1950s, is not in doubt. But its geographical range is limited, for the most part, to the United States and the United Kingdom (with offshoots in some parts of northern and central Europe).

Devotees of Wicca are loosely organized in "covens." Typically these have a local base and small scale, so as to permit a maximum of close, personal interaction. Despite their structural looseness, and an implicit commitment to autonomy and difference, they do share a core of underlying beliefs. One is the efficacy of magic, including charms, chants, spells, image making, and, more generally, the invocation of supernatural power to direct the course of experience. A second is the centrality of a female deity: the Great Goddess, as she is often called. Some Wiccans also embrace a male God, and make much of the pairing, while others espouse a pantheon of many gods. But the Goddess ranks highest overall. A third core belief—in fact, a cluster of beliefs—involves a reverence for the earth and all its life-giving powers; put differently, Wicca, in most of its forms, is Nature worship. Other important elements here—though they are less matters of belief than intrinsic tendency—include a sense of divine immanence (the presence of the Goddess permeates all being) and a feeling of existential community (distinctions between self and other fade into an all-encompassing Oneness).

But in any case, practice matters more than belief. Ritual enactments, performances, and celebrations are truly the heart of Wicca. The most important of these are tightly linked to the seasons: for example, a sequence of eight festivals tracing "the wheel of the year." They include familiar calendrical moments such as "Yule" (Christmas) and Halloween, mixed with others that are more obscure. Gatherings of the coven take place accordingly; its members dance, sing, and invoke a variety of "figures" (circles, pentagrams, elaborate body charts) with sacred significance—all within a frame of joyful self-expression.

Until recently, the entire system has been thought to rest on deep historical tradition. In particular, Wiccans claimed direct descent from traditional witches of pre-modern times. Witchcraft, they believed, was actually an "old religion," indeed, *the* old religion: pre-Christian, not to say prehistoric, and "pagan" in the fullest sense. Its adherents had been forced to endure centuries of terrible persecution, especially during the witch-craze of 1550–1700. Then they had gone underground and had reemerged essentially intact in our own time.

This claim, if valid, would have given Wicca an important place in the larger history of witchcraft. But the surviving evidence will not sustain it. There is nothing to establish a direct chain of connection—between one person, or group, or decade, or generation, and the next—across the several centuries that separate traditional witchcraft from Wicca. The strongest possibilities here would seem to involve the "white witches" of pre-modern times, those "cunning" men and women who cast spells, bestowed charms, told fortunes, and otherwise sought to assist their village neighbors. Their "magic" was widely acknowledged—of that we have solid proof—and occasionally it did seem to turn from "white" to "black," thus creating targets for witch-hunters. Yet, magic aside, their lives and work differed profoundly from the practice of Wicca. First and foremost, theirs was never a system of *devotion,* of *worship,* embracing high purpose and overarching worldview. To the contrary, it was entirely about *utility*—that is, small and specific gains at the level of everyday circumstance (curing an illness, finding a lost object, helping with some important decision). There is no sign that cunning folk engaged together, as a group, in any context whatsoever.

Careful study within the past decade or two has reconstructed another, far more plausible lineage. It now seems clear that Wicca qualifies, at best, as an "invented tradition." Moreover, a single person can be considered its principal inventor: a man named Gerald Broussard Gardner (1884–1964). Gardner was English by birth and education, but traveled widely in other parts of the world (especially the Far East). He made a career in business; became an avid, if amateur, folklorist; and emerged toward the end of his life as a prolific author on "witchcraft today" (the title of his most famous book). A number of his writings, mostly from the 1950s, laid the foundations of Wicca, as understood and practiced ever since. These drew, in a highly eclectic fashion, on various folklore investigations from the past two centuries, including some that had explicitly construed witchcraft as an ancient, pagan religion. Indeed, the ingredients of Gardner's rather steamy brew reached all the way back to classical

Greece and Rome (the goddess Diana, the god Pan, Bacchanalian fertility rites, the adoration of nature) and out toward Eastern religions (Hindu chakras). However, their most important source was the Romantic movement of the 19th century, with its nostalgia for an Edenic past. Seen in full historical context, then, they expressed a deep reaction against the "modernizing" thrust of industrialization, urbanization, mass society, and rapid social change. As such, they would continue to resonate strongly with Wiccans for decades.

In the years since Gardner's work of "invention," Wicca has blossomed in new directions. For example, it has acquired a strongly feminist slant (as a manifestation of specifically female spirituality). It has also, on some of its fringes, been broached by neo-Nazi and skinhead sympathizers in search of an "Aryan" cultural ancestry, and Celtic traditions have become very popular with many Wiccans. These still unfolding developments carry it further and further from any putative roots in pre-modern witchcraft. It remains, then, very much a creation of its own—and immediately preceding—times. And, as noted, a "smiling" one at that.

So the trail of witch-hunting peters out. Or does it? In fact, the term—the metaphor—has survived to the present day. All sorts of human imbroglios may now be characterized as witch-hunts. Political "Red Scares" come quickly to mind. But other more localized, even private, events are also described thus. Police investigations, corporate restructurings, projects to reconstitute schools, churches, and civic organizations, family struggles: the list goes on and on. The metaphor comes easily—perhaps too easily—as a mode (most often) of moral reproach. Wherever appears some allegation of subversive intent, of conspiratorial menace, of concealed betrayal—just there the "witch-hunt" label may be directly affixed.

Is there a genuine continuity between the witch-hunts of the pre-modern era and their supposed equivalents in more recent times? Are some parts of the metaphor, as it is commonly used nowadays, more apt than others? And does this usage help us to understand—

perhaps even to combat—certain darker tendencies in our own social and political system? Such questions can serve to frame a highly
compressed and selective *tour d'horison* of American history since the
mid-18th century. Along the way, six separate episodes will be spot-
lighted for particular attention. Each will be summarized and measured against the profile of traditional witch-hunting. Our spotlight
will also touch broader themes and tendencies that, while lacking
any sharp episodic focus, appear to reflect the same basic mentality.

If the beginnings of modern science helped erode the conceptual basis of witchcraft, they also ironically produced a rise in what might
be called "paranoid thinking." As one historian has written, "the
century or so following the Restoration [of the British monarchy,
in 1660] was the great era of conspiratorial fears." In all parts of the
Anglo-American world, public affairs were increasingly understood
in terms of "plots" and "designs," "cabals" and "schemes," intrigue
and hidden intent. This tendency cannot be explained as individual
pathology, for its prevalence was virtually society-wide. The best
historical accounts attribute it to a convergence of social change (the
early growth of the market economy, a rapid process of political mobilization) and the cultural impact of the Enlightenment. As the natural sciences began to assume their modern importance, life in many
sectors became progressively demystified—with increasing emphasis on chains of very specific cause-and-effect linkage. Some of these
belonged to the realm of nature, but many others embraced human
purpose and action. In effect, a space had opened up on the landscape of experience, to be filled (at least in part) by the agency of particular men and women: *he/she/they have planned, and caused, these
particular events, not "Providence," or fate, or other cosmic forces.* This
relatively novel concept was especially conducive to a focus on conspiracy; *the difficulties we face have been craftily, secretly, wickedly plotted
by our enemies.*

Such was the case, for example, with the political movement leading up to the American Revolution. Patriot leaders stressed a darken-

ing "scheme" against their traditional liberties—even, as Thomas Jefferson put it, "a deliberate, systematical plan of reducing us to slavery." Still, there would be no witch-hunt, actual or metaphorical, as a result. A considerable number of Loyalists—people who rejected the move toward independence—were forced to flee their homes in the colonies, and some were subjected to cruel persecution. Yet many others hung on where they were and managed well enough. Loyalists were cast as individual opponents, no more and no less; they were not demonized as a group. Fears of dire conspiracy pointed overseas toward the British parliament and king. With real, massively consequential, combat under way—with soldiers in the field, including such "demonic" foes as regiments of foreign Hessians—there was little motive to focus on enemies within the patriot community itself. Both now and later on, countersubversive activity would follow—not coincide with—direct experience of warfare.

The Bavarian Illuminati (1798–99)

Revolutionary-era anxiety did help open a way for the first of the many political and social "scares" that would dot the later course of American history: the so-called Bavarian Illuminati crisis of the late 1790s. As with other such events to come, its alleged source lay far from American shores. Some two decades earlier in Bavaria, at the University of Ingolstadt, a small group of "enlightened" reformers had organized themselves as a "society" to counter religious (mostly Jesuit) influence in educational life. Because they maintained a protective shield of secrecy, little is known of their actual doings. But their adversaries would soon identify them as a deeply threatening element—opposed to all religious and governmental authority, espousing "Epicurean" values and the pursuit of "sensual pleasures," and aiming for a wholesale transformation of conventional social arrangements. Though quickly suppressed at its German points of origin, the Society of Illuminati was thought to have spread its malignant cells through other parts of Europe, and to have directly inspired the most shocking excesses of the French Revolution.

Inevitably, its reputation crossed the ocean to America in a series of published exposés. An initial cry of alarm was raised in May 1798, on a national fast day, when a prominent Massachusetts minister, Reverend Jedediah Morse, preached against the imminent threat of "Illuminism." According to Morse, "We have in truth secret enemies . . . scattered through our country whose professed design is to subvert and overturn our holy religion and our free and excellent government." Indeed, he claimed to have identified one specific group of Illuminati in Virginia (through "an official, authenticated list" of members) and another in New York; from these, he declared, "have sprung fourteen others scattered we know not where over the United States." Morse's sermon was published and widely distributed, and then inspired additional sermons, commencement addresses, holiday orations, and newspaper editorials. These, in turn, would disseminate a virtual catalogue of (alleged) Illuminist horrors: espionage, plots against civic order, incitement to class hatred, an "end justifies the means" philosophy, and personal "vices of the most gross, savage, and monstrous complexion"—all shrouded behind elaborate efforts of concealment.

The wider context was a growing sense of peril in American relations with France and a deep revulsion against the "radical" course of the ongoing Revolution there. Conflict between American and French vessels at sea had become endemic; full-scale warfare seemed more and more likely. If it came to that, an internal conspiracy linked to the enemy would be insupportable. Even without war, Illuminism posed a grave threat; having already poisoned one republic, it might easily do the same to another.

To be sure, there was more shadow than substance in these dangers. No actual conspirators were ever accused, Reverend Morse's "authenticated list" notwithstanding. But the Illuminist scare did serve, in conjunction with other forces, to create at least a small group of victims. In 1798, Congress passed the infamous Alien and Sedition Acts, which (among other things) criminalized certain forms of writing and speech about the government or its officers. These laws led to 15 indictments and 10 convictions of offending editors and publishers, at least some of whom would serve time in jail. Fears of the Illuminati helped create the atmosphere in which such actions could be organized and sustained.

Was it a witch-hunt? In many ways it does carry that flavor. Consider: Illuminism was, first and last, imagined as a conspiracy: dark and dire, and hidden behind a veil of secrecy; vast in scope, encompassing both Europe and America; with a fundamental aim to undermine—or even to reverse, in direct counterpoint—all that right-thinking folk would regard as good and true; proceeding through nefarious, covert methods, and thus liable to become a kind of unwitting contagion; creating high stakes around the outcome, if not a threat of apocalypse. All these elements evoke the paradigm of traditional witch-hunting. And even if Satan was not directly implicated (not much anyway), the aspect of moral inversion goes strongly in that direction; religious orthodoxy was heavily mobilized, with clergy playing a leading role. Also pointing in the same direction was the underlying emotional charge: deep anxiety, recurrent distress, horrified outrage.

Yet the fit is not a perfect one. If most witch-hunts served, in one way or another, to entrench or defend the position of elite groups, that does not much appear in anti-Illuminism. Moreover, there was little in the way of specific investigation of supposed perpetrators; there were no confessions (forced or otherwise); and there were only a few actual victims (whose suffering was of limited scope). Very much in contrast to traditional witch-hunts, this was something of a shadow affair. Finally, one element almost everywhere apparent in campaigns against witchcraft was entirely missing: a marked preponderance of female targets. On balance, then, the verdict here has to be mixed: something of a witch-hunt, yes, but not entirely so.

As with many similar episodes, the end of the Illuminati scare came very fast. The election of 1800, bringing defeat for the Federalists and the start of Thomas Jefferson's presidency, left American politics in a radically different place. "Jacobinism" and Revolutionary France no longer gripped the public imagination; the Illuminati were scarcely spoken of anymore. For the next quarter century, the nation moved into, and through, a new set of preoccupations: trade embargoes (in which Britain, much more than France, played the role of villain); the War of 1812; the so-called Era of Good Feelings.

Anti-Masonry (1826–40)

The mid-1820s saw the start of another rampant "scare." The target this time was the Order of Freemasons. In fact, the Society of Illuminati had itself been associated with Masonry, since both seemed tainted with a dangerously modern spirit. But now a huge wave of antipathy toward Masons began to run entirely of its own accord. Its source point was the abduction, disappearance, and apparent murder in upstate New York of ex-Mason William Morgan, who had authored an exposé of the order's "secrets." The resultant anxiety and outrage spread rapidly across the entire northern half of the country. (The South remained largely unaffected.) Individual Masons were thrown heavily on the defensive. Masonry as a whole was vilified as anti-American, anti-republican, anti-Christian, antifamily. Unlike the case of Illuminism a generation before, a political movement was born—with conventions held, candidates nominated, and public officials (including 25 congressmen and 1 state governor) elected. There was an anti-Masonic ticket in the presidential election of 1832. Both judicial and legislative committees, formed for the express purpose of investigating Masonry, unearthed dire evidence of a conspiracy against established institutions and principles. (Or so the investigators believed.) Eventually this movement, too, would run its course, as anxiety about the Masons diminished and public attention shifted elsewhere. But it did take its toll—if not in lives lost, then certainly in careers altered, reputations damaged, friendships broken, communities rent asunder.

Was it a witch-hunt? In many respects, anti-Masonry wears a look quite similar to that of anti-Illuminism: conspiracy; secrecy; huge scope; fundamentally subversive ends; hidden, silently contaminating means; apocalyptic danger; the driving force of strong negative affect—key markers all, in both cases (and in witch-hunting). However: religion seems to have played an inconspicuous part in anti-Masonry. Ministers were found on both sides; for the most part, secular leadership prevailed. But, as with traditional witch-hunts, there was strong incentive to investigate; there were also "trials" (if not in the legal sense, then certainly in the court of public opinion). Indeed, there was much overt reality to galvanize and focus the movement: Masonic lodges were well-established, highly visible institutions, and individual Masons were readily identifiable (as Illuminists, and supposed witches, were not). Many Masons were victimized; at the least, they lost status. And Freemasonry, as a whole, was a victim. But gender—the whole underlying aspect of misogyny—was (again) absent. All in all, then, anti-Masonry makes another partial, but not total, match with witch-hunting.

Anti-Masonry, like the Illuminati scare, was intensely focused and time limited—analogous, in medical terms, to a fast-moving epidemic. Other currents of public alarm, in roughly the same period, are better described as endemic; they waxed and waned, diffused and sharpened—but never disappeared entirely. And they helped to shape the cultural matrix in which new scares might emerge.

For example, anti-Catholicism was a long-established tradition among the largely Protestant population of early America. And starting in the 1830s, it gained new force in response to the arrival of large numbers of Catholic immigrants, especially the Irish fleeing famine. Occasionally this antagonism flared into open violence, as, for example, in the burning of an Ursuline convent in Charlestown, Massachusetts in 1834. A variety of specifically anti-Catholic organizations formed at midcentury, one of which, the American Protective Association, would eventually claim over two million supporters.

Meanwhile, Mormonism—a new and wholly indigenous religious movement, founded by Joseph Smith in the 1820s and growing rapidly thereafter—evoked a similar kind of alarm. Public pressure, up to and including mob violence, soon forced the Mormons to leave their original home ground in upstate New York and New England for the wilderness territory of Utah. En route, Smith was seized and murdered by a lynching party and his followers subjected to repeated harassment.

Both Catholics and Mormons were suspect in the eyes of the Protestant majority for owing their primary allegiance to an external, and highly centralized, system of authority—the papacy in one case, the "prophet" Smith and his church councillors in the other. "The papal hierarchy declares its complete sovereignty over the state, and . . . decrees that the papal fiat is superior to the voice of the people": thus the official view of the American Protective Association. "What, then, is the real strength of Mormonism?" asked a foremost critic of that group. "It is an ecclesiastical despotism ruled by a man who is prophet, priest, king, and pope, all in one." (With the Mormons, to be sure, there were additional issues of "secret rites" and of practices abhorrent to conventional morality, like polygamous marriage.) Such authoritarian structures were thought virtually to require the hatching of conspiracies, of "plots," against the national mainstream.

These anxieties reflected a broader sense that republican governance was fragile and easily subverted. The same theme appeared also in politics; each of the leading parties of the day, Whigs and Democrats, accused the other of threatening core principles and institutions. No less was true of the ripening sectional conflict between North and South. Northerners denounced a "Slave Power conspiracy," while Southerners voiced a similar feeling of threat by abolitionists. In all these different venues, then, the language of conspiratorial menace was pervasive. And so, too, was its emotional substrate—fear, distress, and hatred.

But of public "scares," in the epidemic sense, there was nothing during the long and tumultuous middle decades of the 19th century. In the pre-modern period, warfare and witch-hunting had proceeded largely in alternating sequence—one or the other, not both at the same time. Perhaps something of the same dynamic can be attributed to this later era as well. Sectional conflict, followed by grinding, unimaginably bloody Civil War, consumed energies that might otherwise have gone toward hunting for enemies within.

The Civil War was such a watershed moment that antebellum and postbellum seem, in retrospect, different worlds. Part of the difference was a vast increase in labor organizing—and labor conflict—with the coming of a fully industrial age. To be sure, unions had been formed, and strikes staged, as far back as the 1820s. But none of the previous agitation remotely approached what developed in the century's closing years. This, in turn, set the stage for a new round of reactive (and reactionary) response, some of which invites direct comparison with old-style witch-hunting.

There was, to begin with, an international context here: the rapid growth of trade unionism in Britain and France, the spread of Marxian socialism, anarchism, and other such radical ideologies, the dramatic saga of the Paris Commune (a workers' uprising in the French capital) in the spring of 1871. Together, such events helped raise a specter of foreign-born "Red Revolution"—a modern-day equivalent of Satanism—that would haunt American public life for over a century to come. Moreover, anxiety about overseas developments would mesh very tightly with a range of concerns rooted much closer to home. The as-yet unfamiliar system of factory production, the seemingly chaotic environment of modern cities, immigration on a massive scale, the "tramp menace" (thousands of unmoored men set loose to roam around the country), and a rising homicide rate all played into the mix. "There never was a time in the history of the world when an enemy of society could work such mighty mischief as today," declared clergyman and author Josiah Strong in his immensely popular book *Our Country* (1885). "The more highly developed a civilization is, the more vulnerable does it become."

Such feelings of vulnerability were not altogether illusory;

indeed, they incorporated real events and actual dangers. The actions of the French Communards cast an especially long shadow. That workers could seize control of government, execute bishops and other conservative opponents, requisition property, and abolish debt seemed, in the words of a New York newspaper editorialist, "to uproot society and organize Hell." Perhaps other countries, too—including the United States—might soon be engulfed in "a sudden storm of communistic revolutions," reflecting "the deep, explosive forces which underlie all modern society." The Paris Commune would, in years to come, remain a touchstone for all manner of anti-radical opinion.

The 1870s were, for the most part, a decade of economic depression; as such, they spawned a broad range of worker unrest. There was the Granger movement, organized by cooperative associations of farmers in the Midwest to counter the enormous commercial power of the railroad companies. There were strikes in the coalfields of western Pennsylvania, led by the so-called Molly Maguires (a semisecret organization of mostly Irish miners). There were large protest demonstrations, with accompanying violence, in the major urban centers: for instance, the Tompkins Square Riot of 1874, in New York City, sparked by a parade by laborers carrying the red flag of the Commune.

But most impressive by far was the great railway strike of 1877, prompted by wage cuts and other grievances of railroad workers in no fewer than 17 states. Indeed, this can reasonably be called the first strike, in any industry, of truly national proportions. And it turned violent at numerous points, as police, militiamen, and federal troops were mobilized in opposition. The toll in lives lost ran to over 100; the value of the properties destroyed was incalculable. Chicago, the strike's epicenter, was temporarily paralyzed when workers in other industries walked out in sympathy. The reaction of the "respectable classes," especially the business community, was predictably furious: the strikers were denounced as "ragged Commune wretches," as advocates of a "French Communism, entirely at war with the spirit of our institutions," and so on.

The 1880s brought more of the same: more strikes, more bitter antagonism between the "respectable" and the working classes, more police and military intervention, more property destruction, more deaths. According to one estimate, the year 1886 alone witnessed a total of 1,400 strikes, involving over 600,000 workers.

Haymarket (1886)

That same year, 1886, was also the year of the notorious Haymarket Riot—and then of a full-blown Red Scare. Its immediate precursor was a tide of labor protest in many parts of the country, building through the spring toward a national strike on May 1 for enactment of the eight-hour workday. As part of this larger ferment, a bitterly contested work stoppage at the McCormick Harvester plant outside Chicago led, on May 3, to violent clashes between worker pickets and privately-hired Pinkerton guards, resulting in three deaths and more than a dozen injuries. The following evening, radical leaders called a protest rally in Chicago's Haymarket Square. After some hours of speech making, police arrived with orders to disperse the crowd. At that moment, a bomb was tossed into the ranks of the advancing officers; mayhem ensued, with gunfire from both sides. When peace was finally restored, seven policemen and several demonstrators lay dead; others were mortally injured.

Public reaction was rapid and severe. Business leaders and municipal officials alike struck a pose of horrified condemnation. Some construed Haymarket as the prelude to outright revolution. Others feared a takeover of their city by gangs of criminals and unemployed laborers. And all looked expectantly for signs of underlying "conspiracy." Newspaper comment rose to a highly emotional pitch, with the rally's organizers likened to devouring animals—"hyenas . . .

vermin . . . wolves." Police dragnets brought the arrest of several dozen local activists, many of whom according to one breathless account, "looked like communists."

Failing to identify the actual bomb-thrower, detectives and prosecutors focused on radical leaders who had supposedly "encouraged . . . by print or speech" the resort to violence. Trials were held in late summer. The state's attorney described to the court an "anarchist conspiracy . . . beyond the pale of moral forces." (Even "the firing upon Fort Sumter [at the onset of the Civil War] . . . was," he declared, "as nothing compared with this insidious, infamous plot to ruin our laws and our country secretly.") Ten anarchist and socialist leaders were indicted, eight were tried and convicted, and seven were sentenced to death. In the end, four would actually be executed and a fifth committed suicide, while the sentences of the remaining pair were commuted to life in prison.

The riot itself, the follow-up investigation, and the court proceedings all made sensational news, reported in detail throughout the country. Fears of a similar "uprising" rippled along to other cities and towns, especially those in which radical groups were most active. Police raids on socialist meeting halls became a frequent occurrence. In some communities vigilantes acted on their own to suppress the "traitors" in their midst. Labor groups, too, suffered frequent harassment; union organizing was widely seen as a cover for revolutionary "plots." Many of the Haymarket principals were of German birth (or extraction); thus, in 1888, a Chicago congressman introduced legislation "to provide for the removal of dangerous aliens from the territory of the United States." The link between radical activism and foreign influence would henceforth remain a staple of common belief.

Was it a witch-hunt? In this case we can start with difference. Haymarket activism was real, was visible, was openly challenging toward the status quo. At some points this included explicit advocacy of revolutionary goals; it also included possibly violent tactics, up to and including the use of incendiary bombs. Whereas accused witches had generally denied the char-

acterization given them, the Haymarket leaders acknowledged their radical stance: indeed they were proud of it. (Another difference was the preponderance among these leaders/victims of men. So, once again, gender is a mostly "missing" element.) And yet: the threat they posed was limited. Their numbers were few and their resources pitifully small when compared to the forces arrayed against them. Simply put, the Haymarket episode was an instance of massive overreaction; the word "hysteria" seems not out of place here. Again, there was the sense of vast conspiratorial design, of apocalyptic danger, of alien contagion abroad in the land—all of this infused with wildly overheated emotion.

Reaction to Haymarket helped move the center of the labor movement in a strongly anti-socialist direction. The American Federation of Labor (AFL), founded just months after the riot, would quickly achieve preeminence; most (not all) of its member units embraced "pure and simple unionism," short-term goals, and gradualist methods. But other unions, such as the International Workers of the World (IWW), espoused a more confrontational approach, and labor strife continued into the new century at a generally high level. This, along with the assassination of President William McKinley by a professed (perhaps crazed) anarchist, helped keep antiradical feeling alive. There were also political assassinations of several European heads of state during roughly the same time period. And socialist organizing proceeded apace on both sides of the ocean.

Then came the "Great War" of 1914–18, with all its concurrent suffering and death—and, in its final year, the triumph of Bolshevism in Russia and Marxist-inspired revolts elsewhere across Europe. American participation in the war was limited in time (18 months) but massive in scale (nearly one million men in uniform). Rising military fervor helped spawn a clutch of patriotic organizations like the National Security League and the American Defense Society. Their initial focus was the German enemy in the field, and pro-German "collaborators" at home. (Thanks in part to their efforts, the teaching of the German language was outlawed in many school systems, and some individual Americans of German descent went so far as to adopt new surnames.) When radical activists opposed the war on political grounds, public animus turned in that direction, too. Congress enacted laws to criminalize both action and speech against the government: most notably, the Espionage Act of 1917 and the Sedition Act of 1918. These enabled proceedings against socialist leaders like Victor Berger and Eugene Debs, both of whom were eventually jailed.

The Great Red Scare (1919–20)

With the armistice of November 1918, the American economy began a difficult process of readjustment to peacetime production; there was rapid price inflation, and then a sharp rise in unemployment. And there were strikes, strikes, and more strikes: some 3,600, involving over four million workers, during the year 1919 alone. Several of these attained huge proportions. First came the Seattle general strike of January–February, starting as a walkout by shipyard workers and quickly joined by many from other industries. The city was temporarily paralyzed; federal troops were called in, and police were fully mobilized. The more conservative labor organizations, such as the AFL, declined appeals for support, and most of the strikers returned to work after just a few days. But by then public opinion had been seriously engaged against them, in Seattle and around the country.

In late spring, a series of riveting labor conflicts unfolded across the border in Winnipeg, Canada. These were also of a "general" nature—and, unlike any of their predecessors, led to a virtual takeover of city government by a special strikers' "council." Though outside U.S. territory, the Winnipeg strike was close enough, and violent enough, to frighten many who already sensed a tide of revolution gathering around them. Summer brought the threat of a national strike, and accompanying demonstrations, to the United States itself. Plans to begin were set for July 4; the immediate goal was to force the release of jailed labor activist Tom Mooney. When faced with another massive police mobilization, the organizers drew back; however, the mere prospect served to heighten still further a general feeling of alarm.

Autumn brought an absolute peak in the strike-ridden year of 1919: in early September, a police walkout in Boston; later the same month, the start of a nationwide steel strike; and six weeks after that, a broadscale stoppage by mineworkers in the coalfields of the East and upper Midwest. Each of these three major actions was met by forceful counteraction, both in the courts and on the streets. Each provoked sporadic, occasionally lethal, violence. (The Boston police strike led to citywide outbreaks of vandalism. And clashes between strikers and strikebreakers in several midwestern steel towns produced death, injury, and widespread property damage.) Each aroused fearful, outraged reaction from the public at large. And this, in turn, was effectively exploited—not to say, enhanced—by corporate employers and their politically conservative allies.

Finally, each was immediately, and heatedly, linked with "Red Revolution"—in spite of the fact that all were framed by quite limited, labor-related objectives. Consider some newspaper headlines: BOLSHEVIST NIGHTMARE. LENIN AND TROTSKY ARE ON THEIR WAY. SENATORS THINK EFFORT TO SOVIETIZE THE GOVERNMENT IS STARTED. REVOLUTION IS STAKE RADICALS PLAY FOR IN STRIKE OF MINERS. RED BOLSHEVISM DIRECTS BLOW AGAINST THE NATION. A cartoon in the *New York World,* with the caption "Steel Strike," depicted a heavily muscled arm upthrust from a cluster of factory buildings, and holding high a banner bearing the single word "RED." Another cartoon, in the *Seattle Post-Intelligencer,* portrayed an enormous foot labeled "Coal Strike" about to stomp on the dome of the nation's Capitol building.

In fact, this extraordinary year included many other tumultuous happenings: the discovery of bomb plots (especially in Seattle); the founding of two separate Communist parties; race riots in several cities (Chicago, Washington, Houston) as black citizens, including many recently returned veterans, fought off assault by whites. (Another newspaper headline to mention: REDS TRY TO STIR NEGROES TO

REVOLT.) To list such events—and more could be added—is to acknowledge some genuine cause for alarm. Yet never was there the slightest prospect of actual "revolution"; and official response—including the actions of both federal and local authorities—was, by any measure, extreme.

The "Great Red Scare," as it would later be called, rode atop a wave of angry public opinion. In the press, from church pulpits, in community forums across the land, the cry rang out: "Down with the Reds!" Suspicion turned in many directions—toward avowed radicals, first of all, but also toward labor organizers, teachers, some journalists and social workers, plus a large and more nebulous grouping of so-called parlor Reds (in short, anyone who might be construed as sympathetic to "Bolshevism").

These attitudes would sustain a broad and severe campaign of suppression during the late fall and early winter. Its opening phase came in November, with antisubversive roundups by federal authorities in at least a dozen cities: the total of arrests ran into the hundreds. Local and state governments followed with raids of their own; in New York, for example, a legislative committee headed by state senator Clayton R. Lusk conducted investigations leading to the detention, and deportation, of numerous "alien" radicals. (Deporting those who were noncitizens was often the preferred strategy, since it involved only an administrative proceeding, not a full-blown prosecution in court.)

The climax came just after the New Year. On a single night (January 2) the nation's attorney general, A. Mitchell Palmer, sent federal agents in 23 different states on a massive sweep directed largely at members of the two recently founded Communist parties. The net yield was over 6,000 detainees. Some of these would be quickly deported, while others were prosecuted under the criminal statutes of individual states. Public reaction was, at first, hugely enthusiastic and congratulatory. Opinion-makers across the land saluted Palmer and his corps of enforcers; the raids were seen as tolling the "death knell" of radicalism.

Subsequent events, however, proved anticlimactic. Protests against the treatment of detainees, including the sometimes disgraceful conditions of their incarceration, generated a growing backlash. Proceedings in the courts and the various administrative boards became increasingly bogged down; eventually, many of those held had to be released for lack of evidence. Palmer and his zealous young assistant, J. Edgar Hoover (soon to become the first director of the Federal Bureau of Investigation), sought to fan the flames of alarm by anticipating new conspiracies. But when their prediction of revolutionary violence on May Day failed to pan out, public interest began to fade.

Yet in many ways, the Great Red Scare had already achieved its goal of anchoring anti-radical attitudes at the center of the national mainstream. The rest of the 1920s would bring no reprise of the Palmer raids, but there was hardly any need. Sedition laws had by now gained a place on the statute books of a large majority of individual states. And, at the level of local governance, police "red squads" held political activists on a generally tight leash. The federal government, meanwhile, enacted and enforced a set of massively restrictive immigration measures, with quotas designed to maintain the demographic lead of "old-stock" Americans. Although the famous Sacco-Vanzetti trial of 1921 replayed the familiar "alien radical" theme, in actual fact aliens of all kinds were a rapidly shrinking presence. Culturally, too, the dominant note was a xenophobic brand of patriotism, nicely captured in the popular phrase "100 percent Americanism."

So . . . was it a witch-hunt? The pattern grows familiar with each succeeding case. The strongest points in favor once again involve ideation and imagination—an alien conspiracy, vast in scope and size, with fundamentally subversive goals, and creating an aura of immense danger—all of this enhanced by disproportionately strong emotion. Moreover, the Palmer raids and subsequent court trials expressed the "hunt" aspect with special clarity. And the process, as it went forward, developed the usual "spiral" effect (with one case leading on to others), as well as a powerful drive toward "purification" (by extruding the alien poison). The "missing" parts are, as before, misogyny and overtly religious/moral sponsorship. The overall picture seems broadly similar to what appeared in the previous Red Scare, following Haymarket.

If the 1920s were bounded at one end by the Great Red Scare, they were equally marked at the other by the Great Depression. Now the deck would be reshuffled once again, with large-scale anti-radical campaigns effectively coming to an end. Indeed, the era of the New Deal opened a door—at least partway—to radical change, in the face of ever-deepening, society-wide distress. The Communist Party itself gained a certain legitimacy denied it heretofore, and sought to exploit opportunities for "popular front" alliances with other left-of-center political forces.

Anti-communism retreated, but hardly disappeared. Indeed, the end of the 1930s saw its partial revival—and, in a preview of things to come, the beginnings of its transformation into a potent tool of partisan politics. New Deal Democrats were increasingly painted "pink" by Republican opponents. The House Un-American Activities Committee (HUAC) was born with a mandate to hunt down subversion. And the so-called Smith Act, passed by Congress in 1940, made it a crime to advocate overthrowing the government by force.

The Second World War introduced another abrupt break in this unfolding tableau; the "Reds" became allies, both at home and overseas, in the struggle against fascism. But once more the effect was temporary; and the immediate postwar era brought a rapid resurgence of anti-radical, anti-communist feeling.

The McCarthy Era (1950–54)

The second great Red Scare of the 20th century was born in the aftermath of the 1946 congressional elections. Republicans had gained control of both Houses for the first time in nearly two decades, in part by associating their Democratic opponents with "radical" attitudes. The Cold War, though still in its infancy, was a source of growing public alarm. The administration of President Truman responded to these changed circumstances by instituting "loyalty" programs designed to weed out potential subversives within the federal government and by initiating a series of prosecutions under the Smith Act. Meanwhile, a reinvigorated HUAC undertook a new round of investigations, centering this time on infiltration of the movie industry; eventually these would lead to prison terms for a so-called Hollywood Ten, as well as a "blacklist" to prevent employment of other presumed radicals.

Truman's upset victory in the 1948 presidential elections did not deflect the onrushing anti-Communist tide. In the months to follow, the American side experienced a string of Cold War setbacks: the "fall" of China to Maoist forces, the acquisition by the Soviet Union of nuclear weaponry, and the invasion of South Korea by the Communist-ruled North. By now, too, public suspicion had turned forcefully toward (alleged) Communist penetration of the New Deal, personified in the figure of Alger Hiss (a high official in the Roosevelt-era State Department). Hiss had been linked to espionage, and, in the fall of 1949, was tried, convicted, and jailed on charges of perjury. The Hiss case led to other loyalty proceedings against officials in the State and Justice departments; thus was a spiral of politically fraught investigations set in motion. Local and state governments joined the fray with loyalty campaigns of their own, while liberal groups and unions scrambled to rid themselves of the "Red" taint. The Truman administration was itself obliged to fight off politically damning charges of being "soft on Communism."

With this, a stage was set for the emergence of the single most notorious anti-communist warrior of the entire century: Joseph R. McCarthy, a hitherto obscure Republican senator from Wisconsin. McCarthy's opening salvo was a speech delivered in February 1950, in Wheeling, West Virginia, in the course of which he brandished a list supposedly identifying 205 "card-carrying" Communists then at work in the State Department. The number would vary over time—205 one day, 57 the next—but the very idea of a list, with its implied specificity, was electrifying. Moreover, events soon conspired to lift McCarthy's profile enormously. Actual spies, it seemed, had penetrated to the heart of nuclear development programs both at home and abroad: hence the arrest, in quick succession, of Klaus Fuchs in Britain and Julius and Ethel Rosenberg in the United States. McCarthy had begun by targeting government officials of modest rank but would subsequently raise his aim to the level of Secretary of Defense George C. Marshall. Summing up the entire lot, he decried "a conspiracy so immense and an infamy so black as to dwarf any previous venture in the history of man."

But McCarthy was just the centerpiece—in some respects more symbolic than substantive—of a steadily building, polity-wide "crusade." Elected officials across-the-board, including many Democrats, were following a similar track. In 1950 the Senate passed an Internal Security Act, extending political surveillance from the operations of government to private organizations and individuals. Membership in the Communist Party would henceforth be a crime; and potential "security risk," rather than simple "loyalty," became the disqualifying marker for federal employment. The Senate Internal Security Subcommittee began a new round of investigations, paralleling and occasionally exceeding the efforts of HUAC. Meanwhile, too, the Justice Department stepped up the pace of prosecutions under the Smith Act; eventually, dozens of actual or supposed Communists would be jailed. The FBI under Hoover played an especially important role here, compiling secret dossiers on thousands of American citizens (plus some noncitizens) and selectively releasing the contents to those agencies and officials most fully sympathetic to the anti-communist agenda. And Hoover played an increasingly influential part as public spokesman. "Communists," he declared in a widely noted 1950 address, "are today at work within the very gates of America. . . . They have . . . one diabolic ambition: to weaken and to eventually destroy American democracy by stealth and cunning."

Thus did "McCarthyism" enter the mainstream of political life. And soon it would be augmented by powerful elements within the press, the business community (for example, a number of enormously wealthy Texas oilmen), the churches (especially evangelical Protestants and conservative Catholics), veterans groups, patriotic associations, and even some trade unions. Many of these sought to make a direct contribution to the anti-communist cause by weeding out "subversives" within their own ranks. Still, government itself remained the leading arm of attack. When Republicans triumphed in the 1952 national elections—taking control once again of both congressional Houses and making Dwight Eisenhower president—McCarthy gained a committee chairmanship to use as a forum for further investigation. The campaign had included much anti-communist rhetoric, with Democrats widely denounced for overseeing "twenty years of treason" and McCarthy cast in a central role; a respected political commentator could therefore conclude that "the voting majority indicated approval of . . . McCarthyism." In the weeks and months to follow, the newly vindicated senator and his like-minded colleagues would pluck the fruits of their victory.

Loyalty review boards increased their efforts against security risks in the federal workforce. Over 1,000 such had been discovered and dismissed during the last years of the Truman administration, and another 1,500 would depart in the Eisenhower era. Most were low- or middle-echelon operatives: secretaries, clerks, engineers, supervisors, and the like. But at least a few were distinguished civil servants and diplomats, including several in the State Department held responsible for "losing China" to Maoism. (Of course, the suffering and loss, to families as well as to the individuals directly involved, was huge in all cases—no matter the differences in position.)

Even as this process continued, attention was shifting more and more toward "subversives" in various fields outside the government. There was a growing sense of peril to ordinary citizens from the covert designs of Red-leaning schoolteachers, journalists, social workers and other seeming "do-gooders," and even some in the churches.

Hundreds of teachers would lose their jobs in states like New York and California, and many of those who remained were compelled to sign loyalty oaths. Universities were similarly affected; leading professors resigned in protest or were summarily fired. The Hollywood blacklist expanded to include dozens more actors, producers, and directors—and was extended to the television industry as well. In all this, HUAC, its Senate counterparts, and other investigatory bodies both expressed and intensified deep-seated public anxieties about Communist "indoctrination."

The wave of fear about domestic subversion crested, and began to recede, in 1954. And McCarthy himself was first to fall. His popular support, as measured by opinion surveys, reached its highest level that January, but he would soon make a fatal strategic error. He had already begun, in the previous year, a politically hazardous probe of "disloyal tendencies" among the staff at a military base in New Jersey; in short order this would embroil him with high-ranking officers and then with the secretary of the army, Robert T. Stevens. The subsequent Army-McCarthy hearings degenerated into farce, with McCarthy at the witness table, mixing baldly gratuitous smears of his adversaries with endless procedural interventions. Television covered the entire proceeding, and millions watched as it stretched through one embarrassing week after another. By the end, McCarthy's reputation was shattered. The Eisenhower White House, previously diffident toward nearly all his activities, at last offered direct criticism. A colleague (and fellow Republican) introduced in the Senate a formal motion of censure, which was passed in December by a solid, bipartisan majority; henceforth he was largely ignored by both press and public. With his health undermined by alcoholism, McCarthy would die a scant three years later.

For almost the last time we ask: was it a witch-hunt? Indeed, it was labeled that way far more often, and to more telling effect, than any of the preceding "scares." The reason is obvious. Arthur Miller's remarkable play The Crucible—*holding up the Salem trials as a kind of dark mirror to McCarthyism—was written and performed virtually at its height. Herein lies the chief source of our fondness for the metaphor ever since. But, again: with what basis in the actual events? Let us count the ways, most of them by now entirely familiar. "A conspiracy so immense" (in McCarthy's own words). To be achieved by "stealth and cunning" (Hoover's words). Prompted by "diabolic ambition" (Hoover again). Of alien origin (the Soviet Union). With a highly authoritarian structure (the Communist Party). Liable to infect the unwitting ("dupes" in government and elsewhere). And thus requiring a vigorous purge (blacklisting, deportation, imprisonment). Meanwhile, in those who supported the "hunt": revulsion, outrage, deep anxiety, a will to revenge. And the whole framed in starkly moral, and bipolar, terms: Good versus Evil, the God-inspired versus the Godless. However, there is no particular sign of a gendered element. And the impetus—the sponsorship— seems more overtly political than in our other cases: Republicans seizing a fine opportunity to belabor Democrats.*

McCarthy's personal and political disgrace cast a long shadow over the anti-communist project. And there were broader changes afoot. With a Republican president in office, anti-communism as a partisan tool seemed largely irrelevant. Moreover, the end of the Korean War, the death of the Soviet dictator Stalin, the opening of deep schisms within the Communist bloc, the growing strength of the Western alliance: these factors, separately and together, served to blur the sense of inhabiting a bifurcated world with apocalypse looming. The Cold War was becoming a manageable, livable situation; the siege mentality it had initially fostered began to weaken. Both public opinion and government itself turned away from extreme preoccupation with "security" issues. The Supreme Court, in particular, rendered a series of crucial decisions redefining and restricting the investigative powers of congressional committees, the FBI, and other federal agencies. The very word "McCarthyism" became, for many, a kind of epithet.

Beginning in the late 1950s, a "liberal consensus" would set a new and different tone, and last through the next two decades. In 1980 the pendulum swung back, with the emergence of a "conservative consensus." In neither case did attacks on the weak domestic

Communist Party play a major role. Thus was the "Red" bogeyman, which had so bedeviled American public life for almost a century, finally laid to rest.

We have five cases—or "episodes"—before us. And they do yield a broadly consistent picture.

All began with the aspect of "scare." This is to say that all were fueled by extraordinarily strong, widely shared emotion—fear, most especially, but also anger, distress, contempt. And so, too, were the witch-hunts once fueled.

All produced a vivid idea—an image—of their adversaries that was wildly exaggerated, not to say fantastic. Its chief components were conspiracy, secrecy and deception, vast dimensions, deeply subversive purpose, alien origin, unseen contamination (and contagion), authoritarianism, moral polarities, and potentially apocalyptic menace. (The proportions would vary somewhat from one case to another.) And these were also key components of witch-hunting.

Most, if not all, traced a process that included the following stages: identification (of the enemy), magnification (of his inherent qualities and powers), intense and "spiraling" investigation (where one accusation leads directly to others), and measures, finally, of social exclusion. Here, too, lay evident and important parallels to witch-hunting.

Some, though not all, proceeded under one or another form of elite sponsorship: for example, an economic elite (corporate enterprise), or a political one (partisan leadership). In traditional witch-hunting, the sponsorship typically came from a religious elite—in short, the Church hierarchy.

In each case, the underlying social and psychological vectors included what clinicians call "projection" or "externalization" (attributing to others unwanted parts of oneself), plus a closely related urge toward purity, unity, and inner coherence. No less was true of witch-hunting.

And yet the likeness is not complete. Some differences of degree, and of procedure, must be acknowledged. None of our five modern episodes included outright torture, a notorious feature of many traditional witch-

hunts. And in only one (Haymarket) were death sentences imposed and carried out. Moreover: in no case does a strongly gendered element appear. Men were the principal targets (though not exclusively so). This was, presumably, a function of men's dominant public position since the events themselves belonged to the public domain. Witch-hunting, in strong contrast, was deeply—and lethally—misogynous.

There remains, finally, the difficult issue of "reality"—an "actual" basis, or stimulus, to set the whole chain in motion. There were Communists in America during the McCarthy era, at least a few of whom—we now know—were Soviet spies. There were "Reds" of various kinds at the time of the Palmer raids, some of whom did seek to advance revolutionary goals. There were strident labor activists to spark the Haymarket affair. There were Freemasons galore in the 1820s and '30s, ensconced in their lodges and devoted to their fraternal "rites." There was even a Society of Illuminati in the late 18th century, though perhaps without any significant American membership. In every case, then, the feelings of "scare"—and the image they conjured up—had some relation, however remote, to real people and actual events.

Might one also have found "actual" witches in pre-modern times? Certainly contemporaries thought so. Witchcraft was an assumed part of their cosmological world; its mostly unseen, but strongly felt, presence was to them beyond doubt. Here, then, the boundary between the actual and the imagined grows blurred. The safest conclusion about these various events—witch-hunts in both the literal and the metaphorical sense—is that all included extraordinary forms and levels of exaggeration, misperception, and (at some points) outright fantasy. Put differently: the distance between any actual stimulus, on the one side, and the prevalent imagery (and concurrent emotion), on the other, was huge. In the end, it is this distance—these extreme distortions—that best define witch-hunting.

There is a final commonality here: an intense and pervasive preoccupation with questions of loyalty. In the pre-modern era, this meant loyalty to organized Christianity, with witches cast as a deeply undermining force. In late 18th- and 19th-century America, with both "Illuminism" and the Masons, it meant loyalty to "republican freedom." In the 20th century, with the postwar Red Scares, it meant loyalty to the values of democracy and individualism. In each case, the figure of the accused directly inverted a core allegiance.

In sum, the elements of likeness, all the crosscutting commonalities, do seem to outweigh the differences; the metaphor includes much that justifies it. A version of witch-hunting has indeed survived into the modern era. In fact, it has reached into our own lifetimes, appearing here and there in the very recent past. A striking example comes from the 1980s and early '90s; in many ways it brings this entire history full circle—back even to the workings of Satan and his (supposed) earthly followers.

The Child Sex-Abuse Crisis (1983–circa 1995)

It became, in the blunt words of two prize-winning investigative reporters, "a witch-hunt unparalleled in modern times." Its focal period was 1983–88, though its closing phase stretched on for considerably longer. Its geographic dimensions were nationwide, though individual cases fell disproportionately on the West and East coasts. And its similarity to pre-modern witch-hunting was openly recognized—indeed emphasized—virtually from the start, though mostly by its critics and victims.

In retrospect, one could almost see it coming. The decades of the 1960s and '70s had been famously unsettling with their turbulent "movement" politics and a broad array of challenges to received convention. There was a war fought in the face of massive public opposition, and "lost" (for the first time ever, it was said, in American history). There was a broad-gauge revamping of gender roles, with women entering the workforce in unprecedented numbers. There was a step-by-step relaxation of traditional constraints on personal behavior, including dress, deportment, and common speech. There was a "sexual revolution," in tandem with a new contraceptive technology ("the pill"), and a reversal of legal barriers to abortion. There was a whole galaxy of "liberation" struggles around previously disadvantaged minorities.

Parts of this ferment were pointed straight toward the inner workings of family life. In the early 1960s, the deeply troubling problem of child battering was first "discovered" and publicly acknowledged, setting in motion a train of policy initiatives that would culminate a dozen years later with important congressional legislation (the Child Abuse Prevention and Treatment Act of 1974, also known as the Mondale Act after its chief sponsor, the then-senator Walter Mondale). Another so-called discovery, related but different, was father-daughter incest; this, too, sparked high levels of public alarm. The apparent growth of religious "cults" seemed to present special enticements—and dangers—to young people, prompting parents to form advocacy groups dedicated to the goal of "deprogramming." Concern for "missing children," their numbers estimated as high as 50,000 per year, led to widely publicized campaigns of retrieval. Anxiety descended even to the commonplace level of Halloween crime: apples and candy supposedly laced with razor blades or poisons in order to injure innocent young trick-or-treaters. Finally, the growth (however modest) of Wicca and related "occult" practice generated dark fears of Satanism. (A 1973 survey showed that half of Americans believed in Satan as a literal, personified presence; a decade later, fully 70 percent were found to credit the existence of sexually abusive, Satanic cults.) A spate of books published around 1980 presented, by way of "recovered memory," victim accounts of ritual assault in childhood at the hands of organized Devil worshipers.

The underlying realities here spanned a broad range. Child battering and incest were real enough; perpetrators could be identified in large numbers. Most "missing children" however, turned out to be runaways or the unfortunate victims of custody disputes. Halloween crime was, for the most part, an urban legend. And "recovered memory" remains highly controversial to the present day. Still, all these trends—no matter the reality—helped build a mood of fearfulness around the current state, and future prospects, of the family. Meanwhile, too, the divorce rate continued to rise, reaching a much-noted peak of half of all marriages begun in the 1970s. In sum: community turmoil; family disintegration; children in peril. And fear, guilt, outrage, in fateful convergence: a recipe for crisis if ever there was one.

It began in California, with the apparent exposure of a "sex ring" in Bakersfield (at the lower end of the Great Central Valley) and then of an abusive day-care center in Manhattan Beach (near Los Angeles). The resultant investigations laid down a double template for a nationwide "crusade" to follow.

The Bakersfield case emerged during the spring and summer of 1982, out of the tangled relations of a single family group. Indeed, one person, a 37-year-old grandmother, previously diagnosed by psychiatrists as paranoid and delusional, was the source of all the initial accusations. According to this informant, her two young step-granddaughters had been repeatedly molested by several adult relatives (including their mother) and family friends. In due course the county prosecutor, abetted by staff of the local child protection agency, decided to press charges. The upshot was a trial in May 1984—and the conviction of four defendants, each of whom received a sentence of 240 years in prison. From this point on, events mushroomed astoundingly. Soon investigators had identified no fewer than eight supposed sex rings in and around Bakersfield, involving hundreds of suspects (including a district attorney, a deputy sheriff, and several social workers). Moreover, Satanism was added to the rapidly fermenting mix; new charges included not only child rape, sodomy, and pornographic filmmaking, but also the ritual killing of infants and animals—plus black candles, strange disguises, and other such accoutrements of Devil worship. As the web of accusation spread ever wider, and the substance of the allegations strained all credulity, Kern County leaders turned openly skeptical—and the state attorney general's office chose to characterize the whole affair as an unfounded "panic." There were no further trials; however, several of those already convicted would remain in jail for another decade or more.

Meanwhile, 100 miles to the south, seeds of suspicion began to sprout at the McMartin preschool in the affluent suburban community of Manhattan Beach. As in Bakersfield, there was at first just one accuser: a parent who claimed that her four-year-old son had been sodomized by a male teacher. Local police took her seriously enough to send an official letter of warning to the families of 200 current or former McMartin students. This, in turn, sounded a community-wide alarm, and led some parents to believe that their children, too, had been victimized. Prosecutors, private investigators, and therapists who specialized in detecting child abuse all joined in the subsequent investigation; the children involved underwent round after round of intensive questioning. Their answers—most given after initial denials and under great pressure—ran roughly the same gamut as at Bakersfield, from predatory sex acts to ritualized Satanism. The result was a brace of charges not only against the initial suspect but also including his grandmother (the founder of the preschool), his mother and sister (both of them staff members), and several other teachers as well. (A further result was a string of spinoff investigations, 63 in all, at other day-care centers in the greater Los Angeles area; none of these, however, led to formal charges.) Like Bakersfield, the McMartin case would ultimately collapse of its own weight. But unlike Bakersfield, the legal process was so prolonged and so bitterly fought—at 28 months it became the lengthiest, and at $15 million the costliest, prosecution in American history—that no actual convictions were ever returned.

As noted, Bakersfield and McMartin set the pace for dozens, perhaps hundreds, of subsequent investigations. And McMartin, in particular, got the entire nation's attention: newspapers and network television followed its winding course from start to finish. Most of this early publicity tilted strongly in favor of the prosecution and thus encouraged similar proceedings elsewhere. The final dimensions of the entire sequence—numbers of communities, of suspects, of supposed victims—may never be known. A survey of 36 different prosecutions begun between 1983 and 1988 yielded the following totals: 91 individuals charged, 45 dismissed (without trial), 11 acquitted, 23 convicted, and 12 whose cases (at that time) were still undecided. But clearly this was just a fraction of the whole. The figure for those charged should, for a start, be multiplied several times over in order to approach the total of suspects. And the number of individuals directly concerned, in one way or another, must have gone much higher still.

Some cases were small and quickly resolved; others developed the same lethal spiral evidenced at Bakersfield and McMartin. Among the larger ones—for example, Jordan, Minnesota (1983), Chicago (1984), Memphis (1984), El Paso, (1984), the Bronx (1985), and Malden, Massachusetts (1986)—nearly all fell into either the sex-ring or the day-care abuse category. There were some distinctions between the two. Sex-ring prosecutions, those without linkage to day-care or school settings, most often appeared in lower-middle- and working-class communities. The majority of day-care abuse cases, by contrast, involved white-collar and professional folk. With sex rings, moreover, the emphasis on Satanism was usually much stronger. Yet cases of both kinds showed a core of similar elements: parents taking the lead; children asked (or urged, or coaxed, or cajoled) to produce the crucial accusations; zealous prosecutors and child-abuse "experts" eager to push matters into the courts. And through it all coursed such strong emotional currents that families, friendships, even whole communities, could be bitterly riven apart.

The accusing side maintained an absolute commitment to the sacred cause of child protection. (The flavor here was nicely captured in a comment by the judge who sentenced the Bakersfield defendants: "They have stolen from the children the most precious of gifts—a child's innocence.") The accused, for their part, recoiled in shocked bewilderment. And both sides felt—as deeply as possible, though for different reasons—fear, and rage, and a sense of utter betrayal.

There was, in addition, a certain commonality in the details of the abuse allegations. Sexual assault (rape, sodomy, fellatio) was everywhere the starting point. But much else would be added: ritual acts of urination and defecation; objects (sticks, knives, combs, beads) poked into various bodily orifices; nude photography; animal sacrifice; digging up or burying corpses; the consumption of human blood and flesh; rides in vans, buses, and airplanes; crawling through tunnels and secret passageways; capes and hoods and graveyards; and so on. Much of this was connected—by the adults involved, if not always by the accusing children—with Satanism. Its recurrence in widely different settings was taken by some as the indisputable sign of a nation-spanning conspiracy.

There was another kind of commonality—in the methods used by the various investigators. As with the trials of medieval and early modern times, a deep wish—a compulsion, really—for punitive retribution was the animating core; ends and means were framed accordingly. Many of the children involved were, at first, unwilling to accuse their caretakers; some strongly rejected the whole idea through hours and hours of pointed questioning. But their interrogators persisted, prodded, offered leading suggestions, promised rewards for more "complete" answers, and otherwise pushed toward the desired (not to say predetermined) outcome. An additional, highly unusual, and controversial tactic was the deployment of "anatomically correct" dolls in games designed to elicit stories of abuse. (When videotapes of the interview process were shown in court, the McMartin jury drew back; indeed, this aspect, more than any other, seems to have turned it against the prosecution case.) Legal precedents were also repeatedly modified in deference to the very young age of the witnesses. Testimony might be filmed, rather than given in person, so as to spare them from encountering their (supposed) abusers. And hearsay was sometimes allowed as evidence—for example, in a parent's report of his child's allegations.

These novelties would eventually undermine the entire project of investigation. And the implausibility, the sheer extravagance, of some of the charges would have the same effect. But it all took considerable time. The number, and scope, of abuse cases—having risen dramatically throughout 1984 and peaked the following year—then began an overall decline. Yet even as late as 1995, a sensational sex-ring prosecution was mounted in the city of Wenatchee, Washington. Indeed, the last embers of this extraordinary conflagration are smoldering still; many of the original convicts remain in prison, and a variety of civil suits filed by the wrongly accused remain unresolved. Nonetheless, it should be possible now to take some measure of the whole.

The approach followed by investigators has been largely discredited: their resort to coercive (or at least highly suggestive) questioning of the children involved; their propensity to doubt whenever a supposed victim denied abuse, and to believe—virtually *without* doubt—any and all allegations that fitted their own theories. In these matters "children do not lie": thus the credo they clung to. (However, as both empirical studies and common experience affirm, children *do* wish to please adults, and *will* yield to insistent pressure, including both rewards and threats, and *can* "fabricate"—a more accurate term than "lie"—when the stakes are raised sufficiently high.)

Many of the substantive charges—airplane rides, hidden tunnels, buried corpses, the entire array of supposed satanic practices—have also been discredited. (At some sites investigators carried out large-scale excavations in search of bones, costume fragments, and other physical evidence; their yield, in every instance, was nil.) To be sure a rejection of these more fanciful elements does not mean that sex abuse never happened. But it does throw deep shadows of doubt on all the child testimony. The safest conclusion is that while there may have been actual abusive episodes, the number cannot have been large. And, whatever their basis in fact, the suspicions so widely aroused—and the accusations so loudly voiced—led on to a process of elaboration that soon spun massively out of control.

It remains, finally, to weigh the costs incurred, the damage done, the victims created in the course of this sprawling "crisis." Any list of victims must begin with the supposed perpetrators, most of them (possibly all?) charged with crimes they did not commit. To be sure, none were executed, or tortured, or otherwise injured in a physical sense. However, the psychological toll on them, the financial drain, the wounds to personal and professional reputation—not to mention the years lost to incarceration—all this was immense and incalculable. A list of victims should also include those who tried to defend friends and neighbors wrongfully charged and who then became "suspect" (and legally vulnerable) themselves. More than a few saw their own lives radically disrupted: endured personal threats and harassment, lost work or public office, were driven from their homes and forced to relocate. A final category embraces the child accusers themselves—or, rather, the children who were turned into accusers by the adults around them. Though not victims in the sense initially supposed, they did nevertheless *become* victims in a different sense. Many of them have since gone through an agonizing process of readjustment and reappraisal—disavowing as best they can the roles they were once obliged to play, tormented by the harm they now know they brought on others. Some, indeed, feel a crushing burden of guilt, a kind of inner scarring that warps their lives to the present day.

In truth, the victims were many—and of several sorts. And of victors, there were none. So again we may ask: *Was it a witch-hunt?* Consider, as this book's almost-end, a single case—a virtual epitome of the entire subject.

CHAPTER XII

Fells Acres Day School:
A Question of Abuse

April 1984; Malden, Massachusetts. At the Fells Acres Day School, a care center for young children, a four-year-old boy (newly enrolled) wets his pants during nap time. His teacher asks a fellow staff member named Gerald Amirault to take charge of changing his clothes. The two of them repair to a bathroom; dry clothes are found; the boy is changed and returned to his class.

At home that evening—and on many other evenings, both before and after—the boy seems distressed. He is given to frequent bed-wetting, tantrums, lying and concealment, regression to baby talk. His mother, who is just then in the midst of a painful separation from the boy's father, feels a mounting concern. She wonders whether her son has somehow been molested, as her brother was years ago. She mentions the brother's experience to her son.

Some weeks later the boy is discovered in sex play with a cousin, which further alarms his mother; she questions him closely about it. His uncle (the previously molested brother) also speaks with him, as does a hospital therapist. These sessions continue at intervals throughout the summer. Initially, and for some time thereafter, the boy makes no mention of the Day School and its staff. In late August, however, he tells his uncle that Gerald Amirault took his pants down. This leads to deepening suspicion and more questioning; finally, a direct line of accusation opens up. (Over four months have passed since it all began.) Now—according to his mother and uncle—the boy reports that Gerald has repeatedly put him in blindfold, taken him to a "secret room" containing a bed and "golden trophies," undressed him, and involved him in a variety of sex acts.

On September 2, the mother calls a government hotline to report Gerald for abusing her child. On September 4, local police enter the school to obtain enrollment lists. The next day they arrest Gerald, and announce a meeting with Fells Acres parents the following week at the Malden police station. On September 7, Gerald posts bail, leaves prison, and arrives home just in time for the birth of his third child.

By this point rumor and worry are spreading through the community; other Day School parents have begun asking their own children about the "secret room" and the events to which it is linked. On September 11, state authorities close the school. September 12 brings the much anticipated parents' meeting with the police; more than a hundred attend. The agenda features an elaborate portrayal of abuse "symptoms": bed-wetting, nightmares, appetite loss, and so on. (When reviewed later on, all of these will seem consistent with more or less ordinary childhood experience.) Parents are urged to "go home and question your children, and don't take no for an answer." According to some, the officer in charge also comments: "God forbid you say anything good about these people [the Day School staff], or your children will never tell you anything."

This is more than enough to launch a storm of panic among the families involved. The pace of questioning with the children—by parents, police, and therapists—is drastically increased. In the coming weeks and months, at least 19 three-, four-, and five-year-olds will be subjected to interviews lasting, in some cases, an hour and a half. Not one of them volunteers an accusation on his or her own. Many give firm denials when urged to offer more. Several spontaneously declare their liking for the school, and their wish to go back. But such responses are discounted by the authorities as indicative of a child who is "not ready to disclose." One police investigator will later compare the entire interview process to "getting blood from a stone." Eventually, however, repeated inquiry—and outright prodding— brings the desired result: a web of accusation that grows to envelop all the teachers at the school, plus a few mysterious outsiders. (At least one of the children implicates a policeman, another mentions a therapist, a third describes the occasional presence of robots equipped with flashing lights.)

A sample from the interview of a little girl, identified only as J.O., by a pediatric nurse will serve to illustrate the typical sequence. The nurse produces an "anatomically correct" doll, and says: "Let's pretend this little girl doll is at Fells Acres, okay?" She poses a set of linked questions, ending with: "What would happen if someone touched her [the doll's] vagina? Would she be sad?" She then turns directly toward J.O. and asks whether anyone at the Day School has ever touched her vagina. Receiving no reply, she adopts a somewhat disapproving tone, and suggests that perhaps J.O. feels "too scared to talk." Throughout this entire exchange (if it was an exchange), the little girl has not accused anyone of anything.

Other children, faced with similar questioning, are more responsive:

"Tooky [Gerald Amirault's nickname] took out his peepee and . . . [urinated] in front of us."

A clown came to the school and "spanked us on the bum-bum and on the face, too."

Another clown came and "took out his peepee, and told us to take our clothes off, and put it between our legs." (Investigators will subsequently conclude that Gerald had frequently dressed in clown costume.)

"Miss Vi [Violet Amirault] made me eat a frog. . . . The frog went quack-quack."

"Miss Cheryl [Amirault] took icky pictures of us."

"Tooky . . . was disguised as a bad lobster."

A mysterious man who came to visit looked like "a wicked witch with a mask that doesn't come off."

A teacher "took all the good kids to jail at the police office."

"Tooky was sorry for chopping me into little pieces."

The children played "an elephant game . . . [where] you lick ice cream off the elephant . . . in Tooky's lap."

There were puppet shows, in the midst of which "they made us kids take our pants off and hold each other's peepees."

The children were driven across town to a house, where "from the inside I see monsters."

"There is a forest next to the school with monsters and witches in it."

"Sixteen kids have died from that school. . . . Kids have been killed and hurt."

The investigation will continue through nearly three years. Local news coverage is extensive and generally favorable to the prosecution. Public interest is high, and still growing. There are threats of vigilante action; according to later reports, Gerald is chased on the streets of his hometown, and on two separate occasions shots are fired into his house. (Local police take no protective action.) In January 1985, with the charges still accumulating, grand jury indictments are secured against three of the alleged perpetrators: Gerald; his mother, Violet; and his sister, Cheryl.

Malden is one of the oldest communities in Massachusetts. Originally part of Charlestown, the site of a very early witchcraft prosecution, it gained separate incorporation in 1649. Boston lay across the Mystic River to the south. There were hills and rocky outcroppings to the north. And in between lay fertile meadows and marshland. A visitor in the early 18th century described the town as "fruitful and well cultivated, being entirely cleared and enclosed with stone fences."

From its traditional farm-based economy and orthodox Puritan tone, Malden gradually evolved toward the medium-size, diversified city it is today. Its now nearly 60,000 residents are predominantly, though not exclusively, white, including many of 19th- and 20th-century immigrant stock. Most would qualify as middle- or working-class; only a few are truly affluent. Its spatial configuration is a checkerboard of quite distinct neighborhoods; typically, these are organized around small squares or parks. The housing stock ranges from numerous multifamily dwellings ("triple-deckers"), to occasional clusters of fine old Victorian homes, to some newly constructed redevelopment units. There are many local businesses scattered about and several factories. In spite of its fundamentally urban character, Malden likes to claim a "small-town feel."

It was amid this rather unremarkable environment that the Fells

Acres Day School was founded (1964), when Violet Amirault—then a recently divorced mother of three, eager to escape welfare—decided to open a care center for local toddlers in the basement of her home. From there the school expanded and flourished impressively, moving in short order to its own space and acquiring a strongly positive reputation among hundreds of grateful families. Through almost two decades not a single serious complaint was brought against it.

As Violet's children grew to adulthood, the school itself became a family operation, with daughter Cheryl coming on as a teacher and Gerald serving as a kind of handyman-assistant. In due course, Gerald's wife, Patti, also joined in. By now Fells Acres was serving some 70 pupils, with a staff of around 10 and Violet acting as principal. When Cheryl married in 1983, the entire school was invited to the wedding, and the pews of the Immaculate Conception Church were packed with wide-eyed children eager to support a favorite teacher. The start of the "abuse" investigation was barely a year away.

Gerald's trial begins on April 29, 1986, in Middlesex County Court, with Judge Elizabeth Dolan presiding. From the outset there are some highly unusual arrangements. The Fells Acres children are seated, as a group, on small chairs down in front, with their parents just behind; this means the defendant is out of their line of sight. (One child will testify only by videotape; apparently he is too frightened to be there in person.) The judge removes her official robes, leaves the bench, and sits beside the children.

The prosecution outlines its case and opens the questioning. The children answer in a mostly halting tone; jury and spectators alike strain to hear. Some begin by denying any knowledge of abuse. When that happens, the prosecutors are allowed to reframe, and re-ask, the same question. And sooner or later, they get what they are looking for.

The children's testimony has been carefully rehearsed (as they readily acknowledge). On the whole, it follows the pattern of their many previous interviews with therapists and others—sprawling across a broad range, but returning frequently to the "secret room" (also called the "magic room") and the various sex acts allegedly performed there. The latter include: mastur-

bation, fellatio, anal and vaginal intercourse, plus frequent picture taking in the nude. The prosecutors have struggled from the start to discover a motive behind the crimes at the school. And now they feel they have one: the production, and sale, of child pornography. Thus they make much of cameras and film seized on school property. (When examined closely, however, the photographic subjects seem innocent enough: birthday parties, classroom games, swimming lessons, nothing more.) In addition, they offer graphic descriptions of worldwide "rings" devoted to "kiddie porn." (But none of these can be linked, even remotely, to Fells Acres.)

There is some physical evidence as well—or so the prosecution contends. A pediatrician is called to testify about small signs of hymenal scarring and vaginitis in two or three of the little girls involved. The defense counters that such conditions are relatively common in children, for all sorts of reasons having nothing to do with abuse (soaps, minor infections, even tight-fitting clothes).

Meanwhile, 17 former staff members offer testimony on behalf of the accused. They know of no school space that could conceivably have served as a "secret room." (Nor could the children ever identify—or the police ever discover—any such area.) They saw none of the usual indicators of abusive treatment (bruises, lacerations, emotional stress). Moreover, the school was an open setting, with parents, deliverymen, and others coming and going on a frequent basis; how, then, could so much criminal activity have remained entirely unobserved?

On July 8, the case goes to the jury. Eleven days later, after 64 hours of actual deliberation—the longest such time period in Massachusetts trial history—the jury returns a verdict: guilty on all counts. A month later, Judge Dolan pronounces sentence: Gerald must serve 30 to 40 years in prison.

The prosecution turns next to Violet and Cheryl, who will be tried together. Their case begins on June 1 of the following year, with Judge Paul Sullivan presiding. Once again the children are seated so as not to face the accused. Their testimony covers by-now familiar ground: the "secret room," coercive sex, nude photography. As before, some of it strains the limits of credulity. One child was hung upside down and made to eat white pills.

Another was sodomized by Violet with a 12-inch butcher knife (but apparently emerged without injury). A third watched Cheryl cut the leg off a squirrel. A fourth was undressed and tied to a tree—at midmorning, in front of the school, and facing a busy street. A fifth was accosted by a robot, which twirled her around and bit her on the arm. A baby was murdered, a dog was butchered (with its blood buried in a sandbox), bears and elephants and raccoons wandered by. As with Gerald's trial, the prosecution—and the press coverage as well—tends to ignore these more fantastic elements.

Once again, teachers, teachers' aides, and school visitors are called as defense witnesses. And once again, they report having seen nothing at all untoward. But it makes no difference; the children's testimony easily trumps theirs. The trial lasts 11 days. And this time the jury deliberates for only a few hours. Violet and Cheryl are, like Gerald, convicted on all counts. Their sentences are identical but somewhat less than his: imprisonment for 8 to 20 years.

With the second trial ended, the Fells Acres case moves into a less focused, more protracted phase. The scope of public interest widens considerably as events in the Middlesex courtroom are joined to a "crisis" of national proportions. The final, inconclusive result of the McMartin case in California gives at least some cause for reflection and reconsideration. In this shifting context, the Middlesex district attorney's office reaches an important decision. Even though other teachers besides the three Amiraults have been accused, charges will not be brought against them.

In the meantime, Violet and Cheryl go off to prison. The years to follow will bring a steady stream of appeals, motions for a new trial, and other efforts on their behalf. It is, however, very slow going. In 1992, their parole request is turned down because they refuse demands to acknowledge guilt. In 1995, a judge new to the case, Robert A. Barton, accepts their motion for retrial and releases them on bail. (A similar motion by Gerald, in a different court, is rejected.) Further legal maneuvers lead, finally, to an extended hearing before the state's Supreme Judicial Court (1997).

But this court revokes the previous retrial order, meaning both women will have to return to jail. Chief Justice Charles Fried writes the opinion for a not quite unanimous majority. (One judge stands apart and produces a

long, impassioned dissent.) According to Fried, there were indeed question-
able aspects to the prior legal proceedings, including some encroachment on
constitutional rights. Nonetheless "the community's interest in finality"
overrides all other considerations. "The mere fact that if the process were
redone, there might be a different outcome, or that some lingering doubt
about the first outcome may remain, cannot be a sufficient reason to reopen
what society has a right to consider closed."

That same summer, Violet is diagnosed with terminal stomach cancer;
she will die in September. Cheryl, still temporarily free on bail, looks after
her; Gerald is allowed to leave prison, in shackles, for a single, brief fare-
well. Meanwhile, defense lawyers renew their efforts—and the momentum
begins to shift slowly in their direction. Judge Barton recuses himself from
further participation, saying he can no longer be "fair and impartial" given
his personal belief that the accused "did not receive a fair trial, and justice
was not done." In June 1998, his replacement, Judge Isaac Borenstein, grants
Cheryl a retrial under very different ground rules, noting "serious, over-
whelming errors" in the earlier proceedings. But this, too, will be reversed on
appeal to the Supreme Judicial Court. Finally, in October 1999, Cheryl's
lawyers strike a deal with the district attorney that revises her sentence to
time served and sets a number of highly restrictive conditions for her re-
lease; apparently, it is the best she can hope for.

Gerald will have to wait several years more for a similar opportunity.
In 2001, the state's parole board votes unanimously in his favor, but then-
governor Jane Swift turns down its recommendation. In October 2003, his
renewed application for parole is granted. Yet he remains in jail while
the district attorney determines whether or not to commit him to an institu-
tion as a "sexually dangerous person." That decision will, at long last, be
made in his favor; on April 30, 2004, he goes home on parole. Even so, he is
given official classification as a Level Three (that is, extremely serious) sex
offender—a stigma he will carry, presumably, for the rest of his life.

As events in the courts veered to and fro, the press, the wider legal
community, and professional psychologists began a series of linked
debates about what had really happened (or not happened) at Fells

Acres (and elsewhere). Both major Boston newspapers, the *Boston Globe* and the *Boston Herald American*, supported the prosecution throughout—explicitly on their editorial pages, implicitly in their news coverage. Asked about this after her release, Cheryl answered simply, "What came out of the media lies was a jury that convicted me." Eventually, to be sure, a counter-viewpoint appeared, first and foremost in the *Wall Street Journal*. There, a tenacious reporter named Dorothy Rabinowitz began a series of highly critical articles on Fells Acres. These would win her a Pulitzer Prize and lead to a powerfully written book entitled *No Crueler Tyrannies: Accusation, False Witness, and Other Terrors of Our Times*.

Lawyers and legal scholars also entered the building controversy. Hallway discussion turned into op-eds and articles in the trade journals, and then into full-dress professional conferences. The focus was courtroom procedure—where, time after time, serious "error" had appeared. To begin with, the physical arrangements were flawed: special chairs, judges leaving the bench, and so on. The shielding of child witnesses, however solicitous of their tender years, violated the basic constitutional right of every defendant to face an accuser. Moreover, indictments were unusually broad. And hearsay testimony was freely admitted. Judges declined to intervene when prosecutors engaged in suggestive or downright coercive questioning. Then there was Justice Fried's extraordinary supreme court opinion, elevating "finality" over due process and the right to a fair trial. (In short: justice be damned?) One state official would subsequently call this "the most cold-blooded decision I have ever read."

Psychologists and psychiatrists had been involved right from the start. Some who claimed that status were, indeed, among the lead interviewers of the Day School children. Their own use of suggestive questioning would seem, in retrospect, utterly transparent. At first, and for some considerable time, they helped validate the prosecutors' mantra that "children cannot lie" about abuse. But other psychologists worked hard to discredit this idea. The courts would eventually hear, from professionals describing carefully framed research, how "interviewer bias" might reshape a child's understanding of objectively innocent events and thus "induce" a particular result.

Finally, there was politics. Scott Harshbarger, the first of the hard-charging district attorneys, was a rising star in the Massachusetts Democratic Party. From his post in Middlesex County he would ascend to the office of state attorney general and then run a failed race for governor. Tom Reilly, his assistant and successor in Middlesex, would follow exactly the same path, from DA to AG to not-quite governor. Both used the Fells Acres case as a political stepping-stone. Both rose, then fell, along the changing curve of public attitudes toward it. And neither one ever expressed the slightest doubt, or regret, about participating in it. Three successive governors were pressed to intervene by offering pardons or paroles. All shied away, fearing the possible electoral consequences. Other careers were also affected—those of the key judges, for example. Fried remains a vaunted law school professor (Harvard), but his stature among jurists has been diminished. Barton and Borenstein, by contrast, have emerged as admired figures.

Malden to Salem is barely a dozen miles. A half-hour's drive today, or a morning's cart-ride in the 17th century, might end at Gallows Hill. The distance between the 1692 witch-hunt in the one place, and the 1980s abuse case in the other, is not so far, either. Consider:

Families, as well as individuals, lock together in bitter conflict.

A panic atmosphere builds, with one suspicion leading rapidly to others.

A sense of the demonic—literally so at Salem, figuratively so at Fells Acres—serves as the animating core.

The judicial system is immediately, and fully, engaged. In each case there are "hanging judges" (albeit with the same literal/figurative distinction attached). Chief Justice Charles Fried seems a virtual "specter" of his notorious 17th-century predecessors, magistrate John Hathorne and Chief Judge William Stoughton.

Intense, prolonged interrogation assumes central importance, with professionals in charge—ministers and magistrates at Salem, therapists and
prosecutors at Fells Acres.

Legal and moral precedents are tossed aside in the heat of the moment,
with "the community's interest" superseding justice.

Victim testimony is a key point of controversy, especially "spectral" evidence at Salem, and "induced" charges at Fells Acres. In both cases, inherent evidentiary weakness will lead finally to retreat.

Children are centrally positioned—somewhat older ones at Salem,
somewhat younger at Fells Acres. They play a role that has, in effect, been
assigned them by their elders.

And there remains this question, also bridging the centuries, and cutting to the heart of both "tragedies." By whom have the children been abused?
Not by witches. Nor by pedophiles or pornographers. But rather—however
unwittingly—by the adults around them. By those who would protect them.
By their families, their parents, most of all.

Epilogue

Chelmsford, England, 1582. When Alice Glasscock was charged with practicing witchcraft, the indictment described her also as "a naughty woman."

Marchtal, Germany, 1623. When Ursula Götz was warned away from the village festival by her neighbors because of her supposed status as a witch, they pointedly called her "shitty."

New Haven, Connecticut, 1656. At the court where Elizabeth Godman was tried for bewitching her neighbor's chickens, witnesses assailed her as "a malicious one."

Salem, Massachusetts, 1692. As Martha Carrier stood amidst a pack of howling girls, supposedly her victims, she heard herself denounced as "a very angry woman."

Time after time, these and other witch-hunt targets were charged not just with "entertaining Satan," and not simply with bringing maleficent harm down on their peers, but also with a broad array of characterological and social failings. Here is a further sampling of the traits attributed to one or another accused witch: "spiteful," "maliciously bent," "of turbulent spirit"; "discontented," "impatient," "very intemperate"; "vile," "terrible," "evil"; "light woman," "common harlot," "bad neighbor," "wicked creature." Again, these descriptors spoke less of the formal matter of witchcraft and Satanism than of everyday bits of human experience. Taken together, they set a kind of negative template for entire cultures or historical eras; as such they clearly, and powerfully, identified the enemy within the larger group. Moreover, a similar role and function could also be ascribed to the figurative witches of modern times—to the targets of political Red Scares and of day-care "abuse" investigations.

But this enemy *is*—present tense from here on—not only a social creature, a subversive element poised to ravage community life. He or she also resides within each of the countless persons who fear, and hunt, witches—is, in short, integral to the individual self, to ego, to "I." Moreover, just as communities occasionally seek to excise unwanted persons from within their midst, so, too, does the self strive to extrude troublesome aspects of its own structure. The latter may include sexual impulse (as in much of Catholic Europe during the craze period); aggression and the urge to attack (as with Puritan groups in early modern Anglo-America); or envy, greed, and guilt (depending on the given historical situation). They may also involve, at a much more immediate and mundane level, whatever is meant by "naughty," "shitty," "malicious," "angry," and so on. This is what clinicians call "projection," and it infuses witch-hunting in the deepest possible way. Always and everywhere, the witch is the designated recipient of projection, the carrier, the symbol. He or she stands for—and, in a sense, is made to absorb—an unacknowledged "dark side" from the inner life of the hunters.

On all counts, then, witch-hunting involves process more than any specific content. And it is, finally, this double sense of "within" that invests process with such extraordinary force: *the individual and the group—the I as well as the we—on the hunt, in lethal combination.*

These last reflections may serve to underscore the ubiquity, the near universality of witch-hunting. Each and every one of the witch-hunts described here had a very particular location in time and space. No two were exactly alike; all must be approached as individually distinct events. Yet they bear as well a shared relation to the general, Euro-American, Judeo-Christian, "Western" tradition; none can be fully understood apart from that broadly influential baseline. Finally, they do embody tendencies that cross every frontier of time, place, and culture; hence they qualify, in effect, as part of the "human condition."

But, surely, theirs is a tragic and uniquely destructive part—and witch-hunting, considered whole, is nothing less than a scourge. Which leaves an author, and perhaps his readers too, pondering this question: Is a world without witch-hunts achievable, or even imaginable? In trying to answer, we might consider an ironic distinction. The "witches" we discover around us are molded by extraordinary pressures of distortion, exaggeration, reification; often enough, they are fabricated wholesale. Hence, as a *social* presence they are much more fictive than actual. However, the corresponding psychological element—the fantasy of witchcraft, the concomitant affects, the impulse to projection—is all too real. More than anything else, this constitutes the enemy which has through the centuries exacted such a terrible toll. To reduce its power is no easy task. Yet by deepening knowledge of both self and society, we create at least an opening for change. To that most important process "history" offers its own hopeful, if uncertain, contribution.

Bibliographic Commentary

Because this book is aimed more toward a general than a professional audience, it does not include footnoting or other scholarly apparatus. The commentary below is meant simply to identify its main foundations in research and secondary literature, and to offer suggestions for readers interested in pursuing a specific topical area.

CHAPTER ONE

This account of the Lyon "martyrdom" is based on W. H. C. Frend, *Martyrdom and Persecution in the Early Christian Church* (Oxford, U.K., 1965); see especially chapter 1. Valuable material can also be found in the essays for a 1977 conference (Lyon, France) on the same subject, published under the title *Les Martyrs de Lyon* (Paris, 1978). The most important period source for these events is the Roman author Eusebius; see Eusebius, *The Ecclesiastical History*, Kirsopp Lake, trans. (London, 1926), book 5. For discussion of religion, economy, and other aspects of community life in 2nd-century Lyon, see *Les Martyrs de Lyon*, passim.

CHAPTER TWO

During the past 40 years, the study of European witchcraft has reached levels of sophistication without parallel for any other topical area in the early modern period. By now there are literally dozens of first-rate works, covering many different regions and centuries, and written by historians of uncommon distinction. The following list is necessarily limited to the most valuable (and only to those published in English-language editions). The first of the major contributions was H. R. Trevor-Roper, "The European Witch-Craze in the Sixteenth and Seventeenth Centuries," in *The European*

Witch-craze of the Sixteenth and Seventeenth Centuries, and Other Essays (New York, 1967). This was soon followed by Keith Thomas, *Religion and the Decline of Magic* (New York, 1971), a truly magisterial work that set the agenda for a host of subsequent projects. Other early, broad-gauge accounts include Norman Cohn, *Europe's Inner Demons: An Enquiry Inspired by the Great Witch-Hunt* (London, 1975), and Brian P. Levack, *The Witch-Hunt in Early Modern Europe* (New York, 1985). A somewhat later, summative book of much depth and power is Robin Briggs, *Witches and Neighbors: The Social and Cultural Context of European Witchcraft* (London, 1996). And perhaps the finest single work in this entire array is Stuart Clark, *Thinking with Demons: The Idea of Witchcraft in Early Modern Europe* (Oxford, U.K., 1997), a remarkably compendious joining of social, intellectual, and cultural perspectives. Other studies of more limited focus are as follows. On witchcraft in the medieval period: Geoffrey Burton Russell, *Witchcraft in the Middle Ages* (Ithaca, N.Y., 1972); Edward Peters, *The Magician, the Witch, and the Law* (Philadelphia, 1978); and Richard Kieckhefer, *European Witch Trials: Their Foundations in Popular and Learned Cultures, 1300–1500* (London, 1976). On witchcraft in the British Isles: Alan Macfarlane, *Witchcraft in Tudor and Stuart England* (New York, 1970); James Sharpe, *Instruments of Darkness: Witchcraft in England, 1550–1750* (London, 1996); Malcolm Gaskill, *Witchfinders: A Seventeenth-Century English Tragedy* (London, 2005); Christina Larner, *Enemies of God: The Witch-Hunt in Scotland* (London, 1981); and Christina Larner, *Witchcraft and Religion: The Politics of Popular Belief*, ed. Alan Macfarlane (New York, 1984). On witchcraft in continental Europe, especially during the period of the great witch-hunt: H. C. Erik Midelfort, *Witch-Hunting in Southwestern Germany, 1562–1684: The Social and Intellectual Foundations* (Stanford, Calif., 1972); E. William Monter, *Witchcraft in France and Switzerland: The Borderlands During the Reformation* (Ithaca, N.Y., 1976); Carlo Ginzburg, *The Night Battles: Witchcraft and Agrarian Cults in the Sixteenth and Seventeenth Centuries* (Baltimore, Md., 1983); Ginzburg, *Ecstasies: Deciphering the Witches' Sabbath* (London, 1990); and Lyndal Roper, *Witch Craze: Terror and Fantasy in Baroque Germany* (New Haven, Conn., 2005). Finally, on witchcraft history after the 17th century: Ronald Hutton, *Triumph of the Moon: A History of Modern Pagan Witchcraft* (New York, 1999), and Owen Davies, *Witchcraft, Magic, and Culture, 1736–1951* (Manchester, U.K., 1999).

CHAPTER THREE

Since its publication in 1486, the *Malleus Maleficarum*, by Heinrich Kramer (or Institoris, his Latin name) and Jacob Sprenger has undergone numerous reprintings in many languages. Until recently, the most accessible English version—and the one used for the present chapter—was Montague Summers, ed. and trans. (London, 1928; repr. New York, 1948 and 1971). A new and definitive edition has just appeared: Christopher Mackay, *Malleus Maleficarum* (2 volumes, New York, 2007). Useful comment on the *Malleus* can be found in Sydney Anglo, ed., *The Damned Art: Essays in the Literature of Witchcraft* (London, 1977), and the papers from a 1987 conference (Bayreuth, Germany) published in Peter Segl, ed., *Der Hexenhammer: Enstehung und umfeld des malleus maleficarum von 1487* (Cologne/Berlin, 1988). On the career of Summers, see Joseph Jerome, *Montague Summers* (London, 1965), and Summers's own *The Galanty Show: An Autobiography* (London, 1980). The paragraphs with which this chapter concludes present entries taken from the online bookseller Amazon.com.

CHAPTER FOUR

The Windsor, Connecticut, witchcraft case of 1654 has been pieced together from legal evidence published in *Records of the Particular Court of Connecticut, 1639–1663* (Connecticut Historical Society, *Collections*, vol. 22), passim, and personal documents included in Homer Worthington Brainerd et al., *The Gilbert Family* (New Haven, Conn., 1953). Details in the chapter's opening section—on the training-field accident that claimed Henry Stiles's life—are transposed from what is known generally about early New England militia activities. The final section, imagining the way the town's minister might have preached on this event, is based on actual sermons given in response to similar situations: for example, Deodat Lawson, "Christ's Fidelity the Only Shield Against Satan's Malignity" (2nd ed., London, 1704) and Samuel Willard, "Useful Instructions for a Professing People in Times of Great Security and Degeneracy" (Cambridge, Mass., 1673). On the settlement and early history of Windsor, see Henry R. Stiles, *History of Ancient Windsor, Connecticut* (New York, 1859) and Linda A. Bissell, "Family, Friends, and Neighbors: Social Interaction in Seventeenth-Century Windsor, Connecticut," Ph.D. dissertation, Brandeis University (1973).

CHAPTER FIVE

The bulk of this chapter is rooted in the author's own archival research, much of it carried out in the 1970s and published in *Entertaining Satan: Witchcraft and the Culture of Early New England* (New York, 1982). But newer work has also been incorporated where appropriate. For a useful overview of magic and popular religion in colonial America as a whole, see Jon Butler, "Magic, Astrology, and the Early American Religious Heritage 1600–1760," *American Historical Review*, 84:317–46 (1979); and see also scattered references to the same matters in Butler, *Awash in a Sea of Faith: Christianizing the American People* (Cambridge, Mass., 1990), passim. For recent discussions specific to early New England, see Richard Godbeer, *The Devil's Dominion: Magic and Religion in Early New England* (New York, 1992); Richard Godbeer, *Escaping Salem: The Other Witch Hunt of 1692* (New York, 2005); David D. Hall, *Worlds of Wonder, Days of Judgment: Popular Religious Belief in Early New England* (New York, 1989); Carol Karlsen, *The Devil in the Shape of a Woman: Witchcraft in Colonial New England* (New York, 1987); Elizabeth Reis, *Damned Women: Sinners and Witches in Puritan New England* (Ithaca, N.Y., 1997); and Richard Weisman, *Witchcraft, Magic, and Religion in Seventeenth-Century Massachusetts* (Amherst, Mass., 1984). Scholarly work on witchcraft among the various colonial populations outside New England is quite thin. On Virginia, see Philip Alexander Bruce, *The Institutional History of Virginia in the Seventeenth Century*, vol. 2 (New York, 1893), ch. 25. Materials from the last witch trial in Virginia (or anywhere in the colonies) are published in George Lincoln Burr, ed., *Narratives of the Witchcraft Cases, 1648–1706* (New York, 1914), 435–42. For cases of witch prosecution in New York and Pennsylvania, see ibid., 39–52, 79–88; see also Amandus Johnson, *The Swedish Settlements on the Delaware, 1638–1664*, vol. 2 (New York, 1911), 454–60. For Maryland cases, see Hester Dorsey Richardson, *Side-Lights on Maryland History* (Baltimore, Md., 1908), ch. 31. On colonists' perceptions of Native American witchcraft and "devil worship," see Alfred Cave, "Indian Shamans and English Witches," *Essex Institute Historical Collections*, 128:241–54 (1992); David S. Lovejoy, "Satanizing the American Indian," *New England Quarterly*, 67:603–21 (1994); and William S. Simmons, "Cultural Bias in the New England Puritan Perception of Indians," *William and Mary Quarterly*, 3rd ser., 38:56–72 (1981). On witchcraft, sorcery, and "poison" among African American slaves, and the response of their owners, see Philip D. Morgan, *Slave Counterpoint: Black Culture in the Eighteenth-Century Chesapeake and Lowcountry* (Chapel Hill, N.C., 1998), 610–25 and passim.

CHAPTER SIX

A somewhat different rendering of the story of Mary Parsons, accused witch, appears in John Demos, *Entertaining Satan: Witchcraft and the Culture of Early New England* (New York, 1982), ch. 8. A lengthy file of manuscript depositions from the several Parsons trials is in the Middlesex County, Massachusetts, Court Papers: Original Depositions and Other Materials (Middlesex County Courthouse, Cambridge, Mass.), folder 16, papers 626, 646–74; other testimonies are published in Samuel G. Drake, *Annals of Witchcraft in New England* (New York, 1869), 219–56; and in Joseph H. Smith, ed., *Colonial Justice in Western Massachusetts* (Cambridge, Mass., 1961), passim. Genealogical material for the Blisses, Mary Parsons's natal family, can be found in *The American Genealogist*, 52:193–97 (1976); and in John Homer Bliss, *The Genealogy of the Bliss Family in America* (Boston, 1881); for the Lymans, in Mary Lovering Holman, *Ancestry of Colonel John Harrington Stevens* (Concord. N.H., 1948), 383–87; and in Coleman Lyman, *Genealogy of the Lyman Family in Great Britain and America* (Albany, N.Y., 1872); and for the Bridgmans, in Joseph Clark Bridgman, *Genealogy of the Bridgman Family* (Hyde Park, Mass., 1894). See also Henry M. Burt, *Cornet Joseph Parsons* (Garden City, N.Y., 1898). Other evidence bearing on the intertwined lives of these families appears in *Records of the Particular Court of Connecticut, 1639–1663* (Connecticut Historical Society, *Collections*, vol. 22) and Colonial Records of Connecticut (ms. Archives, Connecticut State Library, Hartford, Conn.), passim. Several local histories include pertinent information; for example, Joseph Russell Trumbull, *The History of Northampton, Mass.* (Northampton, Mass., 1898); Mason A. Green, *Springfield, 1636–86* (Springfield, Mass., 1888); and Stephen Innes, *Labor in a New Land: Economy and Society in Seventeenth-Century Springfield* (Princeton, N.J., 1983). The vignette with which the chapter begins—presenting a conversation among three local women—is imagined.

CHAPTER SEVEN

Materials from, and about, the trial of Rebecca Nurse are plentiful. A full transcript of her examination and indictment, together with witness testimonies for and against her and petitions on her behalf, can be found in Paul Boyer and Stephen Nissenbaum, eds., *The Salem Witchcraft Papers: Verbatim Transcripts of the Legal Documents of the Salem Witchcraft Outbreak of 1692* (New York, 1977), vol. 2, 583–608. Accounts by contemporaries include Deodat Lawson, *A Brief and True Narrative of Some Remarkable Passages Relating to . . . Witchcraft* (Boston, 1692), and Robert Calef, *More Wonders of the Invisible World* (London, 1700). Both are reprinted in George Lincoln Burr, *Narratives of the Witchcraft Cases, 1648–1706* (New York, 1914); see especially 157–60, 357–60. A sympathetic description of her case, with some useful family history, appears in Charles S. Tapley, *Rebecca Nurse: Saint But Witch Victim* (Boston, 1930). Of course, she also figures prominently in all the recent histories of the Salem witch-hunt. (See references for chapter 8.) A Nurse family genealogy is included in Sidney Perley, *The History of Salem, Mass.* vol. 2 (Salem, 1924–28), 143. For material on the long-standing dispute between members of the Towne, Nurse, and Putnam families, see Persis McMillen, *Currents of Malice: Mary Towne Esty and Her Family in Salem Witchcraft* (Portsmouth, N.H., 1990); pertinent legal evidence on the same matters is presented in Paul Boyer and Stephen Nissenbaum, eds., *Salem Village Witchcraft: A Documentary History of Local Conflict in Colonial New England* (New York, 1972), 148–54, 235–37. A lengthy discussion of the vicissitudes of the Putnam family (principal accusers of Rebecca Nurse in the witch trials) can be found in Boyer and Nissenbaum, *Salem Possessed: The Social Origins of Witchcraft* (Cambridge, Mass., 1974), ch. 5. A Putnam genealogy is in Perley, *History of Salem*, vol. 2, 109–11; see also Eben Putnam, *A History of the Putnam Family* (Salem, Mass., 1891). The chapter's concluding section recounts a visit to pertinent sites by the author and Penelope (Demos) Lawrence.

CHAPTER EIGHT

The literature on the Salem witch-hunt is enormous: only a fraction can be noted here. The single most comprehensive treatment—a virtual encyclopedia of the entire affair, referencing hundreds of individual participants—is

Marilynne K. Roach, *The Salem Witch Trials: A Day-by-Day Chronicle of a Community Under Siege* (New York, 2002). Most (not all) of the manuscript trial records are in the Essex County Court Archives, Salem Witchcraft Papers, currently on deposit in the James Duncan Phelps Library, Peabody Essex Museum, Salem, Massachusetts. Most of these, in turn, are published in Paul Boyer and Stephen Nissenbaum, eds., *The Salem Witchcraft Papers: Verbatim Transcripts of the Legal Documents of the Salem Witchcraft Outbreak of 1692* (New York, 1977); a new and fuller edition is forthcoming. A sampling of sermons and other contemporaneous writings on the trials can be found in George Lincoln Burr, *Narratives of the Witchcraft Cases, 1648–1706* (New York, 1914). The rest of these notes will cite the various works discussed in the chapter's concluding section. In order of appearance they are: John Hale, *A Modest Enquiry into the Nature of Witchcraft* (Boston, 1702); Thomas Hutchinson, *The History of the Colony and Province of Massachusetts Bay*, 2 vols. (Boston, 1764; repr. Cambridge, Mass., 1936); George Bancroft, *History of the United States from the Discovery of the American Continent*, 11 vols. (Boston, 1834–75); Charles W. Upham, *Salem Witchcraft* (Boston, 1867); George M. Beard, *The Psychology of the Salem Witchcraft Excitement of 1692* (New York, 1882); James Truslow Adams, *The Founding of New England* (Boston, 1921); Vernon L. Parrington, *Main Currents of American Thought: The Colonial Mind, 1620–1800* (New York, 1927); Samuel Eliot Morison, *The Puritan Pronaos: Studies in the Intellectual Life of New England in the Seventeenth Century* (Cambridge, Mass., 1936); Perry Miller, *The New England Mind: The Seventeenth Century* (Boston, 1939); Ernest Caulfield, "Pediatric Aspects of the Salem Witchcraft Tragedy," *American Journal of Diseases of Children*, 65:788–802 (1943); Marion L. Starkey, *The Devil in Massachusetts: A Modern Enquiry Into the Salem Witch Trials* (New York, 1949); Arthur Miller, *The Crucible* (New York, 1952); Kai T. Erikson, *Wayward Puritans: A Study in the Sociology of Deviance* (New York, 1966); Chadwick Hansen, *Witchcraft at Salem* (New York, 1969); Paul Boyer and Stephen Nissenbaum, *Salem Possessed: The Social Origins of Witchcraft* (Cambridge, Mass., 1974); Linda Caporeal, "Ergotism: The Satan Loosed in Salem," *Science*, 194:1390–94 (1976); Nicholas P. Spanos and Jack Gottlieb, "Ergotism and the Salem Witch Trials," *Science*, 194:1390–94 (1976); Mary K. Matossian, "Ergot and the Salem Witchcraft Affair," *American Scientist* (July–Aug. 1982), 185–92; Matossian,

Poisons of the Past: Molds, Epidemics, and History (New Haven, Conn., 1989); Carol Karlsen, *The Devil in the Shape of a Woman: Witchcraft in Colonial New England* (New York, 1987); Larry Gragg, *The Salem Witch Crisis* (Westport, Conn., 1992); Bernard Rosenthal, *Salem Story: Reading the Salem Witch Trials of 1692* (New York, 1993); Peter Hoffer, *The Devil's Disciples: Makers of the Salem Witch Trials* (Baltimore, Md., 1996); Frances Hill, *A Delusion of Satan: The Full Story of the Salem Witch Trials* (New York, 1995); Laurie Carlson, *A Fever in Salem: A New Interpretation of the New England Witch Trials* (Chicago, 1999); and Mary Beth Norton, *In The Devil's Snare: The Salem Witchcraft Crisis of 1692* (New York, 2002). For a general view of the early history of Salem, see Sidney Perley, *The History of Salem, Massachusetts*, 3 vols. (Boston, 1928), and James Duncan Phillips, *Salem in the Seventeenth Century* (Boston, 1933).

CHAPTER NINE

This account of Cotton Mather's career, emphasizing his involvement in witchcraft cases, is based heavily on two excellent biographies: Kenneth Silverman, *The Life and Times of Cotton Mather* (New York, 1984), and David Levin, *Cotton Mather: The Young Life of the Lord's Remembrancer* (Cambridge, Mass., 1978). See also the judicious appraisal by Richard H. Werking, "'Reformation Is Our Only Preservation': Cotton Mather and Salem Witchcraft," in *William and Mary Quarterly*, third ser., 29:281–90 (1972). Earlier discussions of the same question include: Charles W. Upham, "Salem Witchcraft and Cotton Mather," *Historical Magazine*, second ser., 6:129–219 (Sept. 1869), and W. F. Poole, "Cotton Mather and Salem Witchcraft," *North American Review*, 108:337–97 (April 1869). For an overview of the long debate about Mather's role in the Salem trials, see Chadwick Hansen, *Witchcraft at Salem* (New York, 1969), xi–xiv. Hansen offers his own view of the matter in ibid., 95–102, 171–72, 194–95. Mather's original writings on witchcraft, too numerous to be listed here, are referenced in the aforementioned works.

CHAPTER TEN

The two most authoritative works on anti-Masonry are Paul Goodman, *Towards a Christian Republic: Antimasonry and the Great Transition in New England, 1826–1836* (New York, 1988), and William Preston Vaughn, *The Antimasonic*

Party in the United States, 1826–1843 (Lexington, Ky., 1983); both have been extensively mined for this chapter. See also: Ronald P. Formisano and Kathleen Smith Kutolowski, "Antimasonry and Masonry: The Genesis of Protest, 1826–1827," in *American Quarterly*, 29:139–65 (1977); Kutolowski, "Freemasonry and Community in the Early Republic: The Case for Antimasonic Activities," *American Quarterly*, 34:543–61 (1982); Kutolowski, "Antimasonry Reexamined: Social Bases of the Grass-Roots Party," *Journal of American History*, 71:269–93 (1984); and Michael F. Holt, "The Antimasonic and Know Nothing Parties," in *History of U.S. Political Parties*, Arthur M. Schlesinger, Jr., ed. (New York, 1973), vol. 1, 583–89. These works, in turn, are based on primary research in anti-Masonic newspaper and pamphlet literature, local records, and personal papers; a large file of such material has been gathered by Paul Goodman and deposited at the Library of the University of California, Berkeley.

CHAPTER ELEVEN

The coverage of this chapter is very broad; so, too, are its bibliographical foundations. The opening section, on the survival of witchcraft belief in America after the 17th century, draws on research into folklore and local history; see, for example, Samuel A. Drake, *A Book of New England Legends and Folklore* (Boston, 1902). On the gradual decline in the strength and salience of such belief, see John Demos, *Entertaining Satan: Witchcraft and the Culture of Early New England* (New York, 1982), 387–94, and Herbert Leventhal, *In the Shadow of the Enlightenment: Occultism and Renaissance Science in Eighteenth-Century America* (New York, 1976). On modern-day Wicca and related "neo-pagan" practice, a useful introduction is Sabrina Magliocco, *Witching Culture: Folklore and Neo-Paganism in America* (Philadelphia, 2004). For a detailed, ethnographic portrayal, see T. M. Luhrmann, *Persuasions of the Witch's Craft* (Cambridge, Mass., 1989). On the historical roots of the movement, especially the key role played by Gerald Broussard Gardner, see Ronald Hutton, *The Triumph of the Moon: A History of Modern Pagan Witchcraft* (New York, 1999). For an insider's viewpoint, see Vivianne Crowley, *Wicca: The Old Religion in a New Millennium* (London, 1996). The discussion of "paranoid" elements in 18th-century Anglo-American thought reflects the work of Bernard Bailyn and Gordon S. Wood; see especially Wood's essay, "Conspiracy and the Paranoid Style: Causality and Deceit in the Eighteenth Century," *William and Mary Quarterly*, third ser., 39:401–41 (1982). Two studies of related import are Richard Hofstadter, "The Paranoid Style in American Politics," in *The Paranoid Style in American Politics, and Other Essays* (New York, 1965), and David Brion Davis, *The Fear of Conspiracy: Images of Un-American Subversion from the Revolution to the Present* (Ithaca, N.Y., 1971). The best (indeed the only) substantial work on response to the Bavarian Illuminati is Vernon Stauffer, *New England and the Bavarian Illuminati* (New York, 1918). On anti-Masonry, see the references for chapter 10. The most recent, and authoritative, account of the Haymarket affair is James R. Green, *Death in the Haymarket: A Story of Chicago, the First Labor Movement, and the Bombing That Divided Gilded-Age America* (New York, 2006). Writings on the history of modern Red Scares are voluminous. For a good overview, see M. J. Heale, *American Anticommunism: Combating the Enemy Within, 1830–1970* (Baltimore, Md., 1990). Other works consulted for the present chapter include: William Preston, Jr., *Aliens and Dissenters: Federal Suppression of Radicals, 1903–1933* (Chicago, 1963); Murray B. Levin, *Political Hysteria in America: The Democratic Capacity for Repression* (New York, 1971); David Caute, *The Great Fear: The Anti-Communist Purge Under Truman and Eisenhower* (New York, 1978); Michael J. Ybarra, *Washington Gone Crazy: Senator Pat McCarran and the Great American Communist Hunt* (Hanover, N.H., 2004); Ellen Shrecker, *Many Are the Crimes: McCarthyism in America* (New York, 1998); and David Oshinsky, *A Conspiracy So Immense: The World of Joe McCarthy* (New York, 1983). The chapter's concluding section, on the day-care child sex-abuse "crisis," draws together newspaper reports, magazine articles, legal briefs, psychological evaluations, and other pertinent material. Book-length studies of this topic are as yet relatively few. But, for the McMartin case, see Paul Eberle and Shirley Eberle, *The Abuse of Innocence: The McMartin Preschool Trial* (Buffalo, N.Y., 1993). On McMartin, along with several other cases, see Debbie Nathan and Michael Snedeker, *Satan's Silence: Ritual Abuse and the Making of a Modern American Witch Hunt* (New York, 1995). The latter work includes in chapter 7 an especially effective review of the debate on the validity of child testimony, material that is otherwise scattered through professional journals.

For a brilliant exploration of a single "sex ring" case in Olympia, Washington, see Lawrence Wright, *Remembering Satan* (New York, 1994).

CHAPTER TWELVE

For a passionately written account of the Fells Acres case, see Dorothy Rabinowitz, *No Crueler Tyrannies: Accusation, False Witness, and Other Terrors of Our Times* (New York, 2001), 1–46, 63–95, 123–37, 166–209. Otherwise the relevant material is too recent to have been carefully assembled; much of it is found in court transcripts and day-to-day newspaper coverage. (See especially the *Boston Globe* and the *Boston Herald American*.) Two recent conferences at the Harvard Law School were aimed at unraveling the key legal issues. The first, "The Day Care Child Sex Abuse Phenomenon" (Nov. 17, 2000), was sponsored by the Criminal Justice Institute of Harvard Law School, the Massachusetts Bar Association, the Massachusetts Association of Criminal Defense Lawyers, and the American Civil Liberties Union; its agenda included Fells Acres along with other, similar cases. The second, "The Harvard Law School Forum on Fells Acres" (April 4, 2003), focused on the Fells Acres episode alone.

Index of Names

General Index